Fields of Vision

Frontispiece: Portrait of William Bartram by Charles Willson Peale, from life, circa 1808. (Image courtesy of Independence National Historical Park)

Fields of Vision

Essays on the *Travels* of William Bartram

Edited by
Kathryn E. Holland Braund
Charlotte M. Porter

THE UNIVERSITY OF ALABAMA PRESS

Tuscaloosa

Copyright © 2010
The University of Alabama Press
Tuscaloosa, Alabama 35487–0380
All rights reserved
Manufactured in the United States of America

Typeface: Caslon

∞

The paper on which this book is printed meets the minimum requirements of
American National Standard for Information Sciences-Permanence of Paper for
Printed Library Materials, ANSI Z39.48–1984.

Library of Congress Cataloging-in-Publication Data

Fields of vision : essays on the travels of William Bartram / edited by Kathryn E.
Holland Braund, Charlotte M. Porter.
       p.   cm.
   Includes bibliographical references and index.
   ISBN 978-0-8173-1682-2 (cloth : alk. paper) — ISBN 978-0-8173-5571-5 (pbk. : alk.
paper) — ISBN 978-0-8173-8324-4 (electronic) 1. Southern States—Description and
travel—Congresses. 2. Bartram, William, 1739–1823—Travel—Southern States—
Congresses. 3. Natural history—Southern States—Congresses. 4. Indians of North
America—Southern States—Congresses. I. Braund, Kathryn E. Holland, 1955–
II. Porter, Charlotte M., 1948–
   F213.F53 2010
   917.5′043—dc22

                                                                      2009026109

Cover: *Oenothera grandiflora.* Courtesy of the Sterling Morton Library,
The Morton Arboretum.

As William Bartram would attest, fathers are important.
We dedicate this book to ours:

James E. Holland
and
Harry Boone Porter

Contents

Illustrations

Preface: "Fields of Vision"

In 1791, the naturalist William Bartram (1739–1823) published a long four-part narrative of a 2,400-mile journey made in 1773 to 1777. Raised as a Quaker, Bartram was a child of plain dress, but the title of his book reads like an elaborate eye chart: *Travels through North & South Carolina, Georgia, East & West Florida, the Cherokee Country, the Extensive Territories of the Muscogulges, or Creek Confederacy, and the Country of the Chactaws; Containing an Account of the Soil and Natural Productions of Those Regions, Together with Observations on the Manners of the Indians*. Published in Philadelphia, Bartram's *Travels* recounted Native American homelands, new settlements of colonists in Georgia, and two new British colonies: East and West Florida. He devoted entire sections to natural communities, including many floral and faunal wonders. Bartram was not a stranger to the Southeast. He had attempted livelihood as an itinerant merchant along the Cape Fear River in North Carolina, and in the winter of 1765–1766, he explored part of the St. Johns River, Florida, with his ailing father, the botanist John Bartram.

On his own and in the company of traders, in the 1770s, Bartram traveled the foothills of the Appalachian Mountains to the royal province of East Florida, through the southeastern interior to the Mississippi River. As a travelogue, his book described the frontier, the eighteenth-century environment of eight present states: North and South Carolina, Georgia, Florida, Alabama, Mississippi, Louisiana, and Tennessee. As a form of autobiography, Bartram's published account is a scientific adventure, in which Bartram the late bloomer matures as an advocate for Indian peoples and the species on which they were dependent. An early example of American nature writing, Bartram's *Travels* quickly became a classic, termed in today's literary criticism as a form of genrefusion. History, science, and prose poetry come together in passages that have defied imitation.

A weighty book, Bartram's *Travels* became an immediate success in Europe. The author's vision influenced English romantic poets, French novelists, and German armchair travelers who savored his complex descriptions of the exotic Florida karst, Indian peoples, and landscapes of great beauty. Of special importance were Bartram's accounts of wetlands. To his word pictures, he often added sound tracks—Creek flute music, calling frogs, wind sighing through the trees. Bartram lived a long life, and, during the first quarter of the nineteenth century, he became the grand old man of American natural history. He advised Thomas Jefferson and mentored the first generation of naturalists eager to follow "Bartram's track" and explore the natural wealth of the young nation.

The Bartram Trail Conference, Inc. (BTC), founded in 1976, seeks to identify and mark the corridor of Bartram's southern journey and encourages the study, preservation, and interpretation of the William Bartram heritage at both cultural and natural sites in Bartram Trail states. The BTC works to foster scholarship related to Bartram and his legacy, including biennial meetings of members at selected locations along the Bartram Trail corridor. The papers in this volume are products of BTC meetings and related symposiums held in Gainesville, Florida; Montgomery, Alabama; Augusta, Georgia; Auburn, Alabama; Cashiers, North Carolina; and Spanish Fort, Alabama. The authors of the essays hail from a wide range of scholarly disciplines, including history, literature, archaeology, botany, library science, and education. They represent a variety of approaches to the study of William Bartram's work and his eighteenth-century world. In keeping with the aims of the BTC, they employ new ways of looking at Bartram's *Travels* and disseminate their findings to wider audiences.

Chapters in part 1 of this book follow Bartram the traveler throughout Georgia and across the large royal province of West Florida to the Mississippi River. Edward J. Cashin situates Bartram the colonist in 1773 and the political context of the American Revolution. Robert Scott Davis focuses on a Georgia Quaker community of interest to Bartram, who was raised in the Religious Society of Friends. Bartram had much to say on the zoological food chain, but Kathryn E. Holland Braund reminds us of the traveler's need for repast. Robert J. Malone puts a face and name on scientist William Dunbar, one of the successful planters unidentified in Bartram's account.

Bartram's *Travels* is a dense book. Here, part 2 provides tools for readers of that book. Stephanie Volmer discusses Bartram's expository style with respect to natural history, a term with shifting borders. Burt Kornegay presents the lucidity of Bartram's piety in his vision of nature. Bartram was not the first naturalist hired to observe natural history in the southern colonies, and Arlene

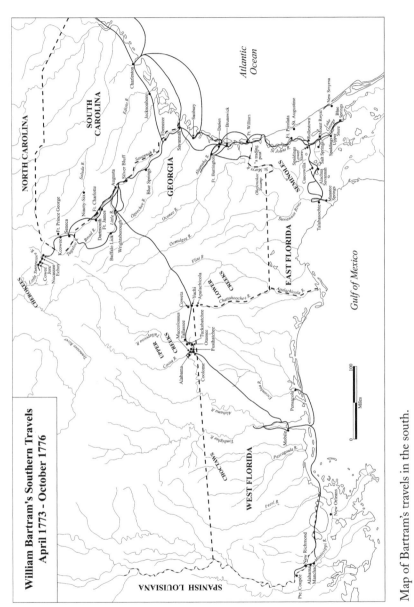

Map of Bartram's travels in the south.

Fradkin and Mallory McCane O'Conner compare him to the competition, an illustrious predecessor from London, Mark Catesby.

In part 3 we return to Bartram's unique observations of Indian communities, data valued by his contemporaries, but published without illustration in the *Travels*. Although Bartram did not excavate sites, he recognized the vulnerability of their contents to vandals and the plow. Jerald T. Milanich examines the grand Florida earthwork, Mount Royal, named and described by Bartram's father and revisited by William in 1774, and, with contemporary expertise, identifies artifacts from organized digs of the late nineteenth century. Craig T. Sheldon Jr. provides a walking tour of an eighteenth-century square ground, the distinctive plan of Creek villages visited by Bartram in 1775. Mark Williams investigates the provenience of Bartram's ethnographic drawings published after his death.

Bartram was an attentive nurseryman as well as an ardent naturalist. Part 4 celebrates the quality of his botanical observations and discoveries. With a gardener's touch, Joel T. Fry narrates Bartram's 1775 discovery near Mobile, Alabama, of an uncooperative wonder, a giant species of evening primrose. Sleuths Marc C. Minno and Maria Minno solve the two-hundred-year-old mystery of the elusive Florida Okeechobee gourd.

Part 5 views Bartram's contributions in a digital age. Stephanie C. Haas, Kent D. Perkins, and Michael Bond demonstrate the research advantages of digital images for Bartram's type specimens, the name bearers of new species. Charlotte M. Porter concludes the volume with an essay on Bartram's environmental sensibilities.

Acknowledgments

This book began long ago as Charlotte Porter's idea to publish outstanding papers presented at a biennial meeting of the Bartram Trail Conference held in Gainesville, Florida. Other papers and discussions from subsequent meetings and symposiums devoted to Bartram scholarship joined the line-up. Thus, the papers collected here were presented in Gainesville, Florida; Augusta, Georgia; Cashiers, North Carolina; and, in Alabama at Montgomery, Auburn, and Spanish Fort.

We would like to thank our contributors for their support of the Bartram Trail Conference, Bartram scholarship, and this book. We would also like to thank our many hosts and sponsors: the University of Florida Museum of Natural History; the University of Florida Libraries; the Alabama Department of Archives and History; the Alabama Historical Commission; Augusta State University's Center for the Study of Georgia History; the Carolyn Marshall Draughon Center for the Arts and Humanities at Auburn University; the Special Collections of the Ralph B. Draughon Library at Auburn University; the Cashiers Historical Society; 5 Rivers: Alabama's Delta Resource Center; the Baldwin County Department of Archives and History and The University of Alabama Museum of Natural History (whose canoes provided a fluvial reward for our presenters on two occasions). And special thanks to some of the special people whose continued generosity and enthusiasm keep Bartram scholars moving along Bartram's Trail: Edwin Bridges, the late Ed Cashin, Mary Ann Cashin, John Hall, Randy Mecredy, John Jackson, Hank Burch, Jan Wyatt, Dwayne Cox, Jay Lamar, and Jacob Lowrey.

Sarah Mattics, of the University of South Alabama's Center for Archaeological Studies, prepared the comprehensive map of Bartram's route (page xiii). A number of Bartram scholars provided assistance and helpful advice on matters ranging from plant identification to stylistic matters. For their good-natured and prompt responses to our many questions, we wish to thank Gregory A. Waselkov, John Hall, Tom Hallock, Jim Kautz, Brad Sanders, and Joel T. Fry.

We especially thank the following repositories that provided illustrations from their collections: the Independence National Historical Park, Bartram's Gardens, and the American Philosophical Society Library, all in Philadelphia; the George A. Smathers Libraries and the University of Florida Herbarium at the Florida Museum of Natural History, Gainesville; the National Anthropological Archives, Smithsonian Institution in Washington, D.C.; the British Natural History Museum, London; the University of Wisconsin Library's Digital Collections; and the Sterling Morton Library, Lisle, Illinois.

Finally, we thank the officers and members of our very special organization, the Bartram Trail Conference. The loyal members who trouped from Alachua to Tensaw always constituted enthusiastic audiences full of eager ears, informed questions, and full-hearted support for scholars from every field. Like Bartram, their curiosity, quest for knowledge, and joy in the exploration of the natural world has sustained and inspired us.

Fields of Vision

I
Encounters along the Trail

I
The Real World of Bartram's *Travels*

Edward J. Cashin

William Bartram would be surprised at the number of his admirers two hundred years after the publication of his book, and he would be pleased that trails named for him lure latter-day adventurers into the wildernesses he loved. In the overlong title of his book, he listed all those places he visited, as if laying claim to them. Scores of historical markers commemorate his passing and link him in memory to those who came after. From the Nantahala Mountains in North Carolina to Pensacola on the Gulf Coast, plaques tell the traveler that William Bartram crossed the southern frontier when it was still relatively pristine.

Even before he died in 1823, he must have been amazed and gratified at the impact his book had on Europeans. It contributed to the romantic movement in literature, the cult of nature, the tradition of the noble savage. It influenced Europeans' perception of America.[1] On a tour I made of the grand archbishop's palace in Wurzburg, Germany, constructed in 1807, the guide pointed to the symbols of the continents on the expansive ceiling. My fellow tourists expressed surprise that the symbol for America was the alligator; I thought—"Bartram." Readers today marvel at his awareness of beauty in simple things, and his sensitivity. In Charles Frazier's *Cold Mountain*, Inman carries his "Bartram" when he carries little else, and reads it for inspiration.[2] Like Inman, one comes away feeling good without quite knowing why.

I shared these feelings when I first read *Travels*, but I realized that his book covered the years 1773 to 1777 and described his journey across the entire southland without mentioning the critical event of the time—the American Revolution. Books about him seem to have exhausted all aspects of his activity, and explored his impact on literature, philosophy, botany, ornithology, zoology, even conchology and crocodilia. At least one has plumbed his psychology—was the snake real, or a Freudian symbol?[3] But none of the library of Bartram books, until recently, has attempted to put his travels in the actual context of events. Would an examination of the world of his travels change the interpretation of his book?

Afficionados know the early details. William Bartram was born in 1739 to America's foremost botanist, John Bartram, at the Bartram home in Kingsessing outside Philadelphia. From his earliest years, he loved to draw. He traveled with his father through the Catskills at the age of fourteen, drawing birds and plants.[4] His father sent some of the best ones to his friends in England, including Peter Collinson, like the Bartrams a Quaker and a naturalist. Unfortunately, Billy did not seem much good for anything but drawing. Family friend Ben Franklin got him a job in a printing shop, but Billy hated being cooped up indoors.

Fortunately, in 1765 John Bartram received a royal commission to explore Florida, Britain's new acquisition, and he invited his son to go with him. They stayed with the Lamboll family in Charlestown. William, now twenty-five, found twenty-year-old Mary Lamboll fascinating. He drew pictures for her and called her "Charming Polly."[5] John Bartram introduced his son to other important persons who would be helpful to William later. The two went on to explore northern Florida and Georgia as far as Augusta. William liked it so much he decided to remain in Florida as a planter. Again he failed miserably, and he might have died if Henry Laurens had not rescued him.[6]

Finally in 1773 William offered his services to Dr. John Fothergill, a wealthy London Quaker. John Bartram's correspondent Peter Collinson had informed Fothergill of William's talent for drawing, and Fothergill needed new specimens of plants for his gardens.[7] In Fothergill's pay, William traveled again to Charlestown and again stayed with the Lambolls. By now Charming Polly was twenty-eight and widowed with two children. It would seem the perfect opportunity for a match. William called her "excellent in goodness" and referred to their relationship as "affable and cordial."[8] Romantics will be disappointed that it went no further.

William learned from Indian superintendent John Stuart that a great Indian congress would meet soon in Augusta, and William resolved to start his journey into the interior there. He had a few weeks to kill in the meantime and decided to revisit the Georgia coast. In Savannah, he renewed acquaintance with Governor James Wright, now enjoying popularity because in the coming Indian Congress that he had arranged Georgia would acquire over two million acres of land, good for settlers and better for speculators. No one, certainly not Bartram, would have thought that the Revolution was only two years away. The governor gave the explorer a letter of reference that began, "To all Persons to whom this May be Shown: Know Ye that the Bearer Mr. Bartram, botanist, is come into this Province to Travel about in Search of and to discover Trees, Shrubs, Plants etc—that may be Uncommon, useful, or curious."[9]

William bought a horse and went off to find the uncommon, useful, or curious in coastal Georgia. Someone, possibly Governor Wright, advised him to call upon Lachlan McIntosh at Darien. The genial Scot could not have been more gracious as Bartram described the meeting, "When I came up to the door, the friendly man, smiling, and with a grace and dignity peculiar to himself, took me by the hand, and accosted me thus, 'Friend Bartram, come under my roof, and I desire you to make my house your home.'"[10] Thus began a lasting friendship. The botanist enjoyed a month of botanizing about the region, familiar to him from his visit with his father, and in the process he rediscovered the Franklinia.[11] Sixteen-year-old Johnny McIntosh begged to go to Augusta with William, and by dint of persuasion, his mother agreed. So far, William's travels were as idyllic in reality as they seem in his written account of them.

On the way to Augusta, Bartram and young McIntosh called upon the influential trader George Galphin at his Silver Bluff plantation where a number of Lower Creek Indians waited for the congress to begin. Some of the Indians accompanied the botanist to Augusta, and Galphin followed soon after. Bartram and young McIntosh lodged with Dr. Humphrey Wells, who had been recommended by friends in Charlestown.[12] Before the Indian meeting began, they had time to visit the Quaker town of Wrightsborough, an Eden-like community as Bartram saw it and described it.

Three hundred Creeks gathered for the congress, along with one hundred Cherokees, including John Stuart's friend Attakullakulla, "the Little Carpenter." Stuart managed the affair. Four royal governors from Virginia, North Carolina, South Carolina, and Georgia attended. In his *Travels* Bartram described how the Creeks berated the Cherokees for agreeing to surrender land that both of the Indian nations claimed. The Cherokees gave up the land in exchange for the cancellation of their debt to the traders. The Creeks too had debt to discharge, but they refused to grant as much land as the governors, settlers, and speculators wanted. By liberal presents, John Stuart persuaded the Creek headmen to agree to a large cession east of the Ogeechee River to the north and south, but the young warriors left the meeting in an angry mood.[13] Stuart warned Bartram that it would not be wise to go exploring in the interior just then. But at least he and Johnny McIntosh could accompany a large surveying party that marked the boundaries of the new cession. It began as a lark for Bartram as he went out ahead of the others discovering new plants and delighting in the scenery.

The Creek delegation left the surveying party when it reached the line separating Creek from Cherokee hunting grounds; the Cherokees continued on to the point where the Tugaloo River joined the Savannah River. With appropriate ceremony the Georgians carved "GR" (for George Rex) on a tree and the Cherokees put their mark alongside.[14] The leader, Colonel Edward Barnard (Bartram confused dozens of chroniclers by referring to him as Barnett in his book), celebrated the completion of the journey with a barbecue. Bartram went fishing with the young Cherokees. They caught dozens of trout and bream by using reeds to harpoon the swimming fish.

The next day, sometime in mid-July, the Georgians began their return downriver to Augusta, and Bartram with them. Bartram chose not to tell us what happened to his Cherokee friends, though the news was soon bruited about in Georgia and Carolina. Two of the Cherokees, one nineteen and one twenty, on their return to their village of Tugaloo, called at the house of one of the squatters on the Indian land. The woman of the house happened to be alone. The Indians indicated that they would like something to drink. The woman let them in, sat them at a table, and brought out milk and something to eat. While the two sat eating, the woman's husband, Hezekiah Collins by name, appeared at the door. Without warning he leveled his rifle at one visitor and pulled the trigger, killing him instantly. He struck the other with his rifle so savagely that the barrel broke away from the stock. While the injured Cherokee crouched in pain, Collins picked up an axe and finished his bloody work. John Collins, father of the murderer, helped drag the bodies to the river. They scalped and mutilated the bodies before throwing them into the water.[15]

John Stuart heard the grim news a few days later and dashed off a letter to Lord Dartmouth reporting the "unprovoked and atrocious murder of two of the party I sent to mark the boundary line."[16] Collins's wife told the whole story to two of Colonel Barnard's deputies. John Collins was arrested, but Hezekiah Collins remained at large. Governor James Wright offered a reward for his arrest, but it was never claimed. Too many squatters considered him a hero.

Trouble continued that winter when some disgruntled Creeks staged raids on the new settlements on the ceded lands in December and January. Wright and the governors of South Carolina and East Florida imposed a ban on Indian trade while the war ensued.[17] With the interior thus closed, William Bartram decided to go to Florida. While residing near the McIntoshes, Bartram met James Spalding of St. Simons, partner in one of the largest companies trading to the Indians. Spalding offered the botanist transportation to Florida on one of his trading boats.[18] Thus began Bartram's Florida adventures that so fascinated Europeans, especially those scenes in which the explorer paddled his canoe through waters roiling with roaring, life-threatening alligators.

Bartram accompanied Spalding's traders to the town of Cuscowilla and met Ahaye, called by the English Cowkeeper. Bartram seemed pleased to be dubbed Puc Puggy, the Flower Hunter, by the chief.[19] At Spalding's lower store on the St. John's forty Lower Creeks under their leader Long Warrior met with Charles McLatchy, Spalding's principal trader. Bartram sat near McLatchy during the negotiations. Long Warrior listed the supplies he wanted and assumed since he was such a good friend of Mr. Spalding that he would get the goods on credit. When McLatchy said that he would like to honor the request, but would have to go ask Mr. Spalding, the chief flew into a rage and threatened to bring down thunder and lightning upon the trader. McLatchy said that he knew Long Warrior's great powers and suggested that he demonstrate by blasting that large oak nearby. They ended by striking a deal and the supplies were delivered.[20] The episode is amusing to the reader; for the governors of East Florida, Georgia, and South Carolina, it was criminal.

The illicit trading—so innocently chronicled by Bartram—created a firestorm of recrimination involving Wright in Georgia, Stuart in Charlestown, General Thomas Gage in Boston, and Lord Dartmouth in London. Wright blamed Governor Tonyn of East Florida for not enforcing the ban on trade. The Indian scare still lay on the land; the rich newly ceded lands remained unsettled. The Georgia Council advised the governor to ask Attorney General Anthony Stokes to prosecute Spalding's firm.[21] Despite the fact that the British government condemned his clandestine activity, and later the Whig government vilified him as a Tory, the trader remained in Bartram's estimation, "the excellent James Spalding."

Fortunately, in late August leading Creeks sent a messenger who walked boldly into Augusta and assured the British that they were for peace. Stuart hurried over to Savannah in order to oversee the treaty signing. On October 18, 1774, the Creek leaders promised to punish their guilty, Wright reopened the trade, and an uncertain peace settled upon the land.[22] It was probably not a coincidence that Bartram returned to Georgia in November 1774. The botanist chose not to mention two dramatic events that occurred a month after his return to the Georgia coast. The most serious slave revolt in colonial Georgia took place in Darien while Bartram was there. The *Georgia Gazette* of December 7, 1774, reported that some slaves belonging to a Captain Morris killed their overseer, his wife, a carpenter named Wright, and an unnamed boy. They then attacked the plantation of Angus McIntosh, appealing to his slaves to join them. They left McIntosh seriously wounded, marched on to Roderick M'Leod's house, killed another boy, and injured M'Leod. The militia of the parish of St. Andrew subdued the rebellious slaves. The magistrates sentenced the two leaders to death.[23] Bartram hated slavery, as we know from his correspondence, but curiously, he rarely mentioned African slaves in his book, other than to note their presence. On one occasion, he described the "sooty sons of Afric" singing songs of their own composition, "contented and joyful."[24]

The second omission of the month of December concerned St. John Parish, neighboring St. Andrew. On December 1, 1774, the residents of St. John voted to join the continental ban on trade with England. The parish elected Lyman Hall to the Continental Congress, and collected two hundred barrels of rice for the people of Boston, suffering from the closing of their port by the British navy. On January 12, 1775, a committee headed by Bartram's friend Lachlan McIntosh passed resolutions expressing sympathy with the people of Boston. The final resolution must have pleased Bartram. By it the parish declared "its detestation and abhorrence of the unnatural practice of slavery, a practice founded in injustice and cruelty, and highly dangerous to our liberties, debasing part of our fellow creatures below men."[25] We do not know whether Bartram participated in the discussions leading to the resolution, but perhaps he did.

In March 1775 Bartram went to Charlestown, then seething with revolutionary fervor. He again resided with the Lambolls. He wrote his father that he intended to explore the Cherokee and Creek country and "please God" to reach the Mississippi.[26] John Stuart wrote letters of reference for him and gave him letters to convey to Alexander Cameron, Stuart's deputy to the Cherokee Indians. Stuart informed Lord Dartmouth that he sent instructions to the Indians to persevere in their attachment to the king and "to be always ready to act in the Service."[27] Stuart copied his correspondence in his letterbook. Neither Stuart nor Bartram could have guessed that in two months' time, the revolutionaries would break into Stuart's home, seize the letterbooks, and accuse Stuart of inciting an Indian war. Bartram left Charlestown on April 22, 1775, carrying the incendiary letters in his knapsack, together with a prayer book given him by Mary Lamboll. That night a group of men, including Henry Laurens, broke into the armory on the second floor of the statehouse and took away eight hundred stand of arms and two hundred cutlasses.[28]

William Bartram proceeded leisurely to Lochaber, Cameron's residence near the present city of Abbeville, South Carolina. On the way he revisited George Galphin and obtained letters of reference to the traders in the Creek country.[29] Galphin and Stuart would soon be on opposite sides in the revolutionary struggle and Bartram had letters from them both. Bartram enjoyed his visit with "the agreeable and liberal Mr. Cameron."[30] He learned that a caravan of traders would leave from nearby Fort Charlotte in two months' time for the Creek country, and he decided to explore the Cherokee mountains and then join the caravan. He left Lochaber on May 15, 1775, a week after the rumor of the Stuart-Cameron conspiracy alarmed Charlestown. He must have known that Cameron summoned the Cherokee chiefs to a conference in Seneca. While Bartram strolled through the mountains, Cameron had to flee to the Indian country to avoid arrest by the revolutionary government.

Bartram's account of his journey through the mountains still delights readers and lures them to the trails named in his honor. It was May and the hills still green with new growth; flaming azaleas and pink mountain laurel decorated the landscape. He crossed the Chatooga River at Earl's Ford, followed Warwoman Creek, admired the falls at Fishing Creek, came to the "crossing" of trails at today's Clayton, Georgia, entered the beautiful "vale of Cowee" at Rabun Gap, passed peaceful Indian villages along the Little Tennessee River, and reached the principal town of Cowee. A young trader there asked him if he would like to see a "curious scene." Of course he would. The two rode their horses over precipitous Leatherman Gap, at times leading them by the bridle, down into the Alarka valley. There they encountered the "sylvan scene of primitive innocence" featuring shy and modest Indian maidens, who with a little coaxing "presented their little baskets, merrily letting us know that their fruit was ripe and sound."[31]

After remaining a few days in Cowee, Bartram resumed his journey, crossing today's Appalachian Trail, and following the trail to the Overhill towns of the Cherokee. On the way he met a band of Indians headed for Cameron's conference at Seneca. He recognized Attakullakulla and drew to one side. The Little Carpenter halted and asked Bartram if he knew who he was. Bartram was diplomat enough to embellish the truth. Rather than saying that he had seen the chief at the Augusta Congress, he said that the name of Attakullakulla was known in far-off Philadelphia. That pleased the chief and he inquired for his friend John Stuart. Bartram did not know that Stuart had fled Charlestown in fear of his life. Continuing on his way another towering range, probably the Snowbird Mountains, blocked his way. He decided that he had collected enough specimens in this part of the world and returned to Cowee, then to Seneca. He does not say that he attended Cameron's conference, and perhaps he did not. One who was there said that Cameron allowed one of the traders to tell the Cherokees to be ready to fall upon the Carolinians, but to spare the Georgians.[32] In any case, Bartram went to Fort James, on the Georgia side of the river, to await the organization of the caravan from Fort Charlotte.

Bartram tells how he joined "a company of adventurers" headed by Captain George Whitfield at Fort Charlotte, and how they were entertained at New Bordeaux by its founder, Mesnil du St. Pierre. He does not say that both Whitfield and St. Pierre went no farther on the journey because both men were detained under suspicion of disloyalty by the Carolina Council of Safety headed by Henry Laurens.[33] Bartram's account of his western adventure reads as though he traveled through a vast garden peopled by peaceful Indians. Actually the frontier was in turmoil as competing agents of Stuart and Galphin struggled for the allegiance of the tribes. Bartram did reach the Mississippi, as he had hoped he would. Along the way he encountered loyalists fleeing from the Revolution. No matter how far he retired into the hinterlands, the Revolution snapped at his heels.

By the time he returned to Savannah by way of Augusta he could no longer escape the Revolution. He found Savannah in near panic that January 1776. A fleet of British ships lay at the mouth of the Savannah River, and everyone expected an attack. If Bartram wanted to pay a courtesy call on Governor Wright, he would have found him under house arrest. The Georgia Council of Safety had put Lachlan McIntosh in charge of the defense of the city. McIntosh later wrote to George Washington, "In this desperate state of affairs, I ventured to take command of the militia, lest the colony should be tamely given up."[34] No one could be neutral, not even a Quaker. William Bartram joined the Revolution. Because he was swallowed up in the violence, Bartram said very little in this chapter of his travels. He wrote, "After my return from the Creek nation, I employed myself during the spring and fore-part of the summer in revisiting the several districts in Georgia and the east borders of Florida." Except for a description of a few plants, there is nothing more in the chapter of one and a half pages.[35]

The British warships came upriver to seize vessels loaded with rice and Georgia's first battle of the Revolution followed. In his letter to Washington, McIntosh claimed for Georgia the honor of being the second province, second to Massachusetts, to resist a British invasion.[36] Bartram's casual mention of spending time on the "east borders of Florida" is interesting. The Florida borderlands were a battle zone during the spring and summer of 1776. Though he said nothing about any military engagement in his book, in a postwar essay ultimately directed to Secretary of War Henry Knox, Bartram described an encounter between the British and the Georgia militia commanded by Captain William McIntosh, Lachlan's brother. He meant the letter to be a plea to the Washington administration for a humane Indian policy, but it revealed his own involvement in the revolutionary war.[37]

Bartram's account of the engagement is worth quoting since it does not appear in his *Travels*. Noting that when he:

> was at Gen¹ McAntoshes, on the Alatamaha, the English attempted to invade Georgia . . . They advanced to the Banks of St Mary's, possess'd themselves of it, & took Shelter in the old Indian trading House. A few Indians were in company. A Small party of Georgians marched from the Alatamaha, to oppose them, & they gain'd the banks before the Enemy had pass'd the Flood. Hostilities commenced by the Parties firing at each other across the River. The British were under cover of the evacuated trading Houses, & the Georgians sheilded themselves behind the Trees,

on the River Banks. . . . The conflict had continued for some time, when the Chief of the Indians threw down his Gun & boldly stepping out from the corner of a House, he took off his Hat, & whirling it up in the Air, as he advanced to the River Side, amidst showers of Bullets, he spoke aloud to the Georgians, declaring that they were Brothers & friends and that he knew not any cause why they should spill each others Blood. Neither I (said he) nor my Companions the Red-Men, will fire another Gun. He turned about, shouted, & immediately led off the Indians. This put an end to the contest at that time.[38]

The Indian chief was almost certainly the Cowkeeper, whom Tonyn had sent to the frontier to bolster the body of troops.[39] Is it too fanciful to suppose that Cowkeeper, who had given the name Puc Puggy to the explorer, recognized Bartram among the Georgians and decided not to continue the battle? It probably is. Whatever the chief's reason, it was not his dislike of killing Georgians. In subsequent battles along the Florida border, Cowkeeper proved to be the most warlike ally of the British. Lachlan McIntosh reported the engagement to General Charles Lee. He told how two hundred Indians engaged the Georgians. Captain McIntosh "obliged them to desist."[40] However the Georgians thought it prudent to retire to the Satilla where they constructed Fort McIntosh. Bartram lingered with the McIntoshes at Darien until an American army under the command of General Charles Lee destroyed the farm rather than let it fall into the hands of the enemy. The explorer decided that he had had enough of war and returned to his father's house in Kingsessing, reaching that place early in 1777. He spent a satisfying eight months with his father before the latter's death.

William wrote his book while America's great men assembled in Philadelphia to frame the Constitution. Several delegates visited him in his garden, among them George Washington, James Madison, Alexander Hamilton, George Mason, and John Rutledge of Carolina. It must have been a happy reunion when Henry Laurens and Lachlan McIntosh came to see him.

Readers of *Travels* are free to conjecture about Bartram's motives for writing the book. Those who are unaware of the omissions might come to different conclusions than those who know the context of the times. If his travels were understood to be a walk through a primitive garden and a visit with peaceful Native Americans, moderns would consider his philosophy of nature, his lists of plants and birds, his influence on the various sciences, his impact on Europe, and issues growing out of that context. Indeed all those aspects have been studied over the years. However, if we realize that the world of *Travels* was a world of hatred of Indians, slave uprisings, and civil war among one's friends, we can ask why he chose to omit the ugly and violent?

Perhaps the key to his reason for writing his book is a phrase he expressed to his friend Benjamin Smith Barton in 1791, "I foresee the Magnificent structure and would be instrumental in its advancement—tools and instruments you know are as necessary as materials in the hand of the Architect."[41] Bartram saw the hand of Providence guiding events. The successful trial by combat in the Revolution and the work of the framers of the Constitution suggested a new beginning for America. He would be the instrument, and his book the tool for shaping the structure. He depicted an America as he hoped it would be, purged of wars and ugliness, filled with wonderful plants and animals for the betterment of mankind. If his countrymen treated Native Americans with the respect they deserved; if they ended the evil of slavery; if Americans responded to the innate moral laws endowed by their Creator, and lived in communion with nature, the "Magnificent structure" might be realized.

He dwelt upon the good in the hope of advancing the good. Because he omitted specific places and events, the book is timeless. The time may be right, two hundred and more years after the appearance of *Travels*, to study Bartram in the world in which he lived, in addition to the one he wrote about.

Notes

1. Josephine Herbst, *New Green World* (New York: Hastings House, 1954), 150.

2. Charles Frazier, *Cold Mountain: A Novel* (New York: Atlantic Monthly Press, 1997), 100.

3. Thomas P. Slaughter, *The Natures of John and William Bartram* (New York: Alfred A. Knopf, 1996), 154.

4. John Bartram, *Observations on the Inhabitants, Climate, Soil, Productions, Animals and Other Matters Worthy of Notice* . . . (London: printed for J. Whiston and B. White, 1751).

5. John Bartram to William Bartram, April 9, 1776, Bartram Papers, New-York Historical Society.

6. William Stork, *An Account of East Florida, with a Journal Kept by John Bartram of Philadelphia, Botanist to His Majesty for the Floridas* . . . (London: W. Nicoll, 1766). Henry Laurens to John Bartram, August 9, 1766, William Darlington, *Memorial of John Bartram and Humphry Marshall* . . . (Philadelphia: Lindsay and Blakiston, 1849), 438–442. Henceforth, Darlington, *Memorial*.

7. John Fothergill to John Bartram, 1772, Darlington, *Memorial*, 343–345.

8. William Bartram to John Bartram, March 27, 1775, in Edmund Berkeley and Dorothy Smith Berkeley, eds., *The Correspondence of John Bartram, 1734–1777* (Gainesville: University of Florida Press, 1992), 768–770.

9. Sir James Wright, "To All Persons . . . ," Bartram Papers, New-York Historical Society.

10. William Bartram, *The Travels of William Bartram,* Naturalist's Edition, ed. Francis Harper (New Haven, Conn.: Yale University Press, 1958), 9–10.

11. William Bartram to Lachlan McIntosh, May 31, 1796, Bartram Papers, New-York Historical Society; Bartram, *Travels,* ed. Harper, 337.

12. Humphrey and George Wells were sons of Dr. Richard Wells of Queen Anne County, Maryland; communication of John Britton Wells III to author, February 28, 1997.

13. Bartram, *Travels,* ed. Harper, 307–308; Kathryn E. Holland Braund, *Deerskins and Duffels: The Creek Indians, Anglo-America and the Deerskin Trade, 1685–1815* (Lincoln: University of Nebraska Press, 1993), 150–152.

14. Bartram, *Travels,* ed. Harper, 29; William Bartram, "Travels in Georgia and Florida, 1773–1774: A Report to Dr. John Fothergill," annotated by Francis Harper, *Transactions of the American Philosophical Society,* new series, vol. 22, part 2 (Philadelphia: APS, 1943), 143, hereafer cited as "Report to Fothergill."

15. Stuart to Dartmouth, August 5, 1773, K. C. Davies, ed. *Documents of the American Revolution 1770–1783,* 21 vols. (Shannon: Irish University Press, 1972–1981), 6: 200–201.

16. Ibid.

17. *Georgia Gazette,* February 2, 1774.

18. Spalding to McLatchie, August 15, 1773, Bartram Papers, Historical Society of Pennsylvania.

19. Bartram, *Travels,* ed. Harper, 118.

20. Ibid., 163–164.

21. Council Minutes, August 30, 1774, Allen D. Candler et al., eds., *The Colonial Records of the State of Georgia,* 30 vols. (Atlanta: various printers, 1904–1916, 1979–1982), 12: 408–409.

22. Original treaty enclosed in Stuart to Gage, November 29, 1774, Gage Papers, William L. Clements Library, Ann Arbor, Michigan.

23. Betty Wood, *Slavery in Colonial Georgia, 1730–1775* (Athens: University of Georgia Press, 1984), 191–192.

24. Bartram, *Travels,* ed. Harper, 198.

25. "In the Darien Committee, Thursday, January 12, 1775," Allen D. Candler, *The Revolutionary Records of the State of Georgia,* 3 vols. (Atlanta: Franklin-Turner Company, 1903), 1: 41–42.

26. William Bartram to John Bartram, March 27, 1775, Bartram Papers, Historical Society of Pennsylvania.

27. Stuart to Dartmouth, March 28, 1775, British Public Record Office, Colonial Office, 5/76.

28. William Bartram to Mary Lamboll Thomas, July 15, 1786, Bartram Papers, New-York Historical Society; John Drayton, *Memoirs of the American Revolution,* 2 vols. (1821; reprint, New York: New York Times and Arno Press, 1969), 1: 222.

29. Galphin to Messrs. Graham et al., April 30, 1775, Bartram Papers, New-York Historical Society.

30. Bartram, *Travels*, ed. Harper, 208.

31. Ibid., 226.

32. Deposition of Robert Goudey, sworn before James Mayson, July 9, 1775, Miscellaneous Collections, South Caroliniana Library, Columbia, S.C.

33. Laurens to Col. William Thomson, July 16, 1775, Philip M. Hamer et al., eds., *The Papers of Henry Laurens*, 14 vols. (Columbia: University of South Carolina Press, 1968–1994), 10: 225–227.

34. McIntosh to Washington, March 8, 1776, *Collections*, 20 vols. (Savannah: Georgia Historical Society, 1840–1980), 12: 1–4.

35. Bartram, *Travels*, ed. Harper, 295.

36. McIntosh to Washington, March 8, 1776, *Collections*, 20 vols. (Savannah: Georgia Historical Society, 1840–1980), 12: 1–4.

37. For a discussion of the essay, "Some Hints & Observations, concerning the civilization, of the Indians, or Aborigines of America," see William Bartram, *William Bartram on the Southeastern Indians*, ed. Gregory A. Waselkov and Kathryn E. Holland Braund (Lincoln: University of Nebraska Press, 1995), 187–198.

38. William Bartram, "Some Hints and Observations . . . ," Henry Knox Papers of the Gilder-Lehrman Collection (on deposit at the New-York Historical Society).

39. Governor Patrick Tonyn to Sir Henry Clinton, June 8, 1776, British Public Record Office, Colonial Office, 5/556.

40. Lachlan McIntosh to General Charles Lee, July 29, 1776, Georgia Historical Society *Collections*, 12: 10–11.

41. William Bartram to Benjamin Smith Barton, March 1791, Benjamin Smith Barton Papers, American Philosophical Society Library, Philadelphia.

2

William Bartram, Wrightsborough, and the Prospects for the Georgia Backcountry, 1765–1774

Robert Scott Davis

Any extensive list of famous naturalist explorers to Georgia would certainly include William Bartram, an adventurer into the natural world whose well-known travels took him through the province in 1765 and in 1773–1776.[1] On the first trip, William accompanied his famous father, John Bartram, who used the small stipend given to him as a royal botanist to explore East Florida, one of Britain's new mainland American acquisitions from the Seven Years' War.[2] John also sought to collect new specimens for his family nursery business in Philadelphia, the first real botanical gardens in America. On the second journey, William traveled on his own, under a commission from English Quaker naturalist and medical scientist Dr. John Fothergill to add to the latter's gardens. Partially through the additions provided by John Bartram, Fothergill's collection became second only to the royal gardens at Kew.[3] William Bartram's work with soil, plants, and animals has long been recognized although his important notes on the peoples he encountered should not be overlooked, including what he recorded about the settlement of the Georgia backcountry north and west from Augusta. Writings from these two journeys document wilderness aspects of that frontier following years of war and then the extraordinary beginnings of its agricultural economy.

Essentially en route from the Carolina backcountry to the new British colonial acquisition of East Florida, John and William Bartram first entered Georgia on September 3, 1765, as they neared the Savannah River crossing at Purysburgh, South Carolina. They crossed the river on a bateau, a small boat, and noted that, even that high up the river, alligators could still be seen. Without much more to mention, they proceeded on to Savannah, the colonial capital, of which John only recorded its distance from the sea.

Even by colonial American standards, the province that they now entered remained largely undeveloped wilderness. Founded on February 12, 1733, as a social experiment that offered middle-class Britons a chance at new lives in the New World as small farmers, by 1765, Georgia existed as little more than the scattered physical and human ruins of the Georgia Trustees' great experiment. The Trustees, a board of the prominent British upper class, had transplanted thousands of English, German, and Highland Scot settlers to the new land to populate a province in which they deliberately banned those elements popularly blamed for Britain's societal ills: debt, rum, lawyers, slaves, religious conflict, and property ownership. The Trustees sought reform through social control within the existing system, not by such later Enlightenment ideas as classless individual freedom and unfettered markets. This "Georgia Plan" deviated from what the colonial observer and later governor of North Carolina, Arthur Dobbs, earlier criticized as the excessive personal and economic liberty that Great Britain had hereto allowed in the twelve earlier mainland colonies. Ideally the new colony would benefit the empire as a whole with an economy based in the government subsidized production of such exotic, otherwise imported, products as silk and wine rather than the slave-produced products of the free-enterprise economy practiced in neighboring South Carolina. The Trustees established the river/seaport capital of Savannah, a settlement of German Salzburgers at Ebenezer, a military community of Highland Scots at Darien, and the frontier village of Augusta. The latter, at the navigable head of the Savannah River, became the passage for most of the trade with the neighboring Cherokee and Creek Indian tribes. Dobbs saw government control of the business with the Native American peoples through such places as critical to a long-term, orderly, and peaceful government-managed development of the American frontier.[4]

The Trustees tried to control the lives of these settlers at long distance. Of their board, only James Oglethorpe actually lived in the colony. He left forever in 1742 but, during his time in Georgia, he demonstrated his thorough lack of knowledge of farming, exotic or otherwise. Settlers who followed the Trustees' restrictive agenda failed and many died, contributing to the orphanage at Bethesda, which became the original colony's most successful institution. The specialty crops tried also failed, leaving little behind by 1765 beyond the remains of the silk operations. Many of the immigrants to the new land gave up on the province and migrated to North and South Carolina where fewer restrictions gave individuals opportunities to survive and even prosper. The Trustees had lifted almost all of the limitations placed upon the remaining Georgians by 1752, when Parliament's decision to cease funding the project compelled the surrender of the colony to the Crown. A royal governor, sea captain John Reynolds, arrived in 1754 but his inability to work with the Georgians and military threats from Spanish Florida to the south and French Louisiana to the west stymied growth. His successors, Henry Ellis and James Wright, respectively, worked hard to promote the colony and, by 1765, as Georgia's largest land and slave owner, Governor Wright entertained the Bartrams in Savannah. This thirteenth colony, however, had not been a success by any standard, vindicating the later ideas of the economics pioneer Adam Smith and other men of the Enlightenment on the virtues of individual initiative and an uninhibited market-based economy.[5]

The Bartrams' initial journey into the Georgia frontier began that September 1765. They passed the settlement of Ebenezer, in present-day Effingham County, where John only noted it as having some twenty houses and one hundred mulberry trees that were remains of the early experiment in silk production. They then proceeded across Briar Creek, a body of water that he called a fine creek. Having traveled as far north as Augusta, the Bartrams returned to the village of Savannah, where John made more detailed observations of its few public buildings and the homes of its gentlemen. They traveled south, passing through what remained of Georgia's Highland Scot community, to newly acquired British East Florida, where they arrived in early October 1765. During this journey, John created an exact and credible listing of the types of soil, geography, plants, and wildlife, which contrasts with the few other but less-detailed descriptive accounts of Georgia's frontier at that time. His two reports of that journey do make extremely favorable remarks about people and accommodations, but contain hardly anything more about the few settlements encountered.[6] John Bartram added significantly to information on the place and period while also discrediting rumor and myth that survived in place of firsthand accounts by a professional observer. For example, even fourteen years later an anonymous Hessian officer made a report from Savannah of how he and his comrades enjoyed local beans, peas, lettuce, and "white and yellow turnips," but he understood that further inland: "Wild ducks, geese, turkeys, pheasants, parrots, large and small game, as well as domestic fowls, are plentiful. Bears, wolves, tigers, and similar wild beasts are also met with. Buffaloes, likewise are to be found in the forests further inland. Rattles-snakes and even more deadly animals abound, and are as you may well imagine, most disagreeable."[7]

The Bartrams encountered no such dangers, or even buffalo, illustrating that even among contemporary accounts, fact and myth could become confused in describing the southern frontier. (William Bartram would find such wildlife in his later journeys deeper into the American wilderness, however.) Even as early as the time of their travels, the reality, as encountered by the Bartrams, often conflicts with backcountry stories.[8] John Bartram could also repeat myth. When the wealthy trader, planter, and rancher George Galphin took them to see the various natural wonders of Silver Bluff, for example, John recorded the story that it drew its name from a Spanish mine that had once been worked there. A more credible explanation would be the glistening pyrites and mica that John did note.

On this journey, father and son did not see the area of the frontier that would later include Wrightsborough. They reached Augusta on September 12 and found it to be a town of some eighty buildings, two wooden forts, and a church with the remains of silk plantations nearby. John wrote that he found the soil fertile but that local agriculture proved too expensive for the nearest market, especially when added to the cost of defending a plantation against Indian attacks. He found the "greatest curiosity that this country affords" to be only George Galphin's cowpen, near the present site of Louisville, Georgia. It

> being a kind of house, or hut, near a good spring, in which four or five negroes, with one white man, generally live to look after a number of cattle of various kinds, that occupy a range of country of six to ten miles round; the chief employment of these herdsmen, as they might be called, is to tend the calving of the cows, and the foaling of the mares, and to bring those to the pen that stand most in need of assistance and care; several of the inhabitants have two or three of the cow pens at ten miles distance from each other, and the cattle are kept in distinct herds, and feed, both summer and winter in their respective walks. These herdsmen are very dexterous in catching and training the wildest horses, and great profit is made to their masters by the sale.[9]

The literary scholar Thomas Hallock wrote that John Bartram's diary of this journey "scarcely rises above the occasion of a promotional tract" and only as "duty bound prose" on "the practical uses of a recently ceded territory."[10] Bartram saw no potential for serious development ventures on the frontier, although later, upon reaching Savannah, he did comment on how Georgia frontiersmen used floods and drained ponds to produce extensive crops of corn that they shipped down the Savannah River in ten-ton cargo bateaus that required crews of seven men each.[11]

Some efforts at development on the northwest frontier had been tried but economic prosperity in the Georgia frontier remained more hope than hard reality. A land cession in 1763, at the end of the Seven Years' War, had officially extended the colony's borders to the Little River on the north and to the Ogeechee River to the west. Settlers could also take up the colony's free (headright) lands within five miles along the Savannah River, north of the mouth of the Little River.[12] A few persons took advantage of that particular exception to make settlements deep into Indian lands. Patrick Clark of Augusta, for example, took over Gregory Hains's land claim on the north side of the Broad

River and even included a drawing of his cabin on the 1754 plat. Although he never received a formal colonial grant, Thomas Lee likewise took out a warrant for a survey in 1759 on what became the junction of Soap Creek and the Savannah River.[13] A settlement by Edmund Gray and his followers from North Carolina existed at Brandon, or the "Quaker Spring," west of Augusta in 1755, on the frontier with the Indian territory that would become the Ceded Lands. Governor Henry Ellis ordered that settlement recalled in 1759 and, by the time of the arrival of the Bartrams, nothing remained of it beyond the names of its members given to local creeks.[14]

Passing through the same area eight years later for his patron, Dr. John Fothergill of London, William Bartram would document but fail to fully recognize a very different situation. He arrived in Savannah from Charleston, South Carolina, in mid-April 1773 before traveling to an announced conference with the Creek and Cherokee Indians in Augusta.

The province must have seemed like a new world compared to what he had witnessed as a young man. A new lighthouse, replacing the Trustees' ruined one, now stood at the mouth of the Savannah River. The colonial capital had been a sleepy village of a few public buildings and houses in 1765 but now it bustled with people and commerce. Communities like Sunbury, Midway, and Darien on the coast that had barely existed before now had thousands of residents, both black and white, prospering on the colony's primary business, the rice trade. This new economy had been imported from South Carolina, along with many of that colony's new rice producers.[15]

William Bartram soon discovered equally great changes had occurred on the colony's northern frontier. On May 1, 1773, he set out with Governor Wright's retinue for the treaty meeting in Augusta. Along the way, he revisited Ebenezer, where the local people had erected a brick church that still stands. He found the Salzburgers prosperous with numerous mills, orchards, and gardens, while still trying to make a profitable crop from silk. At Augusta, the Indians had not yet arrived for the scheduled conference and so Bartram set out to explore the neighborhood, including a visit to Wrightsborough.[16]

As William Bartram returned to Georgia in 1773, a man who set out from England at about the same time that John Bartram had come there in 1765 wrote of his life near Augusta. Styling himself "An American," he claimed that in those intervening years he had come to possess 6,340 acres, twenty-five slaves, and five white servants. He made his first profits from the timber that he had to clear to create the fields for his successful crops of potatoes, wheat, barley, and Indian corn. His holdings profitably produced beef, pork, indigo, and hemp for market. With great exuberance, he wrote of how others of all classes could repeat his success. Ironically, in view of the original purpose of the colony, he also produced silk and his French neighbor planned to revive the experiment of making a marketable wine. His countryman and contemporary Dr. Thomas Taylor would similarly write specifically from Wrightsborough of how "most of the Settlers having arriv'd within this eight years from the back parts of Pennsylvania & Virginia. The Land here bears pretty good Wheat, Rice, Oats, Pease, Indian Corn, Indigo, Cotton &c. Peaches are pretty plentifull but no other Sort of Fruit, merely (I believe) for Want of Culture."[17]

The Scottish engineer William Mylne, hiding nearby after a bridge he built in Edinburgh partially collapsed, left an equally positive account of the new frontier, however, but from the perspective of the greater number of settlers who were of more modest means. Living at Stevens Creek in South Carolina, but only a few miles from Augusta, he described himself as living alone in the woods in a rented house that consisted of a sixteen-by-twenty-foot enclosure made from stacked pine logs and covered with a clapboard roof. When not keeping snakes and the resident cat from eating his chickens, he subsisted by hunting and fishing. He observed that the stout and well-made men around him lived like Indians and by following their livestock while the women planted a wide variety of grains, vegetables, and fruits, as well as doing the spinning and weaving. These colorfully dressed and largely Baptist frontiersmen raised tobacco that they took to distant cities like Charleston and Savannah for sale. That product would travel on to Europe, before returning as snuff for purchase by the original growers. The people of the backcountry bartered for goods from local merchants but they found the prices in such stores to be too high.[18]

Economic development had come to the frontier north and west of Augusta for a variety of reasons that defied the obstacles seen by the Bartrams in 1765. On the neighboring South Carolina frontier, settlers known as "Regulators" forced that colony's government to establish rule of law in the form of local courts and jails, giving the area the kind of stability that could encourage investment on a large scale.[19] Georgia's governor James Wright had little use for Regulators or the large numbers of landless and sometimes lawless frontiersmen, whom he referred to derisively as "Crackers" and "Virginians." He did use what he learned from that conflict in his plans for new social engineering in his province.[20] While contemporary observers and those for generations to come would write of founding a new society and even civilized empires on the frontier, Wright envisioned expansion of the coastal economy and society into the backcountry, while maintaining government control as it grew and spread. He hoped, even as early as the 1763 land cession, to populate the new lands with a peaceful frontier middle class of families who had few if any slaves, people in a society similar to what had been the earlier ambitions of the Trustees. Georgians, therefore, did not have to take up arms to force the colonial government to bring rule of law to the province's frontier. James

Wright endorsed the successful effort among the people he termed as being of "the better sort" in his backcountry to bring courts to the Augusta and Briar Creek areas.[21]

Even if by well-endowed gentlemen, however, Wright did not want his frontier to be settled as isolated communities, or projects like Edmund Gray's Brandon settlement. A 1758 settlement by Gray on the coast between then British Georgia and Spanish Florida illustrated to Wright how such ventures could become colonies within a colony that had no economic ties to the whole, acting independently of the colonial government and attracting gangs of the lawless who infested the areas between these ventures.[22] This new era of peace and stability on the Georgia frontier, however, inspired impresarios with great and very different ambitions who did receive encouragement from Wright. George Galphin, his fellow Irishman Robert Rae, and Scotsman Lachlan McGillivray had dominated trade with the Indians for many years and they felt safe in establishing, with the governor's help, the Queensborough Township around the previously mentioned Galphin cowpen. From 1768 to 1774, they brought at least six ship-loads of emigrants from Ireland to settle on this frontier reserve.[23]

More significantly, although for reasons beyond just the area's agricultural potential, North Carolinians created the Wrightsborough Township west and north of Augusta. Joseph Maddock (or Mattox) and other future leaders of that community had moved from what is today's state of Delaware to Orange County, North Carolina, in the 1750s, forming a clique even within their local Quaker meeting. By supporting the famous radical Herman Husband's views in a dispute over the disowning of a certain female member, Maddock and other later Wrightsborough settlers risked disownment. A religious and political explorer, Husband served as the spiritual inspiration to North Carolina's failed frontier Regulators, some of whose leaders had met at Maddock's mill.

Georgia's Trustees had planned for the colony to be a home for select oppressed Protestant groups including the Religious Society of Friends, known as Quakers, but until Maddock created the Wrightsborough community in 1767, other than the remote possibility that Edmund Gray's followers in 1755 did actually include, as Gray claimed, some Quakers, no real community of that faith had been tried before in Georgia. This new settlement, however, had many of the traits that Wright feared would exist in such private frontier communities. It consisted of Maddock's core following, rebels against their meeting and supporters of the Regulator rebellion in the North Carolina colonial government, although this isolated new meeting drew members from many colonies. Named for Governor Wright, and with public squares named for Maddock, Galphin, and McGillivray, Wrightsborough village became the nucleus of a township of the same name that covered more than 31,000 acres. The pacifist Quakers suffered theft and raids, especially of livestock, from persons of all local races. Despite the meeting's efforts to keep in discipline all known members of its faith in the area, Wrightsborough Meeting's minutes omit any mention of over 80 percent of the families who lived in the township, indicating that the vast majority of the settlement did not consist of "Friends" but of sympathetic persons without religious qualms about using violence to defend the settlement. Wrightsborough even had a fort by the time of William Bartram's arrival.[24]

Bartram, himself a Quaker, described this community in 1773 as a pleasant village of some twenty houses occupied largely by the followers of a still active and healthy seventy-year-old Joseph Maddock who, like Maddock, were usually Quakers from North Carolina. These people, Bartram found, brought northern style agriculture to the South that included the profitable production of wheat, barley, flax, hemp, oats, corn, cotton, and indigo. They bred cattle, raised sheep, and made excellent butter and cheese. Fruit trees and berries proved plentiful, including apples, pears, peaches, plums, nectarines, cherries, and raspberries. In Maddock's own garden, Bartram found large apples on trees and grapes on vines that, respectively, the settlers claimed had been seeds and cuttings two years earlier. The village had a number of traders who sold goods as cheaply as could be had in Augusta. Mills now ran on many of the area's fast-moving creeks.[25]

In the years between John and William Bartram's visit in 1765 and William Bartram's return expedition in 1773, Galphin and Maddock had thus made spectacular government-supported beginnings at developing the frontier. Private efforts had also begun that William would witness and record. For example, he saw something of how activities like those he and his father had witnessed in 1765 at George Galphin's cowpens had metamorphosed into Galphin controlling a vast living corporation that centered on slaves, crops, herds, and trade with the Indians in animal skins and pelts. This operation gave special meaning to "in house," since he literally produced his administrators in the form of his children by different women who were of African, Indian, and Caucasian descent, respectively. The early Creek historian Thomas Woodward wrote of Galphin that "of the five varieties of the human family; he raised children from three, and no doubt would have gone the whole hog, but the Malay and the Mongol were out of his reach."[26] Bartram also encountered a nearby cowpen where women, children, and men, both free and enslaved, emulated Galphin's success at a settlement where they milked forty cows. They also had an operation where logs were squared and hauled by wheel to the river for eventual sale in the West Indies. In a famous passage of his memoirs, he wrote of the people as gracious, happy, and healthy as represented by hospitable newlyweds he met whom he described as a Venus and an Adonis.[27]

William Bartram also witnessed the greatest success of the frontier's unique entrepreneurs in a scheme that included debts, social engineering, and class in ways that echoed both the much earlier failures of Georgia's original Trustees and their ambitions for their colony. George Galphin and his partners had made an agreement with the Cherokees to exchange a vast area of land north and west of Augusta for debts held by the British firm William Greenwood and William Higginson that were owed by Galphin and others involved in trade with the Indians. Governor Wright preempted this plan, in part because the Cherokees planned to only transfer lands that they had lost in war to the Creeks. Under the May 1772 treaty held in Augusta, the Creek leaders reluctantly assented to a plan whereby all debts owed by both Indian nations would be repaid from proceeds of the transfer and sale of 1.5 million acres of land north and west of Augusta. Bartram noted how many of the three hundred Creek Indians present had doubts about the debts and the necessity of giving up more land to the Georgians. Many of the Creek leaders recognized the gradual shrinkage of their traditional lands and opposed any further cessions to the encroaching white and black cultures. Aside from personal and spiritual attachments to this country, the Indians also needed this land for the animal skins that had become their sole tradable asset and the lack of which, in part, had brought about their credit problems.[28]

Governor Wright, eventually made a baronet for his efforts in procuring these lands, did not gain all that he sought but he had plans that went far beyond acquiring territory. To guarantee a significant increase of population on the colony's Indian frontier at a time when the Crown ended the free colonial headright grants everywhere else, he chose to have the land sold at below market value in an attempt to try to attract middle-class families of means who would develop the territory before it could be overrun by landless Crackers who would try to settle on these same grounds. He also officially limited the purchases to only non-Georgians and he hoped that the Virginians among the newcomers would introduce tobacco as a large-scale crop in Georgia. A troop of provincial rangers, financed from the sale of the lands, would maintain law and order among the white settlers and between them and the neighboring Indians. Forts at Wrightsborough on the Little River and the new settlement of Dartmouth at the mouth of the Broad River served as headquarters for these rangers. The government would thus enforce peace and order from the beginning instead of being compelled to take action at some future time.[29]

William Bartram witnessed the treaty and then, on June 7, 1773, set out to explore the new territory as part of an expedition headed by Edward Barnard, captain of the newly created company of rangers. The naturalist wrote of this "caravan," consisting of some seventy to eighty surveyors, astronomers, artisans, chain-carriers, guides, and hunters, both white and Indian, along with their horses and pack animals. Problems arose between the Creeks and the surveyors over the direction of lines but the warriors also provided food for men and animals. At least once the work stopped when the Indians proved too drunk to continue. As the survey succeeded marking the boundaries of the new acquisition, the surveyors also produced what has become a classic map of the territory and of its potential for agriculture.[30]

Bartram, the naturalist, however, had come to see the frontier undeveloped by the Europeans and so sought to study it before white and black families transformed it into farms and cowpens. This journey proved to be everything he could have hoped for. Bartram found the new acquisition to be a land of gentle streams, rolling hills, remains of past Indian settlements, and a wide variety of plants. He visited the local curiosity known as the Great Buffalo Lick, a natural clay deposit that attracted the local wildlife. The sheer beauty of the Ceded Lands would remain with him for the rest of his life. He wrote in a typical passage:

> The day's progress was agreeably entertaining, from the novelty and variety of objects and views; the wild country now almost depopulated, vast forests, expansive plains and detached groves; then chains of hills whose gravelly, dry, barren summits present detached piles of rocks, which delude and flatter the hopes and expectations of the solitary traveller, full sure of hospitable habitations; heaps of white, gnawed bones of the ancient buffaloe, elk and deer, indiscriminately mixed with those of men, half grown over with moss, altogether exhibit scenes of uncultivated nature, on reflection, perhaps, rather disagreeable to a mind of delicate feelings and sensibility, since some of these objects recognize past transactions and events, perhaps not altogether reconcilable to justice and humanity.[31]

Bartram, the man, however, did not lament the loss of this wilderness but wrote of its agricultural potential, especially for the type of frontier settlement envisioned by Governor Wright and even by the Georgia Trustees:

> The new ceded country promises plenty and felicity. The lands on the [Broad] River are generally rich & those of the almost innumerable branches agreeable and healthy situations, especially for small farms, every where little mounts & hills to build on & beneath them rich level land fit for corn & any grain with delightful glittering streams of running water through cain [sic] bottoms, proper for meadows, with abundance of water brooks for mills. The hills suit extremely well for vineyards & olives as nature points out by the abundant produce of fruitful

grape vine, native mulberry trees of an excellent quality for silk. Any of this land would produce indigo & no country is more proper for the culture of almost all kinds of fruits.[32]

Most of William Bartram's remaining time on the northwest Georgia frontier took him through unsettled forests where he duly recorded the soils, plants, and animals. He did note as he entered the new lands that a public house already existed on the Little River and, upon crossing the Broad River en route back to Augusta, he encountered a new plantation, likely that of Thomas Waters, going up even before the land had been formally opened for settlement.[33]

Bartram's host in Wrightsborough, Joseph Maddock, served as one of the commissioners for selling the new lands and, as such, between 1773 and 1774, he helped to compile a record of most of the subsequent land sales that gave the area a new population of almost 300 families, 85 percent of which were almost equally divided between the Carolinas and 11 percent from Pennsylvania and Virginia. Aside from an intrusion by hundreds of squatters, Wright's goal of limiting the new lands to only persons of means failed, largely due to the generosity of ranger Thomas Waters. He loaned money to arriving families with which they could make their initial payments.[34]

The Ceded Lands that William Bartram explored also drew many entrepreneurs who wanted to develop the individual, almost self-sustaining European settlements that Wright had disdained. Former British sergeant Farquhar Malcomb, for example, claimed that he had owned 760 head of cattle, 300 hogs, fourteen breeding mares, and eight horses at the cowpen he established on Coal's Creek and the Oconee River. Witnesses swore that they saw more than 1,500 head of cattle there.[35] The English-born Thomas Waters had been a resident of both Georgia and South Carolina since at least 1760. The map of the Ceded Lands showed his South Carolina plantation adjoining the new acquisition. Around the mouth of the Broad River and along the Savannah River, as well as near Wrightsborough, he established plantations of some 4,500 acres where he and his slaves raised Indian corn, oats, peas, wheat, indigo, sheep, hogs, horses, and cattle. His operations included a large two-story house, three mills, a blacksmith shop, and a fort.[36] On Thomas Lee's 1760 land claim, near Waters's holdings, John Dooly, deputy surveyor in South Carolina and Georgia, created an ambitious but smaller plantation.[37] Other settlements on the Little River, near Wrightsborough, included one by Scotsman William Manson and another by the English partners Thomas Brown and James Gordon, all newcomers to Georgia. For their respective Friendsborough and Brownsborough projects, these entrepreneurs brought with them indentured servants from northern England and Scotland.[38] Martin Jollie, a sometimes Georgian claiming residence in Barbados, acquired 3,500 acres of land in the area for a scheme that he promised would include black and white servants. Before the Revolution, he brought thirty-three slaves to Georgia to develop his new holdings.[39]

In July 1773 William Bartram left the Ceded Lands to explore the Cherokee nation, the Creek Confederacy, and East Florida. He would briefly return to Georgia before leaving the southern provinces forever in 1776. By that time, the Ceded Lands had already become embroiled in battles between dissident Creek war parties and the Georgians that came about over the transfer of the new territory. After the local militia suffered a humiliating defeat at the hands of the warriors, Wright managed to save the situation with diplomacy. As hundreds of the type of hard-edged frontier squatters whom the governor had tried to discourage moved into the new acquisition, these troubles undid Wright's plans to fund a peaceful and orderly acquisition of the lands by middle-class families. Even without repaying any debts, subsequent land sales failed to cover the government's costs of maintaining the rangers and selling the lands.[40] During the years 1779 to 1782, the American Revolution deteriorated into a violent class war between many of those families Wright would have wanted as settlers and those he did not. As a writer observed about the Ceded Lands revolutionaries who followed Elijah Clarke: "Clarke's party is said to have consisted of men, whose restless dispositions, or whose crimes prevented their living in any country where even the resemblance of government was maintained, and therefore taking themselves to the vacant lands on the frontiers; living without any control; they made inroads upon the industrious inhabitants of the back settlements, and have frequently involved the Province in wars with the Indians."[41]

Warfare by such men in and between independent settlements occurred as Wright had feared. Ironically, most often their victims were ethnic communities like Wrightsborough that, despite very different backgrounds, banded together to aid the British in a counterrevolution against the frontier mainstream majority that supported the Revolution.[42]

Overall, this last attempt at social engineering in colonial Georgia failed when confronted with the realities of frontier life and economics. The American Revolution also contributed to the eventual failure of the ambitions of Wright, Maddock, Waters, Manson, Brown, Dooly, and others for the Ceded Lands. During that war, the pacifist George Galphin tried to maintain peace between the Americans and the Indians. He died in 1780 and it would be decades before his heirs and partners received the money due to them from the sale of the Ceded Lands.[43] After many harrowing adventures, Wright, Waters, Malcomb, Manson, Taylor, Gordon, and Brown found themselves as Loyalist exiles.[44] Joseph Maddock, for his controversial acts to try to protect some of his followers, would find himself investigated and disenfranchised from the Quaker community he had founded. Forgotten, he died in Columbia County in 1796.[45] John Dooly was murdered for political reasons during the war. The state of Georgia ordered the confiscation of his Leesburg property and its return to Thomas Lee.[46]

John Bartram and his contemporaries looked farther than the fauna, flora, fossils, soils, and rocks to see the bigger events around them. As Kathryn E. Holland Braund has pointed out, they fully appreciated the forest disappearing by looking closely at the many types of trees that they carefully identified, recognizing that as the habitat disappeared, the native plants and animals did as well.[47] Even in 1791, when he wrote his memoirs, William Bartram missed the broader implications of what he had witnessed, that the land's potential he had noted in 1775 would not be denied. In 1780, after two years of war, the new territory still had 723 white male inhabitants.[48] In the midst of a local holocaust so brutal that murdering prisoners came to be cynically called "granting a Georgia parole," the English-born William Lee would still regard Georgia as "a fine country, healthy in the back parts" that produced extraordinary crops of corn, all kinds of fruit, and vast herds of a thousand or more animals each.[49]

Between 1783 and 1794, soldiers who had come to Georgia during that war to guard the frontier returned with their neighbors from the Carolinas and Virginia, and the development that had been started and encouraged by Wright, Galphin, Maddock, and other visionaries now became the beneficiary of the greatest period of Georgia's growth. Despite continued troubles with the Indians, the population grew rapidly and, for a time, prospered on the tobacco industry that Wright had hoped they would transplant in Georgia. In 1790, the former Ceded Lands, by then original Wilkes County, Georgia's first county, had more than 40 percent of the overall population and over 45 percent of the white population of the entire state. The descendents of those peoples would contribute much to the settlement of the later American frontiers.[50] Thus the Bartrams documented how a frontier evolved into a full settlement, during a revolutionary era, when the best laid plans of a well-intentioned establishment failed in attempts at societal controls but when individual efforts and cultures succeeded.[51]

Notes

1. For background on the Bartrams, see Ernest Earnest, *John and William Bartram: Botanists and Explorers* (Philadelphia: University of Pennsylvania Press, 1940); Edmund Berkeley, *The Life and Travels of John Bartram from Lake Ontario to the River St. John* (Tallahassee: University Presses of Florida, 1982); and Thomas P. Slaughter, *The Natures of John and William Bartram* (New York: Knopf, 1996).

2. Thomas Hallock, *From the Fallen Tree: Environmental Politics and the Roots of a National Pastoral, 1749–1826* (Chapel Hill: University of North Carolina Press, 2003), 151. For the significance of these acquisitions to British colonial America, see Colin G. Calloway, *The Scratch of a Pen: 1763 and the Transformation of North America* (New York: Oxford University Press, 2006).

3. John Bartram, "Diary of a Journey Through the Carolinas, Georgia, and Florida, from July 1, 1765, to April 10, 1766," edited and annotated by Francis Harper, *Transactions of the American Philosophical Society,* new series, vol. 33, part 1 (Philadelphia: APS, 1942), 1–3; Edward J. Cashin, *William Bartram and the American Revolution on the Southern Frontier* (Columbia: University of South Carolina Press, 2000), 2–3, 12.

4. Julie Anne Sweet, "The Thirteenth Colony in Perspective: Historian's Views on Early Georgia," *Georgia Historical Quarterly* 85 (Fall 2001): 435–460; Robert Shig Porter II, "The Noblest Offspring: Concerning the British Origins of the Eighteenth-Century Colony of Georgia" (Master's thesis, Armstrong Atlantic State University, 2005), 96–143; Milton L. Ready, "Philanthropy and the Origins of Georgia," in Harvey H. Jackson and Phinizy Spalding, eds., *Forty Years of Diversity: Essays on Colonial Georgia* (Athens: University of Georgia Press, 1984), 46–59; Arthur Dobbs, "A Scheme to Increase the Colonies and Commerce of Britain," Cholmondeley Houghton 84 Collection, 18–19, Ms. No. 68, University Libraries, Cambridge, England. The colony of Georgia also had connections to another alternative to the Enlightenment, the religious revivalism of the Great Awakening led by colonial Georgia minister George Whitefield and former Georgia minister John Wesley. Sweet, "The Thirteenth Colony," 448–450.

5. For particularly graphic discussions of the failures of the Georgia Trustees, see Sarah B. Gober Temple, *Georgia Journeys: Being an Account of the Lives of Georgia's Original Settlers and Many Other Early Settlers from the Founding of the Colony in 1732 until the Institution of Royal Government in 1754,* ed. Kenneth Coleman (Athens: University of Georgia Press, 1961), and Webb Garrison, *Oglethorpe's Folly: The Birth of Georgia* (Lakemont, Ga.: Copple House Books, 1981). For efforts to revive the colony's economy after the Trustees, see Edward J. Cashin, *Governor Henry Ellis and the Transformation of British North America* (Athens: University of Georgia Press, 1994), and Harold Davis, *The Fledgling Province: Social and Cultural Life in Colonial Georgia, 1733–1776* (Chapel Hill: University of North Carolina Press, 1976). For Augusta's early years as a center for the business of trade with the Indians, see Edward J. Cashin et al., *Colonial Georgia: "Key of the Indian Country"* (Macon, Ga.: Mercer University Press, 1986).

6. John Bartram, "Diary," 23–24. No references to John Bartram's Georgia journey appears in John Bartram, *The Correspondence of John Bartram, 1734–1777,* ed. Edmund Berkeley and Dorothy Smith Berkeley (Gainesville: University of Florida Press, 1992).

7. S. D. H——u to ?, January 14, 1779, in William L. Stone, trans., *Letters of*

Brunswick and Hessian Officers During the American Revolution (Albany, N.Y.: Joel Munsell's Sons, 1911), 236–237.

8. See John H. Goff, "The Buffalo in Georgia," *Georgia Review* 11 (January 1957): 19–29.

9. John Bartram, "Diary," 25–26. A frontier cowpens of that place and period usually included cabins, riflemen armed to hunt game, and even crops, surrounded by a broad meadow. Sometimes such a settlement would evolve into a town. John H. Logan, *A History of the Upper Country of South Carolina from the Earliest Period to the Close of the War of Independence,* 2 vols. (Charleston, S.C.: S. G. Courtney & Co., 1859), 1: 152–53. For more on a cowpens, see Richard D. Brooks, Mark D. Groover, and Samuel C. Smith, *Living on the Edge: The Archaeology of Cattle Raisers in the South Carolina Backcountry* (Columbia: University of South Carolina Press, 2000).

10. Hallock, *From the Fallen Tree,* 151.

11. John Bartram, "Diary," 28–29.

12. Alex M. Hitz, "The Earliest Settlements in Wilkes County," *Georgia Historical Quarterly* 40 (1956): 261–265.

13. Ibid., 261–263; Colonial Plat Book C (1748–1771), 43, Gar; Marion R. Hemperley, comp., *English Crown Grants in St. Paul Parish in Georgia, 1755–1775* (Atlanta: State Printers, 1974), 35; Robert S. Davis, "A Frontier for Pioneer Revolutionaries: John Dooly and the Beginnings of Popular Democracy in Original Wilkes County," *Georgia Historical Quarterly* 60 (Fall 2006): 321–322, 342, 347.

14. Cashin, *Governor Henry Ellis,* 62–63; Hitz, "The Earliest Settlements," 261.

15. Cashin, *William Bartram,* 22–37. For South Carolinians and the change in Georgia's economy, see David R. Chesnutt, *South Carolina's Expansion into Colonial Georgia, 1720–1765* (New York: Garland Publishing, 1989), and Alan Gallay, *Jonathan Bryan and the Southern Colonial Frontier: The Formation of a Plantation Elite* (Athens: University of Georgia Press, 1989), 84–108.

16. William Bartram, *The Travels of William Bartram: Naturalist's Edition,* ed. Francis Harper (New Haven, Conn.: Yale University Press, 1958), 138–140; George Fenwick Jones, *The Salzburger Saga* (Athens: University of Georgia Press, 1984), 120.

17. Robert S. Davis, "Letters from St. Paul Parish," *Richmond County History* 10 (Summer 1978): 19–35. Robert S. Davis, "A Georgia Loyalist's Perspective on the American Revolution: The Letters of Thomas Taylor," *Georgia Historical Quarterly* 81 (1997): 128.

18. William Mylne, *Travels in the Colonies in 1773–1775,* ed. Ted Ruddock (Athens: University of Georgia Press, 1990), 25–33.

19. For the history of the South Carolina Regulators, see Richard Maxwell Brown, *The South Carolina Regulators: The Story of an American Vigilante Movement* (Cambridge, Mass.: Harvard University Press, 1963).

20. Edward J. Cashin, "Sowing the Wind: Governor Wright and the Georgia

Backcountry on the Eve of the Revolution," in Jackson and Spalding, *Forty Years of Diversity*, 233–250. For the meanings of the word "Cracker," see Delma E. Presley, "The Crackers of Georgia," *Georgia Historical Quarterly* 60 (Summer 1976): 102–116.

21. Hallock, *From the Fallen Tree*, 2–3; Porter, "The Noblest Offspring," 105; Allen D. Candler, comp., *The Colonial Records of the State of Georgia*, 39 vols. (Atlanta, 1907–1941), 14: 524, 527–528, 545–546; Wright to Board of Trade, December 27, 1771, in Kenneth Coleman and Milton Ready, eds., *Colonial Records of the State of Georgia* (modern publication of the unpublished Candler volumes, Athens: University of Georgia Press, 1979), vol. 28, pt. ii: 379; Calloway, *The Scratch of a Pen*, 100–108.

22. Cashin, *Governor Henry Ellis*, 99–102; Wright to Board of Trade, December 27, 1771, in Coleman and Ready, *Colonial Records*, vol. 28, pt. ii: 378–379.

23. For the history of the Queensborough Township, see Loris D. Cofer, *Queensborough or the Irish Town and Its Citizens* (Louisville, Ga.: Author, 1977).

24. Stephen B. Weeks, *Southern Quakers and Slavery: A Study in Institutional History* (New York: Bergman, 1896), 180–181; minutes of the Cane Creek Monthly Meeting (1760–1900), 29–30, 32–33, 38–39, 47, Friends Historical Collection, Hege Library, Guilford College, Greensboro, N.C.; Mark H. Jones, "Herman Husband: Millenarian, Carolina Regulator, and Whiskey Rebel" (Ph.D. diss., Northern Illinois University, 1982), 84–88, 104–105, 107, 110, 116–118. For the history and the records of the Wrightsborough Township, see Robert S. Davis, comp., *Quaker Records in Georgia* (Augusta: Augusta Genealogical Society, 1986).

25. William Bartram, "Travels in Georgia and Florida, 1773–1774: A Report to Dr. John Fothergill," annotated by Francis Harper, *Transactions of the American Philosophical Society*, new series, vol. 33, part 2 (Philadelphia: APS, 1943), 139, hereafter cited as "Report to Fothergill" and *Travels*, ed. Harper, 23–24.

26. Owen Fendly, "George Galphin," in Kenneth Coleman and Charles Stephen Gurr, eds., *Dictionary of Georgia Biography*, 2 vols. (Athens: University of Georgia Press), 1: 335–337; Robert S. Davis, "George Galphin and the Creek Congress of 1777," *Proceedings and Papers of the Georgia Association of Historians 1982* (Atlanta: GAH, 1982), 14–15, 24–25 n. 10; Thomas Woodward, *Woodward's Reminiscences of the Creek, or Muscogee Indians* (Montgomery: Barrett & Wimbish, 1859), 91–92. For information on Galphin's descendants, see Theresa M. Hicks, *South Carolina Indians and Indian Traders* (Spartanburg, S.C.: Reprint Company, 1998), 107–16.

27. Bartram, *Travels*, ed. Harper, 196–198.

28. Hitz, "The Earliest Settlements," 265–273; Kathryn E. Holland Braund, *Deerskins & Duffels: The Creek Indian Trade with Anglo America, 1685–1815* (Lincoln: University of Nebraska Press, 1993), 54–55, 218.

29. Edward J. Cashin, *Lachlan McGillivray, Indian Trader* (Athens: University

of Georgia Press, 1992), 271–275; memorandum of Wright to the Earl of Hillsborough, December 12, 1771, in Coleman and Ready, *Colonial Records*, vol. 28, pt. ii: 356–358.

30. Bartram, *Travels*, ed. Harper, 23; Hallock, *From the Fallen Tree*, 165; Louis De Vorsey Jr., *The Indian Boundary in the Southern Colonies 1763–1775* (Chapel Hill: University of North Carolina Press, 1966), 175–80; William P. Cumming, *The Southeast in Early Maps* (3rd ed., Chapel Hill: University of North Carolina Press, 1968), 441.

31. Bartram, *Travels*, ed. Harper, 204.

32. De Vorsey, *The Indian Boundary*, 170–171; Bartram, "Report to Fothergill," 144.

33. Bartram, *Travels*, ed. Harper, 203–204; Cashin, *William Bartram*, 44.

34. Robert S. Davis, *The Wilkes County Papers, 1773–1833* (Easley, S.C.: Southern Historical Press, 1979), 1–21, 45–46; Grace G. Davidson, comp., *Early Records of Georgia: Wilkes County*, 2 vols. (Macon: Burke, 1933), 1: 2–29.

35. Peter W. Coldham, comp., *American Migrations* (Baltimore: Genealogical Publishing Company, 2000), 772.

36. Davis, *The Wilkes County Papers*, 25; Peter W. Coldham, comp., *American Loyalist Claims* (Washington, D.C.: National Genealogical Society, 1980), 515.

37. Davidson, *Early Records of Georgia*, 1:12, 18; Allen D. Candler, comp., *The Revolutionary Records of the State of Georgia*, 3 vols. (Atlanta: Franklin, 1908), 2: 117, 223, 225–226, 359.

38. Davis, *Quaker Records*, 177–182; Edward J. Cashin, *The King's Ranger: Thomas Brown and the American Revolution on the Southern Frontier* (Athens: University of Georgia Press, 1989), 17–19.

39. Davidson, *Early Records of Georgia*, 1: 15–16; Coldham, *American Migrations*, 767.

40. For Bartram's subsequent time in the South and the fate of the Ceded Lands, see Edward J. Cashin, *William Bartram and the American Revolution on the Southern Frontier* (Columbia: University of South Carolina Press, 2000).

41. Untitled story, *South Carolina and American General Gazette* (Charleston), September 27, 1780, p. 2, c. 3.

42. "Colonel Robert Gray's Observations on the War in Carolina," *South Carolina Historical and Genealogical Magazine* 11 (1910): 153; John Shy, *A People Numerous and Armed: Reflections on the Military Struggle for American Independence* (rev. ed., Ann Arbor: University of Michigan Press, 1990), 232; Robert M. Calhoon, *The Loyalist Perception and Other Essays* (Columbia: University of South Carolina Press, 1989), 11; Wallace Brown, *The Good Americans: The Loyalists in the American Revolution* (New York: William Morrow, 1969), 46. For more on the ethnic frontier settlements networked to support the British cause, see Robert S. Davis, "Lessons from Kettle Creek: Patriotism and Loyalism at Askance on the

Southern Frontier," *Journal of Backcountry Studies* 1, 1 (May 2006): n. p. (online journal): http://www.uncg.edu/~rmcalhoo/jbs/.

43. William P. Brandon, "The Galphin Claim," *Georgia Historical Quarterly* 15 (1931): 113–141; Davis, *The Wilkes County Papers*, 5–7, and "George Galphin and the Creek Congress," 13–24.

44. Coldham, *American Migrations*, 754, 762, 772–773, 787–788, 790–791; Candler, *Revolutionary Records*, 1: 371–397. For the records of confiscation of the Georgia Loyalist estates, see R. J. Taylor Jr. Foundation, *An Index to Georgia Colonial Conveyances and Confiscated Land Records, 1750–1804* (Atlanta: Author, 1981).

45. "Notice," *Augusta Chronicle and Gazette of the State of Georgia*, December 10, 1796, p. 1, c. 2.

46. Davis, "A Frontier for Pioneer Revolutionaries," 344, 347.

47. For a study of how the Bartrams and others saw America, see Hallock, *From the Fallen Tree*.

48. Heard Robertson, "The Second British Occupation of Augusta," *Georgia Historical Quarterly* 58 (1974): 432.

49. William Lee, *The True and Interesting Travels of William Lee* (York, England: T. & R. Hughes, 1818), 22. In 1767, Thomas Griffiths visited the backcountry South Carolina plantation of Andrew Williamson and wrote of Williamson's peaches as "enumerable" and having filled three thousand bushel baskets. This fruit, Griffiths continued, fed the poor of the backcountry and the hogs. William L. Anderson, "Cherokee Clay from Duché to Wedgwood: The Journal of Thomas Griffiths, 1767–1768," *North Carolina Historical Review* 63 (1986): 501.

50. Hitz, "The Earliest Settlements," 273–274; Frank Parker Hudson, comp., *A 1790 Census for Wilkes County, Georgia* (Spartanburg, S.C.: Reprint Company, 1988), 1. For accounts of life in the postwar settlement of Wilkes County, see the John Newton diaries (1781–1790), Hargrett Rare Books and Manuscripts Library, University of Georgia, Athens; Thomas Grant Reminiscences (1757–1828) and George Willis Journal (1784–1785), University of Virginia, Charlottesville; Jeremiah Evarts Diary (1822), Bureau of American Ethnology, Smithsonian Institution, Washington, D.C.; and Garrett Minor Papers (1764–1798), Library of Congress.

51. For more on such views, see Charles S. Maier, *Among Empires: American Ascendancy and Its Predecessors* (Cambridge, Mass.: Harvard University Press, 2006), and Robert V. Hine, *Community on the American Frontier: Separate but not Alone* (Norman: University of Oklahoma Press, 1980).

3
William Bartram's Gustatory Tour

Kathryn E. Holland Braund

In the introduction to *Travels,* William Bartram wrote that "the attention of a traveller, should be particularly turned, in the first place, to the various works of Nature."[1] Yet like all travelers, his first concern was frequently his daily bread. In fact, travelers frequently find the most memorable part of their trip to be the new cuisine they encounter along the way. And this was certainly true in Bartram's case. Bartram scholars have been very remiss by almost completely ignoring this basic facet of Bartram's daily life as a traveler. His writings, though often vague on ingredients and preparation techniques, are an incredibly valuable source for information about foodways across the eighteenth-century South, particularly those of the southeastern Indians. And, true to his purpose, Bartram showed great interest in exotic dishes based on both wild and cultivated "vegitable productions." Close attention to Bartram's plate reveals products of a landscape already changed by imported plants and animals—and by new settlers and slaves.[2]

Bartram began his travels with plenty of dinner invitations to the best houses in Charleston and Savannah, yet he rarely recorded what he ate there. Dr. Chalmers "received" him "with perfect politeness."[3] On the Georgia sea islands he "supped" with "genteel and polite ladies and gentlemen," but neglected to say what exactly he supped.[4] Later in his southern tour, while traveling from Charleston to Augusta, he found lodging and food at public houses and a ferry as well as private residences. The cuisine was neither novel—nor perhaps foul enough—to receive further note in his commentary, even if at one stop he did admit that he "refreshed [his] spirits with a draught of cooling liquor."[5]

In fact, Bartram failed to describe his meals with any detail at all until he reached the backcountry and the less-populous coastal regions of Georgia and East Florida. It was at the Georgia plantation of Donald McIntosh, whom he memorialized as "the venerable grey headed Caledonian," that Bartram discovered his talent as a food writer. McIntosh served Bartram venison, the staple meat of the backcountry—in this case, "excellent venison."[6] Bartram's culinary adventure was just beginning, and his observations on southern foodways provide a glimpse into the impact that native foods made on settlers' tables as well as the impact of imported foodstuffs on traditional Indian fare.

Venison, of course, was the most common meat of the backcountry, and wherever he went—to Indian villages, traders' stores, or even the plantations of leading Georgia citizens—venison was usually placed before him, no matter the time of day, from breakfast to supper. Bartram reports venison "stewed with bear's oil," venison steak, "bucanned" venison, "sodden venison," as well as broiled venison and venison broth. Bartram's use of cookery terms is sometimes unclear, as in the case of "sodden" venison, which implies that the venison was boiled, presumably producing a gravy, while "bucanned" venison was likely roasted or smoked on a rack or spits.[7]

In addition to venison, Bartram encountered wild turkey from the Broad River to the Mississippi River and most points in between, usually without comment as to its condition when it reached his plate.[8] The naturalist did report that the wild turkey was "nearly thrice" the "size and weight" of the domestic variety, usually weighing between twenty and thirty pounds, although he encountered one that tipped the scales at almost forty pounds.[9] Given his lack of elaboration on turkey dinners, it seems clear that venison was his favorite game meal. When he visited the great Alachua savanna (now modern Paynes Prairie near Gainesville, Florida) in 1774, Bartram was regaled with a meal of "venison, stewed with bear's oil, fresh corn cakes, milk, and homony."[10] The meal was chock full of southeastern Indian food staples, and it was a meal he would see repeatedly throughout his southern travels.

When on the trail, Bartram made do with foods he could hunt or collect, but he also carried cooking supplies and condiments in his pack. Bartram reveals little about his peripatetic pantry, but he did see fit to record that in Florida, just after the great alligator fight, he broiled the trout he caught and accompanied them with the rice he brought along and stewed it in his kettle. He seasoned his dinner with the "oil, pepper and salt" that he carried. Bartram's true sense of gastronomic genius is apparent, for he recognized the value of a handy, albeit nonnative Florida ingredient: the orange. Bartram wrote that he found "excellent oranges hanging in abundance over my head," which served as "a valuable substitute for vinegar."[11] By the next day, his "barbecued trout" remained in "tolerable good order, though the sultry heats of the day had injured them; yet by stewing them up afresh with the lively juice of Oranges, they served well enough for my supper." Bartram did concede that his constant alligator watch (and no doubt the odor of the day-old fish) left him with "little relish or appetite for my victuals."[12] As he traveled to the Cherokee mountains, his viaticum included cheese, dried beef tongue, and hard biscuits, providing the weary traveler "a frugal repast."[13]

Bartram clearly enjoyed life on the trail, with all of nature for his larder. When recalling the Alachua savanna, he mused, "How supremely blessed were our hours at this time! plenty of delicious and healthful food, our stomachs keen, with contented minds; under no control, but what reason and ordinate passions dictated, far removed from the seats of strife!"[14] But meal times were not always so peaceful. In addition to rainstorms, hurricane force winds, and stifling heat, Bartram frequently had to compete with others for his supper. His alligator fight is perhaps his most celebrated victory, but on occasion, Bartram lost a fish dinner to wolves, found himself competing with lynx for turkey, and had to resort to superior firepower to frighten bears from his camp.[15] And it sometimes happened that Bartram *was* dinner, as when he and his camping companions on Fort George's Sound were dismayed to find their after-dinner "repose . . . incompleat, from the stings of musquetoes." The "roaring of crocadiles, and the continual noise and restlessness of the sea fowl" roosting nearby contributed to the general unpleasantness of what had seemed an idyllic spot earlier in the day.[16]

As befitted a botanist, Bartram welcomed native plants onto his plate when he encountered them along the trail. North of Mobile, he encountered "a delusive green wavy plain" of water chinquapin (*Nelumbo lutea* [Willd.] Pers.), commonly known as the American lotus, majestically floating on the quiet waters of a lagoon of the Tombigbee River. Native to eastern North America, Bartram reported he had seen this aquatic plant from New Jersey to West Florida (see Figure 7.1). He informed readers that "the seed vessel when ripe, is a large truncated, dry, porous capsule, its plane or disk regularly perforated, each cell containing an oval osseous gland or nut, of the size of a filbert; when these are fully grown, before they become quite hard, they are sweet and pleasant eating, and taste like chesnuts." Bartram related that he "fed freely on them without any injury," but confided to his readers that he "found them laxative."[17] In Florida, he found bears "feeding on the fruit of the dwarf creeping Chamerops" (saw palmetto). Like the bears, Bartram thought that the date-shaped fruit was "delicious and nourishing food."[18] He was so taken with the "tallow nut" or wild lime (*Ximenia americana*) that he drew a sketch for his patron Dr. Fothergill and forwarded it to London.[19] The "Thorny evergreen shrub" produced a fruit that reminded Bartram of a "large yellow plumb, the pulp when ripe is of the cons[is]tance, looks & tastes like a custard having a little tartness." He declared it "the most agreable wil[d] fruit in the Itmous."[20] Bartram called it a tallow nut because his father had: it was among John Bartram's discoveries on his 1765 journey to East Florida. The name derived from the fact that the fruit's pit, or nut, had "the consistence and taste of the sweet Almond, but more oily and very much like hard tallow."[21]

Perhaps Bartram's greatest disappointment while traveling was his inability to identify and procure specimens of an unusual plant that he had "but a slight opportunity of observing," on the Mobile River. He first tasted the fruit of the plant at the Upper Creek town of Otassee, when Indian hunters returned home with clusters of the plants' fruit. According to Bartram, this unusual plant "has no stalk or stem above ground—The leaves spread regularly all round . . . in the centre is produced a kind of dense panicle or general receptacle of the Fruit—of the form & size of a Sugar Loaf, or the figure of an obtuse cone—a vast collection of plums or drupes of the size & figure of ordinary plums which are covered with a fibrous farinaceous pulpy coating of considerable thickness." The "delicious & nourishing" fruit reminded him of "manna in texture colour & taste, or of the consistence of moist brown sugar, with lumps or particles of loaf Sugar mixt with it." He recalled the food was "a little bitterish & stingy on the palate on first using it; but soon becomes familiar & desirable." The exotic sweet fruit, most likely Spanish bayonet (*Yucca aloifolia* L.), was, Bartram told his readers, "diligently sought after" by Indians.[22] Another wild plant Bartram encountered while traveling along the trade path from the Creek towns to Mobile was "a tall species of Silphium," sometimes called rosin weed. Bartram wrote that the "semi-pellucid drops" of resin produced when the flowers of the plant were broken off the stem had "a very agreeable fragrance and bitterish taste, somewhat like frankincense or turpentine, which is chewed by the Indians and traders, to cleanse their teeth and mouth, and sweeten their breath."[23]

Amazingly, Bartram did not report a meal of cabbage palm (*Sabal palmetto* Rein), today still considered a native Florida delicacy, despite its unappetizing name of swamp cabbage. He sighted the tree repeatedly in Florida and south Georgia, but never referred to the fact that Indians and settlers alike chopped down the trees to uncover the "heart."[24]

In addition to native plants, Bartram encountered transplanted animals and insects on his journey. All across Florida, Bartram found honey, produced by imported European honeybees from both well-maintained and feral colonies.[25] Like other travelers, when Bartram found a bee tree along his trail, he took advantage of the situation. When traveling with Charles McLatchy in the Alachua savanna, Bartram and his party "regaled" on the honey they harvested from a tree, then left a member of the party standing guard while they returned to McLatchy's store to procure a tub in which to collect their "sweet booty."[26] On at least one occasion, Bartram traded with Indians for a "fawn-skin of honey."[27] Besides its obvious use as a sweet treat and a condiment for breads, Bartram frequently encountered "honeyed water," which he reckoned "a very refreshing and agreeable liquor."[28] The "very cool and agreeable" beverage was offered to the thirsty traveler by both whites and Indians. Honeyed water became more potent in the hands of some hosts, who strengthened it with brandy.[29]

Like bees, cattle were also relatively new to the South, and Bartram noted the "chearing social lowings of domestic herds" along the Altamaha as well as elsewhere.[30] Bartram reported that dairy products—milk, butter, and cheese—were a "novelty in the maritime parts of Carolina and Georgia" but were often plentiful around the cowpens and range lands of the backcountry.[31] Bartram found the backcountry produced "very good cheese."[32] Near the Savannah River, Bartram quizzed a stockman on his operation and found that the man had fifteen hundred head of cattle, only forty of which were milk cows. Like other backcountry cattlemen, his main income came from the export of beef, while the milk, cheese, and butter he produced were consumed by his household, including the slaves who helped run his operation. As Bartram reported, the coastal South continued to rely on imports of cheese and butter from Europe and the northern colonies.[33] As these free-range operations spread, so did cattle keeping.

Deerskin traders were often responsible for the spread of cattle into the Creek and Cherokee towns, and Bartram was frequently offered dairy products and beef by such men when he visited their establishments. For example, among the Cherokee, the Indian wife of his English host served him "cream and strawberries." The breakfast that followed included "bucanned venison, hot corn cakes, excellent butter and cheese."[34] By Bartram's day, a number of Indians had also begun to keep cattle. The most famous Indian stockmen were in the Alachua savanna, led by Ahaye, better known to the British as Cowkeeper. The Seminole cattle had been imported by the Spanish and taken over by the Seminoles, who had waged almost continuous war against the Spanish and their mission Indians throughout the eighteenth century. Although they incorporated beef into their diets, most Indian cow keepers eschewed the collection of milk and production of dairy products, although at Cuscowilla, Bartram was treated to "a Kettle of boiled Milk & another kettle of boiled Corn, with dryed Venison & Bears meet, Honey & Water."[35] In fact, outside the Alachua savanna, most Indians were hostile to the introduction of cattle, and many noted the competition for food resources they presented to deer. As cattle moved into cane breaks and natural grasslands and congregated at salt licks, Indians observed the environmental degradation that resulted as well as the disappearance of deer, which were valued for their hides as well as their meat.[36]

During his travels, Bartram encountered many fruit trees and food crops that had been introduced to the New World by Europeans and were spreading across the South due to the efforts of settlers and Indian horticulturalists alike. While in Mobile, he found a plant he identified as "Discorea bulbifera," commonly known as air potato. He reported that this "curious plant" was noted for its "large kidney shaped root[s]" (actually aerial tubers), which when either "boiled or roasted" tasted like the cultivated yams and was "esteemed a pleasant wholesome food."[37] Not all imported food plants were so exotic. Near the Tensaw River, he was delighted by large fig trees, originally planted by French settlers. Bartram found the ripe figs "the shape of pears and as large, and of a dark bluish purple colour." He reckoned the plump fruits "a very acceptable desert after the heats and toil of the day."[38]

Bartram noted with approval the numerous orange groves across Florida and reveled in both the trees' fruit and the "fragrant bloom." Florida's groves, he reported to his readers, were capable of "gratifying the taste, the sight and the smell at the same instant."[39] According to Bartram, there were two "sorts or varieties" of oranges growing wild in Florida: the "large sour Orange & the Bitter-swett both of which the Indians are emoderately fond of, they sometimes roast the sower oranges in the ashes, which eats something like a roasted apple."[40] Groves of both sorts could be found on prime land, which the British settlers were then clearing for more profitable crops such as indigo, and in the wild. The origin of these oranges puzzled Bartram and he questioned "old spaniards at Augustine" who told him that they "were first bro't in by the spaniards & spread over the Country by the Ind[ians]." Their assertion failed to convince him, and Bartram's journal records his uncertainty as to whether the fruit was "exotick" or native.[41]

Likewise enjoyable were the "cool, exhilarating" nonnative watermelons he feasted on in late September near Mr. McLatchy's trading store in Florida.[42] Bartram also sampled southern pears, peaches, plums, and apples—all brought by European settlers. At the ruins of abandoned Fort Toulouse, Bartram noted the "two or three very large Apple trees, planted here by the French," were still "thriving."[43]

Peach trees he found in abundance throughout the southeast. He described those on the St. Marys River as "large, healthy and fruitful."[44] And, he noted that the Indians had "some extraordinary fine Peaches" in their towns.[45] Perhaps no imported fruit tree spread so rapidly to the Indian nations or was so well adapted to the southern climate. In his report to Dr. John Fothergill, Bartram provided one of the most comprehensive accounts of the manner that southeastern Indians used to preserve various native fruits, including maypops, persimmons, and pumpkins. Indian women applied the same techniques to the new arrivals. Bartram's account is instructive: "Peaches, they slice, take out the stone, & marsh up with parch't corn[,] beating all to dry flower, this they mix with other corn flower & bake loaves or Cakes or barbecue the Peaches whole on hyrdles over a gentle fire & smoke, in this manner they do Grapes, Patates, sliced Pumkins & all other such fruites & roots & keep in dry stores, & when they want to cook or make use of them[,] they stew them in a little water, they plump up & look & taste as when fresh. Green corn, Pe[ase] & Beans they use this way &c."[46]

Along East Florida's St. Johns River, Bartram encountered the papaya, a plant introduced by the Spanish from the Caribbean basin. It was, to Bartram, an "admirable tree . . . certainly the most beautiful of any vegetable production I know of; the towering Laurel Magnolia, and exalted Palm, indeed exceed it in grandeur and magnificience, but not in elegance, delicacy and gracefulness." The plant, which claimed his "whole attention" was both in flower and fruit, and some of the pear-shaped fruits were ripe. But the botanist, although he provided a detailed description, failed to note if the taste of the fruit was as delightful as its "charming appearance."[47]

Bartram helped himself to fruits indigenous to North America too—both in the wild and when offered by his Indian hosts. He missed the season for grapes, but did observe them ripening on large vines spreading over shrubs and "low trees" along trade paths in both the Cherokee and Creek country. These, the Indians pressed for "excellent juice" or dried "by first sweating them on hurdles over a gentle fire, and afterwards dry them on their bunches in the sun and air and store them up for provisions."[48] In West Florida, on Pearl Island, Bartram was impressed by the native plum, which had "large oblong crimson fruit in prodigious abundance; the fruit though of a most inticing appearance, are rather too tart, yet are agreeable eating, at sultry noon, in this burning climate, they afford a most delicious and reviving marmalade, when preserved in sugar, and make excellent tarts."[49] One of the most memorable scenes from *Travels* recounts Bartram's leisurely progress through the famous and "fragrant" wild strawberry patches in the Cherokee towns, where the "rich juice" from the native berries turned the hooves and ankles of Bartram's horse scarlet.[50]

Bartram also managed to find java in the Indian country, usually associated with British deerskin traders or Indians involved in the trade. At Apalachicola, a leading town of the Creek Indians on the Chattahoochee River, he was served one of his most memorable meals. He wrote in his "Observations," that he was served "excellent Coffee served up in China Dishes by Young Negro Slaves—We had plenty of excellent Sugar, Honey, Choice Warm Corn Cakes, Venison Steak, & Barbacued."[51] Bartram's Indian host procured his coffee, sugar, china cups, and slaves through trade with Georgians. And Bartram's testimony is valuable evidence of the spread of English cultural traditions and their adaptation by Indians.

The trade was not one-sided. In addition to the deerskins, which were the staples of the Anglo-Creek trade, Creeks and other tribes traded venison, medicinal roots and herbs, nuts, and corn to deerskin traders and settlers alike. By the time of Bartram's visit, the Seminole Indian trade with Cuba was well established, and Florida's Indians, traveling in huge canoes, regularly traded dried fish, honey, and bear's oil for Cuban coffee, sugar, and liquor.[52] Bear oil, rendered from slabs of fat by heating in large pots, was a highly prized condiment, as well as a cosmetic and lubricant for all southeastern Indians.[53] In season, fresh foods were eagerly accepted by deerskin traders, and Bartram's watermelon feast with Mr. McLatchy had been preceded by a commercial transaction, for the Indians brought a canoe load of the melons and oranges to McLatchy's store to exchange for imported manufactured goods.[54]

Along his way, Bartram encountered a variety of fresh and salt-water fishes, as well as oysters, crabs, and shrimp, but usually failed to comment on their taste, with the exception of clams from the Georgia coast, which were "large, their meat white, tender, and delicate."[55] The bowfin, which Bartram called "mud fish," yielded white, tender meat, but was aptly named and Bartram recalled it "tastes of mud, and is not much esteemed."[56] The "great black or blue bream," however, was "delicious."[57] Indeed, he considered bream (bass) "my favourite fish" and on one occasion, exchanged trout that he had caught "with the bob" for bream with a canoe load of passing Seminole fishermen.[58] While participating in the survey of the New Purchase cession along the Broad River, Bartram seemingly enjoyed observing the manner in which his Indian companion caught a fifteen-pound salmon trout "with a reed harpoon, pointed very sharp, barbed, and hardened by fire" more than he did the resultant dish, which failed to elicit recorded comment.[59]

Bartram's writing reveals that eighteenth-century southerners frequently combined sea fish and fowl, as happened on Talbot's Island, when Bartram's party caught "curlews, willets, snipes, sand birds and others: we had them dressed for supper and seasoned with excellent oysters, which lay in heaps in the water." The meal was spiced with a native capsicum, which grew "in abundance" and provided "a very good pepper" for the fishermen.[60]

But not all water fowl were so delectable. Bartram declared that the snake bird (a species of cormorant) was "scarcely to be eaten unless constrained by insufferable hunger."[61] Near the Alachua savanna, at a place Bartram dubbed "bird isle," Bartram's traveling companions beat young nestling of various species out of their roost with sticks. The squabs, which Bartram described as "almost a lump of fat," were variously prepared, with some roasted and others "made into a pilloe [pilau] with rice." Bartram ate with little "relish," as most of the varieties were "so excessively fishy in taste and smell" that they proved a disappointment to his palate.[62] Most every dish with rice was termed a pilau (pilaf) by southerners, an adaptation of an exotic dish from Turkey that usually included meat, rice, fruit, and spices. Where there was rice, every conceivable ingredient found its way into a pilau. Unlike squabs, Bartram found that raccoons produced "excellent meat" when prepared in a "pillo."[63] His Indian hosts used rice "for thickening their <u>soups, ragouts, pilaus</u> &c.—"[64]

Rice was a low-country staple, cultivated by both settlers and Florida's Indians. At the Georgia rice plantation of Benjamin Andrews, Bartram observed the manner in which most of the British colonists grew rice, using a flooded field method.[65] The Indians, Bartram reported, employed a different technique and planted "on hills on high dry ground in their Gardens—By this management a few grains in a Hill (the hills about four feet apart) spread every way incredibly, & seems more prolific than if cultivated in water . . . the heads or Panicles are larger & heavier & the grain is larger, firmer, or more farinaceous, much sweeter & more nourishing."[66]

Among the more exotic dishes served up to Bartram by various Florida hosts either in Indian towns or in camp on the trail were gar fish, soft-shelled turtles, savanna crane, manatee, and rattlesnake. Bartram's rattlesnake dinner occurred during his first Florida venture, at the 1765 Congress of Picolata, which he attended with his father, John Bartram. In his book, Bartram recalled killing the monstrous snake, which he reported was six feet long and "as thick as an ordinary mans leg." He dragged his catch back to camp, and East Florida governor James Grant had his cook prepare the snake in a variety of dishes. Bartram reported that Grant was fond of rattlesnake, but as for the naturalist, "I tasted of it but could not swallow it."[67] This was among the few things that Bartram did not swallow on his sojourn, for he found the meat of the gar fish, which was baked whole in hot embers, to be "white and tender" once the skin and scales were peeled away.[68] He thought the "large and fat" soft-shelled turtle served up for supper was "excellently well cooked."[69] And manatee flesh he counted "wholesome and pleasant food."[70] When hunters returned to his camp in the Alachua savanna with a crane, he opined that it "made excellent soup; nevertheless as long as I can get any other necessary food, I shall prefer their seraphic music in the ethereal skies, and my eyes and understanding gratified in observing their economy and social communities in the expansive green savannas of Florida."[71]

If he could not swallow snake, he did at least manage to gulp down a portion of tripe soup, served to him at a feast near Cuscowilla. His description of this "very singular dish" is worth recalling. He wrote, "it is made of the belly or paunch of the beef, not overcleansed of its contents, cut and minced pretty fine, and then made into a thin soup, seasoned well with salt and aromatic herbs; but the seasoning not quite strong enough to extinguish its original savour and scent. This dish is greatly esteemed by the Indians, but is, in my judgment, the lest agreeable they have amongst them."[72]

3.1. Great soft-shelled tortoise.
Bartram supplied two illustrations
of the great soft-shelled tortoise for
Travels (1791): this full figure as well
as a detail of the head. It is likely
that the model for the sketches later
appeared on his plate.

Fortunately, Bartram did find favor—and good flavor—in most of his Indian hosts' other offerings. At the same feast as the unfortunate tripe soup, Bartram was actually the special guest of the chief of the town, who slaughtered "some of his best steers . . . for a general feast for the whole town, in compliment of our arrival, and pacific negotiations."[73] These cattle were an introduced species, and usually at such feasts, Bartram was treated to more traditional fare, as at Talahasochte, where the White King prepared a feast of barbecued or broiled bear ribs. Bartram reported that a fully grown and fattened black bear, weighing from five to six hundred pounds, provided ample food for a village feast. Southeastern Indians—and their guests—found the tender flesh delectable.[74] At the White King's town, the bear ribs were served with hot corn bread and "honeyed water."[75]

On another occasion, the White King, his Seminole host, provided "a noble entertainment and repast" and bear ribs accompanied by "venison, varieties of fish, roasted turkeys (which they call the white man's dish), hot corn cakes, and a very agreeable, cooling sort of jelly, which they call conte: this is prepared from the root of the China briar."[76] In *Travels,* he described in detail the exacting preparation required for this "very nourishing and wholesome" food: "they chop the roots in pieces, which are afterwards well pounded in a wooden mortar, then being mixed with clean water, in a tray or trough, they strain it through baskets, the sediment, which settles to the bottom of the second vessel, is afterwards dried in the open air, and is then a very fine, reddish flour or meal." When this powder was mixed with "warm water and sweetened with honey, [it became] when cool . . . a beautiful, delicious jelly." Doubtless Bartram also enjoyed it when it was mixed with corn meal then "fried in fresh bear's oil" to produce "hot cakes" or "fritters."[77]

Coontie was a Florida specialty. Bartram also found favor with a more northerly delicacy: hickory nut milk, produced from the nuts of the shell bark hickory. He reported that he had "seen above a hundred bushels" of hickory nut belonging to just one family and recorded the process whereby the nuts were transformed into a true southern delicacy: "They pound them to pieces, and then cast them into boiling water, which, after passing through fine strainers, preserves the most oily part of the liquid: this they call by a name which signifies Hiccory milk; it is as sweet and rich as fresh cream, and is an ingredient in most of their cookery, especially homony and corn cakes."[78] He likewise found the maypop (passion fruit) had "an agreeable taste" and described how Indians pounded the dried pulp of the fruit to a dry flour and employed it as a thickening agent that produced "an agreeable whole[some] kind of jelly."[79]

Hickory was not the only tree that produced a valued nut. In Florida, the live oak produced an acorn that was "small, but sweet and agreeable" when roasted in coals. The practice reminded Bartram of roasting chestnuts. Oil extracted from the acorn was used to flavor a variety of dishes; Bartram mentioned rice and hominy in particular.[80] Nutmeats were widely eaten by the Indians both whole and after being pounded into a flour. In a report to Dr. Fothergill, Bartram reported that both the chestnuts and chinquapins were "used for common food by the Floridian[s]. they roast & boil them & make very good Bread of them."[81]

Bartram's observations on Indian foodways are exceedingly important, and Bartram provides a wealth of information on size and location of fields, usually planted in corn, squash, beans, peas, and potatoes, as well as information on horticultural practices.[82] In addition he offers firsthand observations on a variety of cultural practices associated with food production, preparation, and consumption.[83] Two are particularly important—one involving corn and the other the produce of the hunt.

Corn, the staple of southeastern Indian agriculture, formed the backbone of the native diet. Bartram described in detail the communal town fields in both his *Travels* and his "Observations" manuscript.[84] He also noted the ubiquitous corn cakes and hominy in the meals he enjoyed among the Indians. But Bartram's knowledge of the exact methods of preparation seemed to have been gleaned from conversations with his fellow male travelers, for his descriptions of the tedious and laborious process by which Indian women converted corn into meal and dried hominy are cursory at best. Not once in *Travels* does he mention the omnipresent wooden mortars and pestles employed by native women for this task, completely omitting them from his list of manufactures.[85] It is clear that Bartram spent his time among men, discussing manly pursuits such as trade, hunting, and war. In passing, while in Florida, he happened upon a group of young Seminole warriors whose dress and demeanor he described in detail, merely noting that "their Wenches [were] at some distance cooking."[86]

Even if he missed a visit to workplaces of Indian women, he did recognize that "the most favorite dish the Indians have amongst them is Corn thin Drink seasoned with hicory nut Oil."[87] In the manuscript version of his travels, Bartram wrote that the "thin drink" was "a cool thin hommony." Bartram was actually tasting sofkee, which seemingly stumped his powers of description, but was best remembered by him as "a sort of grewell made of Corn flower [corn meal] & hicory Nut Oil & water boild together."[88] Sofkee, the Creek name for a dish common to every southeastern Indian cuisine, was not only a staple, but a dish offered as hospitality to travelers. Among the Seminole, Bartram was treated to "thin drink," served from a bowl placed on a low table. He wrote: "in this bowl is a great wooden ladle; each person takes up in it as much as he pleases, and after drinking until satisfied, returns it again into the bowl, pushing the handle towards the person in the circle, and so it goes round."[89]

The same ceremony took place in conjunction with a "refreshing repast," provided by the headman of Watauga, a Cherokee town. In addition to the "sodden venison," already mentioned, Bartram was provided a "simple but healthy and liberal collation" consisting of "hot corn cakes, &c. with a pleasant cooling liquor made of hommony well boiled, mixed afterwards with milk; this is served up, either before or after eating, in a large bowl, with a very large spoon or ladle to sup it with."[90] Here again, Bartram was served traditional food in a traditional manner: all diners sharing not only the same serving vessel, but also the same spoon.

Equally interesting and of immense value to ethnohistorians are Bartram's careful descriptions of the chief's role in establishment and control of a public granary. In the historic period, the granary served as a repository for surplus in times of need and the source of provisions for the communal feasts such as Bartram enjoyed at a number of Indian towns. Anthropologists have pointed out that the practice of a communal granary is a clear remnant of chiefly prerogative associated with Mississippian redistributive economies in which the ruling elite controlled food surpluses.[91] In answer to questions posed by his friend Benjamin Smith Barton, Bartram explained the practice in historic times: "When the Fruits of their labours are ripe, and in fit order to gather in, they all on the same day repair to the plantation, each gathering the produce of his own proper lot, brings it to town & deposits it in <u>his own crib,</u> alotting a certain proportion for the <u>Publick Granary</u> which is called the <u>King's Crib</u> because its contents is at his disposal, tho' not his private property, but is to be considered the Tribute, or Free Contribution of the Citizens for the State, at the disposal of the King."[92]

Bartram witnessed an important feature of southeastern Indian ceremonial life when he attended a town feast as a guest of the White King of Talahasochte—a ritual feast to honor hunters and warriors. His published account differs from his journal entry, which was forwarded to Dr. John Fothergill in London shortly after the event. Taken together, the two accounts provide a very detailed portrait of the proceedings. The communal feast featured two staples of southeastern Indian diet: meat, provided by hunters, and corn, the product of women's labor. Bartram's party missed the preparations that preceded the departure of the town's hunting party, but they were present when the White King and his men approached the town and sent a messenger ahead with news that "three great fat bears" had been slain and that the town should begin preparations for the feast.[93] The hunters also were "loaded with Venson" and honey.[94] As the White King and the other leading men and warriors of the town gathered in the town square, where the "royal standard" was displayed, a drum beat, according to Bartram, "to give notice to the town of the royal feast."[95] The White King, as host, sent a messenger to invite Bartram's party, and Bartram explained to Fothergill that "they never eat the Ribs when out but bring them to the Town, where they make a feast in the square to the Warriors & hunters."[96] With this, the "ribs and the choice pieces" of the "well barbecued" bears were "brought to the banqueting house in the square," together with hot corn bread and honeyed water.[97] In his report, Bartram recorded the method of service: "the barbecued Ribs were served up in large Platters or wooden boles in One of the Chief houses of the Square[.] We had Kettles of honey & water, with a great wooden family Spoon in each Kettle, every one in turn took a sup or quaff, discoursing of cheerfull subjects as he liked[,] as hunting adventure, jokeing, News of love, intreagues &c., The Youth and Young fellows dancing[,] singing & wrestling about the Fire."[98]

When the chief and other men and their white visitors were finished, the "chief priest, attended by slaves, came with baskets and carried off the remainder of the victuals &c. which was distributed amongst the families of the town."[99] With that, the men of the town and their guests (all male) partook of tobacco and black drink or cassine, in a highly ritualized manner. In his report to Fothergill, Bartram indicates that the "remains of the victuals" were not removed until after the men had smoked and once again "returned to the feast,

& after taking another whet at the Bear ribs."[100] The affair culminated with the participation of all members of the town, "the young of both sexes . . . as well as the old and middle aged" in an all-night dance.[101]

The feast, which Bartram seems to have regarded as a "frolic" for the benefit of the visitors to the town, was actually a highly stylized ritual celebration that highlighted and celebrated the gendered divisions of labor and the relative contributions of men (meat and honey) and women (corn) to the subsistence of the town. In this case, the feast celebrated the male role as hunter and provider and evidence indicates such feasts and dances were designed to ensure continued success at the hunt.[102] The major southeastern Indian ceremony, the annual Busk (*póskita* in Muskogee) or Green Corn Dance, was of a similar nature and represented the importance of corn to Indian life. Although Bartram describes the Busk in limited detail, he did not personally attend one.[103] Far from being unique to the people of Talahasochte, such harvest feasts were widespread throughout the Southeast and continue to our own time.[104]

Many of Bartram's meals—as at Talahasochte—were preceded or followed by the black drink ceremony. The drink or tea, offered in highly ritual fashion to the men of the town and visitors, was brewed from the leaves of yaupon or cassine (*Ilex vomitoria* Ait.). The plant was carefully cultivated and ceremonially harvested and prepared by spiritual leaders Bartram mistook for "waiters." The hot, frothy beverage was loaded with caffeine, and Indian men frequently and voluntarily regurgitated the beverage on occasion. Bartram failed to faithfully report this aspect of the black drink ceremony, but he did note in his "Observations" that the "infusion is perhaps the most active & powerful Diuretick of any vegetable yet known." He noted that the plant was "celebrated, indeed venerated by the Creeks, and all the Southern maritime nations of Indians."[105]

In reading Bartram's works, it becomes clear that his musings about the foods he encountered during his travels are not only interesting, but basic to his work, providing, as they do, one of the most valuable sources for the study of Indian and early southern foodways. Bartram's meals reveal his travels took him to farms as well as forests; to fields cultivated expertly by Indian horticulturalists and increasingly claimed and put to cultivation by settlers. And they testify that the landscape he visited was far from "pristine," but had already been changed by myriad nonnative plants, animals, and peoples. His reports of imported plants and animals and the use of native products by settlers testify to the power of the Columbian exchange broadly construed to include not simply biological exchange between the old and new worlds, but associated cultural practices. More important, the careful Bartram reader cannot help but believe that it was the quality of the food and hospitality of his various southern hosts that sustained Bartram during his arduous journey, and inspired him to immortalize his adventure and recall, with such fondness, the days he spent in the South.

Notes

1. William Bartram, *The Travels of William Bartram,* Naturalists's Edition, ed. Francis Harper (New Haven, Conn.: Yale University Press, 1958), li, hereafter referred to as Bartram, *Travels,* ed. Harper.

2. William Bartram, *William Bartram on the Southeastern Indians,* ed. Gregory A. Waselkov and Kathryn E. Holland Braund (Lincoln: University of Nebraska Press, 1995), 236.

3. Bartram, *Travels,* ed. Harper, 2. For an extended discussion of domestic hospitality: "the offering of food, drink, lodging and entertainment to unknown and familiar persons of varying status," see Cynthia A. Kierner, "Hospitality, Sociability, and Gender in the Southern Colonies," *Journal of Southern History* 62 (August 1996): 449–480.

4. Bartram, *Travels,* ed. Harper, 3.

5. Ibid., 196.

6. Ibid., 8. The McIntosh plantation was on the South Newport River. Edward J. Cashin, *William Bartram and the American Revolution on the Southern Frontier* (Columbia: University of South Carolina Press, 2000), 34–35.

7. Bartram, *Travels,* ed. Harper, 29, 39, 119 (first quotation), 221 (second quotation), 222 (third quotation). The venison in broth and broiled venison were reported to Dr. Fothergill. See William Bartram, "Travels in Georgia and Florida, 1773–74: A Report to Dr. John Fothergill," edited and annotated by Francis Harper, *Transactions of the American Philosophical Society,* new series, vol. 33, part 2 (Philadelphia: American Philosophical Society, 1943), 157, hereafter cited as Bartram, "Report to Fothergill."

8. Bartram, *Travels,* ed. Harper, 14, 29, 70, 71, 127, 168.

9. Ibid., 9. The turkey is native to North America. The bird was first introduced to Europe by the Spanish and the domesticated breed developed from these birds was then reintroduced to North America. Bartram refers to the domesticated turkey as "European" turkey. Generally, the North American wild turkey (*Meleagris gallopavo* L.) is divided into a number of subspecies and Bartram was describing the eastern wild turkey (*Meleagris gallopavo americana* Bartram or *Meleagris gallopavo silvestris* Vieillot). He also spotted the Florida wild turkey (*Meleagris gallopavo osceola* Scott) during his sojourn along the St. Johns River, at Lake George, in Alachua and at Talahasochte. For a full examination of the subject, see A. W. Schorger, *The Wild Turkey: Its History and Domestication* (Norman: University of

Oklahoma Press, 1966), and Andrew F. Smith, *The Turkey: An American Story* (Urbana: University of Illinois Press, 2006). See Bartram, *Travels*, ed. Harper, 654–655 for more details on Bartram's turkey sightings.

10. Bartram, *Travels*, ed. Harper, 119.

11. Ibid., 79.

12. Ibid., 85.

13. Ibid., 217–218, 228 (quotation on 217).

14. Ibid., 71. Bartram was writing in early 1774. The strife to which he referred began with a large cession of land to Georgia by the Creek and Cherokee Indians. The cession, made under duress in order to eradicate the Indian trade debt, had sparked an attack by a group of Creek warriors on new settlements along the Georgia frontier. Other attacks, perhaps unrelated, had taken place in Florida. Although the Creek leadership sought to mend the breech, tensions were still high as Bartram set off for Florida. For a fuller account of events surrounding Bartram's travels, see Cashin, *William Bartram and the American Revolution.*

15. Bartram, *Travels*, ed. Harper, 70, 79, 101, 157.

16. Ibid., 46. On this occasion, identified as present Nassau Sound, Bartram had feasted on sea fowl, served with oysters and seasoned with native pepper.

17. Ibid., 259. Bartram identified the plant only as "Nymphaea Nilumbo," which Francis Harper correctly identified as water chinquapin, see ibid., 576.

18. Bartram recorded the fruit "is of the form and size of dates, and is delicious and nourishing food." Ibid., lvii. The saw palmetto is more properly identified as *Serenoa repens* [Bart.] Small.

19. Bartram's color portrait portrayed the flowers as well as the ripe fruit, with a morning glory vine twining around the stem. The original is in the British Museum.

20. Bartram, "Report to Fothergill," 170.

21. Bartram, *Travels*, ed. Harper, 73.

22. Bartram, *William Bartram on the Southeastern Indians*, ed. Waselkov and Braund, 166 and 277–78. The identification of this plant is problematic. Bartram did observe Spanish bayonet or Spanish dagger, which he called "Palmettto royal (Yucca gloriosa) or Adam's needle," near Nassau Sound, Florida. See Bartram, *Travels*, ed. Harper, 47.

23. Bartram, *Travels*, ed. Harper, 252–253. Bartram provides an expansive description of "Silphium," but to date, the exact species has not been conclusively identified by botanists. Francis Harper thought it might be *S terebinthinaceum* Jacq. var. *pinnatifidum* (Ell.) Gray. See Bartram, *Travels*, ed. Harper, 626. Perhaps it was *Silphium perfoliatum* L., which is found in Alabama.

24. See Bartram, *Travels*, ed. Harper, 74, for a description of the tree. See Ginger M. Allen, Michael D. Bond, and Martin B. Main, "50 Common Plants

Important in Florida's Ethnobotanical History," Circular 1439, Wildlife Ecology and Conservation Department, Florida Cooperative Extension Service, Institute of Food and Agricultural Sciences, University of Florida, 2002.

25. For example, Bartram counted "fifty or sixty" healthy hives along an avenue of live oaks and palms on St. Simons Island. Bartram, *Travels,* ed. Harper, 39. Elsewhere, he noted that the hollow knees of cypress trees make excellent natural hives. Ibid., 59.

26. Ibid., 193.

27. Ibid., 154.

28. Ibid., 148–149 (first quotation, 149), 39 (second quotation).

29. Ibid., 39, 119 (quotation), 149.

30. Ibid., 32.

31. Ibid., 13 (quotation), 193.

32. Ibid., 13.

33. Ibid., 196. The man had forty cows penned in a two- to three-acre fenced enclosure or cowpen.

34. Ibid., 221.

35. Ibid., 117–119, 121, 132. Bartram, "Report to Fothergill," 147 (quotation).

36. For Bartram's observations on cattle's adaptation to the southern environment, see Bartram, *Travels,* ed. Harper, 14, 26, 38, 43, 56, 238, 263.

37. Ibid., 277. *Dioscorea bulbifera* is regarded as a non-native invasive vine today, introduced from West Africa. Francis Harper identified this plant as the wild yam root (*Dioscorea* sp.), distinct from the Asiatic plant. However, its place in a Mobile garden—and Bartram's failure to mention it elsewhere—suggests it was an introduced variety.

38. Ibid., 258.

39. Ibid., 127.

40. Bartram, "Report to Fothergill," 170.

41. Ibid., 170. Like Bartram, later writer John Lee Williams believed that "Seville, or Bitter Sweets, are common forest trees, indiginous to the eastern and southern districts." See *The Territory of Florida: or Sketches of the Topography, Civil and Natural History, of the Country, the Climate, and the Indian Tribes from the First Discovery to the Present Time* (New York: A. T. Goodrich, 1837), 113. Yet the bitter orange (*Citrus aurantium*), like the sweet orange (*Citrus sinensis*), is a native of Asia.

42. Bartram, *Travels,* ed. Harper, 192.

43. Ibid., 282.

44. Ibid., 16.

45. Bartram, "Report to Fothergill," 142.

46. Bartram, *William Bartram on the Southeastern Indians,* ed. Waselkov and

Braund, 237. Bartram's full account of "Vegitable productions which the Florideans use for food" is found on 236–239. His comments regarding food preservation and preparation techniques are applicable to most southeastern Indian tribes.

47. Bartram, *Travels*, ed. Harper, 83. The *Carica papaya* L. Perhaps he did not taste it. In his journal to Dr. Fothergill, he wrote merely that the "Floridians eat this fruite when ripe." Bartram, *William Bartram on the Southeastern Indians*, ed. Waselkov and Braund, 238.

48. Bartram, *Travels*, ed. Harper, 208 (first and second quotation), 254 (third quotation). Francis Harper identified these low-growing vines as fox grapes (V. *labrusca* L). Bartram, *Travels*, ed. Harper, 521. In his report to Fothergill, he also reported that grapes were "barbecue[d] in bunches." See Bartram, *William Bartram on the Southeastern Indians*, ed. Waselkov and Braund, 236. The material is taken from Bartram, "Report to Fothergill," 169–170.

49. Bartram, *Travels*, ed. Harper, 268 (quotation). According to Francis Harper, Bartram's Pearl Island was not the island now known by that name, but was most likely Prevost Island. See Harper commentary, ibid., 407–408.

50. Ibid., 219.

51. Bartram, *William Bartram on the Southeastern Indians*, ed. Waselkov and Braund, 156. The coffee was likewise "excellent" among the Cherokee. Bartram, *Travels*, ed. Harper, 221.

52. Bartram, *Travels*, ed. Harper, 143.

53. Bartram, *William Bartram on the Southeastern Indians*, ed. Waselkov and Braund, 120, 151, 271. For information on southeastern Indian trade, see Kathryn E. Holland Braund, *Deerskins and Duffels: Creek Indian Trade with Anglo-America, 1685–1815* (Lincoln: University of Nebraska Press, 1993).

54. Bartram, *Travels*, ed. Harper, 192.

55. Ibid., 44. See also 168.

56. Ibid., 111. This is the bowfin (*Amia calva* L.); 570.

57. Ibid., 111–112. Harper identifies the fish as the copper-nosed bream (*Lepomis macrochirus purpurescens* Cope); 456.

58. Ibid., 144. Bartram fully describes fishing for trout with a bob in *Travels*. See ibid., 69–70.

59. Ibid., 29. In his report to Dr. Fothergill, Bartram recorded that the trout was almost two feet long. Bartram, "Report to Fothergill," 144.

60. Bartram, *Travels*, ed. Harper, 46; Harper identified the pepper as C. frutescens L. var. and cited an 1879 published report that noted the presence of the shrub in the location Bartram had found it. Ibid., 464. Red or chile pepper was originally domesticated in the Caribbean and widely distributed in the tropics, most likely by birds, who are attracted to the red fruit. Various wild peppers are commonly known as bird pepper. Paul W. Bosland and E. J. Votana, *Peppers: Vegetable and*

Spice Capsicums, Crop Production Science in Horticulture, #12 (New York: CABI Publishing, 2000), 17–18.

61. Bartram, *Travels,* ed. Harper, 85.

62. Ibid., 157. Francis Harper has identified "bird isle" as Watermelon Pond, Alachua County, Florida, and further noted that in his list of birds found there, Bartram "furnishes here an interesting illustration of his lack of uniformity in nomenclature." Most of the birds Bartram describes are herons, and appear with alternate names on his bird list. See ibid., 375. These "various tribes of water fowl" mentioned were "ardea alba, ar. violacea, ar. cerulea, ar. stellaris crestata, ar. stellaris maxima, ar. virescens, colymbus, tantalus, mergus and others." Francis Harper variously (and in some cases tentatively) identifies these as the American egret (*casmerodius albus egretta* [Gmelio]), yellow-crowned night heron (*Nyctanassa violacea violacea* [L.]), little blue heron (*Florida caerulea caerulea* [L.]), Ward's heron (*Ardea herodias wardi* Ridgway), the eastern green heron (*Butorides virescens virescens* [L.]), Florida water-turkey (*Anhinga anhinga colubrina* [Bartram]), wood ibis (*Mycteria americana* L.) or white ibis (*Eudocimus albus* [L.]), and hooded merganser (*Lophodytes cucullatus* [L.]). See ibid., 442–443, 478, 642, 563.

63. Bartram, *Travels,* ed. Harper, 41.

64. Bartram, *William Bartram on the Southeastern Indians,* ed. Waselkov and Braund, 165.

65. Bartram, *Travels,* ed. Harper, 7.

66. Bartram, *William Bartram on the Southeastern Indians,* ed. Waselkov and Braund, 165.

67. Bartram, *Travels,* ed. Harper, 170.

68. Ibid., 111.

69. Ibid., 114. The turtles (called tortoises by Bartram) weighed between twenty and forty pounds, and Bartram reported that he and his party were only able to consume one-half the carcass. He noted, perhaps from personal experience, that "if eaten to excess," the dish was "apt to purge people not accustomed to it."

70. Ibid., 146.

71. Ibid., 140.

72. Ibid., 122.

73. Ibid., 121.

74. Ibid., 232. Creeks rendered a clear and tasty oil from bear fat. They managed this by separating the fat from the lean meat and cooking the fat in earthen pots until the oil was extracted. Bear oil was stored in either pots or gourds and was not only used as a cooking oil, but also as a favorite condiment and was also used for cosmetic purposes, including anointing the hair and skin.

75. Ibid., 148–149.

76. Ibid., 152. Bartram provided the following botanical identification: "(Smilax

pseudo China; Smilax aspera, fructu nigro, radice nodosa, magna, laevi, farinacea. Sloan, tom 1. p. 31. t. 143. f. 1. habit. Jamaica, Virginia, Carolina and Florida)." Francis Harper noted the plant was "apparently either *Smilax pseudo-china* L. or *S. bona-nox* L." Ibid., 480.

77. Ibid., 152. Bartram's China briar is *Smilax bona-nox* L. Bartram also described the preparation of coontie in his "Observations." See Bartram, *William Bartram on the Southeastern Indians,* ed. Waselkov and Braund, 165–166. In the nineteenth century, when the Seminoles were forced into southern Florida out of range of the saw greenbrier or China briar (*Smilax bona-nox* L.), they turned to another plant, a cycad, also known as coontie (*Zamia floridana* A. DC). For more on coonti, see John R. Swanton, "Coontie," *American Anthropologist,* New Series 15 (January–March 1913): 141–142 and Harold D. Cardwell Sr., "Coontie Root: The Dangerous Blessing," *Florida Anthropologist* 40 (1987): 333–335.

78. Bartram, *Travels,* ed. Harper, 25. See also Bartram, *William Bartram on the Southeastern Indians,* ed. Waselkov and Braund, 238.

79. Bartram, *William Bartram on the Southeastern Indians,* ed. Waselkov and Braund, 236.

80. Bartram, *Travels,* ed. Harper, 55. See also Bartram, *William Bartram on the Southeastern Indians,* ed. Waselkov and Braund, 238 n. 27.

81. *William Bartram on the Southeastern Indians,* ed. Waselkov and Braund, 238 n. 27.

82. Bartram, *Travels,* ed. Harper, 193, 221, 325.

83. Bartram frequently commented on the practice of taking "black drink," which was more properly a ceremonial beverage rather than a food. He also noted many vegetable and herbal medicinal plants, also omitted from consideration here.

84. For references to town plantations and methods of planting, see Bartram, *William Bartram on the Southeastern Indians,* ed. Waselkov and Braund, 158–159; Bartram, *Travels,* ed. Harper, 325–326.

85. His description of manufactures is woefully inadequate, and he noted he found "scarcely any thing worth observation." Bartram, *Travels,* ed. Harper, 326. He does mention wooden mortars twice in reference to food preparation in his "Observations" and in his manuscript report to Fothergill. See Bartram, *William Bartram on the Southeastern Indians,* ed. Waselkov and Braund, 166, 236–238. For a more complete examination of corn as food, see Muriel H. Wright, "American Indian Corn Dishes," *Chronicles of Oklahoma* 36 (1958): 155–166.

86. Bartram, "Report to Fothergill," 160.

87. Bartram, *William Bartram on the Southeastern Indians,* ed. Waselkov and Braund, 238.

88. Ibid., 243 n. 46.

89. Bartram, *Travels,* ed. Harper, 118.

90. Ibid., 222.

91. See Bartram, *Travels,* ed. Harper, 148–149, for the White King's bear feast. For a fuller examination of feasts in southeastern society, see Vernon J. Knight, "Feasting and the Emergence of Platform Mound Ceremonialism in Eastern North America," in *Feasts: Archaeological and Ethnographic Perspectives on Food, Politics, and Power,* ed. Michael Dietler and Brian Hayden, 311–33 (Washington, D.C.: Smithsonian Institution Press, 2001).

92. Bartram, *William Bartram on the Southeastern Indians,* ed. Waselkov and Braund, 159.

93. Bartram, *Travels,* ed. Harper, 149.

94. Bartram, "Report to Fothergill," 157. The account sent to Fothergill is also included in Bartram, *William Bartram on the Southeastern Indians,* ed. Waselkov and Braund, 246 n. 68.

95. Bartram, *Travels,* ed. Harper, 149.

96. Bartram, "Report to Fothergill," 157.

97. Bartram, *Travels,* ed. Harper, 149.

98. Bartram, "Report to Fothergill," 158.

99. Bartram, *Travels,* ed. Harper, 149.

100. Bartram, "Report to Fothergill," 158.

101. Bartram, *Travels,* ed. Harper, 149.

102. See Louis Capron, "Notes on the Hunting Dance of the Cow Creek Seminole," *Florida Anthropologist* 9 (1956): 67.

103. For Bartram's observations on the Busk, see Bartram, *William Bartram on the Southeastern Indians,* ed. Waselkov and Braund, 124–125, 149.

104. Bartram, *Travels,* ed. Harper, 148–149. The Seminole continued to celebrate their hunting dance long after Bartram's sojourn: see Louis Capron, "Notes on the Hunting Dance of the Cow Creek Seminole," *Florida Anthropologist* 9 (1956): 67–78. More recently, Jason Baird Jackson, *Yuchi Ceremonial Life: Performance, Meaning, and Tradition in a Contemporary American Indian Community* (Lincoln: University of Nebraska Press, 2003), has explored the similarity of the Seminole hunting dance to other southeastern Indian ceremonies; see 260–261.

105. Bartram, *Bartram on the Southeastern Indians,* ed. Waselkov and Braund, 147 (first and second quotations), 82 (third quotation). For yaupon groves among the Cherokee, see 82. For Bartram's description of the preparation of the tea and drink ceremony at the Creek town of Autosse, see ibid., 102–104; see also 147.

4
The Two Williams

Science and Connections in West Florida

Robert J. Malone

Bartram's journey through West Florida differed in several ways from his travels in East Florida, Georgia, and the Carolinas. He found no Choctaw or Chickasaw counterparts to the relationships formed with Creeks and Cherokee in the eastern colonies, relying primarily on the hospitality of white settlers and the labor of slaves.[1] Many of the colonial settlements he visited were either new or on the fringe of ruin, few of them possessing the stability of a Charles Town, Augusta, or St. Augustine, and their inhabitants struggled to survive in this area beyond the edge of empire. One of these settlers, identified by Bartram simply as a gentleman from New Richmond (Baton Rouge), had settled in West Florida in 1774, the year before Bartram's visit. This friend of Bartram's, who was most likely William Dunbar (ca. 1749–1810), had received a superior education in the sciences, including advanced astronomical training in London. He would assist Bartram through a combination of intellect and hospitality unmatched in the *Travels*. Bartram's visit with Dunbar, and the circumstances surrounding the encounter, cast light on the whole of the *Travels*, providing a novel context for Bartram's narrative, and demonstrating the challenges in examining the extent of scientific networks in West Florida. Because Bartram never names the gentleman from New Richmond, he left us scant evidence that Dunbar is indeed that person. The fact that there are other gentlemen who could have served as Bartram's host provides clues to the rapid ascent of science in West Florida.

William Bartram's emphasis on the Carolinas, Georgia, and East Florida has led historians to focus on these sections, and rightfully so. Bartram's *Travels*, for example, arguably the most powerful passages, immortalize the flora, fauna, and people of these regions. Indeed, the first 375 pages of his 481-page opus dwell on these eastern colonies. When he at last announces in the summer of 1775 that a "company of adventurers" will take him to West Florida for a "long and hazardous" journey, it appears almost as an afterthought.[2] Of course, had not illness forced him to curtail his trip, the scope of his narrative would have grown considerably, but as it turned out, even his abbreviated narrative of the lower Mississippi River Valley provides a glimpse of a nascent scientific network forming west of the Apalachicola and Chattahoochee rivers, the boundary between East and West Florida. Bartram spent little time in West Florida but benefited from the hospitality and training of unnamed naturalists. These naturalists, many of them Scottish immigrants, would eventually form a network from Philadelphia to the southern latitudes of the Mississippi River.

West Florida

As Bartram prepared to visit the interior of North America, readers of the *Travels* sense his excitement over the westward phase of his journey, a journey that would take him into unfamiliar lands. This was country that he and his father had been unable to visit during their trip together ten years earlier, and Bartram had been looking forward to exploring West Florida for many years, the colony playing an important part in his master plan to discover "rare and useful productions of nature."[3] In fact, the trip west to the Mississippi River would fulfill a dream of his father's: "Oh! if I could but spend six months on the Ohio, Mississippi, and Florida, in health," the elder Bartram had exclaimed, "I believe I could find more curiosities than the English, French and Spaniards have done in six score of years."[4] John Bartram probably guessed correctly what he could have discovered in this verdant country, but in the 1760s the area still lacked the stability needed for exploration—at least the stability required by an aging Quaker botanist. By 1775, British dominance provided enough security to allow the son to explore where the father could not.

What awaited Bartram in West Florida? Land along the Mississippi River boasted some of the richest loess in the world, its deep soil able to nurture an astonishing variety of plants. But in the 1770s, North American boundaries remained ill defined, even though Spanish, French, and English surveyors and cartographers had produced numerous maps throughout the century. Many of these charts, based on second-hand information, reflected national desires more than accurate coordinates. With British domination following the French-Indian War, scores of British surveyors, sometimes with Bartram in tow, attempted to furnish the empire with first-hand knowledge of the southern colonies.

Spanish control of New Orleans, an increasingly important entrepôt for North America, became one of the motivating factors behind Britain's desire to learn more about West Florida's contours. The British became obsessed

with finding a route around New Orleans and into the Gulf of Mexico, trying everything from clearing log-choked riverbeds to building roads. Underlying this obsession was the British hope that it could colonize the lower Mississippi River Valley, although France and Spain had largely failed to sustain
colonies for over two hundred years. Dunbar personified this optimism as he
made his way to West Florida, purchased slaves and land, and started a plantation in 1774.

West Florida, created by royal proclamation, was "bounded to the South-
ward by the Gulph of Mexico, including all islands within six leagues of the
coast, the river Appalachicola to Lake Pontchartrain" with a "line drawn due
East from the part of the Mississippi, which lies in the 31st degree of North lati-
tude, to the river Appalachicola, or the Catahouchee." Negotiators used John
Mitchell's "A Map of the British and French Dominions in North America"
(1755), to set the northern boundary. To their dismay, the British soon realized
that the boundary line fell below the fertile lands of Natchez and other important communities. Subsequently, in 1764, officials quietly moved the boundary north to where the Yazoo River spills into the Mississippi just north of
present-day Vicksburg.[5]

The British redrew the boundary line for good reason. The tangle of trees
and cane brush in the lower Mississippi River Valley sprang from soil that settlers described as a thick, black mold, one and a half to three feet deep. Many
varieties of trees flourished here: oaks, especially the massive and sprawling
live oak, cypress, black walnut, hickory, white ash, cherry, plum, and poplar,
along with a wide variety of shrubs and medicinal roots. Settlers grew indigo,
rice, tobacco, Indian corn, and some wheat while raising livestock of black
cattle, horses, mules, hogs, sheep, and poultry. The agricultural potential of the
area seemed enormous.[6]

Promoters of this land believed that this black mold could produce "Wine,
Oyle, Wheat, Barley, Rice, Rie, Buckwheat, Oates, Hemp, flax, Cotton, Indigo, Hopps, & Tobacco."[7] The Board of Trade moved quickly to encourage
settlements, instructing the new governor of West Florida, George Johnstone,
to allow "one hundred Acres of Land be granted to every Person being Master
or Mistress of a Family, for himself or herself, and fifty Acres for every white
or black Man, Woman or Child, of which such Person's Family shall consist."
To ensure that the grants received wide notice, the board published announce-
ments in the *London Gazette* as early as November 14, 1763.[8]

Unfortunately, as the misplaced northern boundary illustrates, settlers had
to rely on faulty maps, setting up points of conflict with Native Americans that
would echo throughout the century. For example, a 1772 map by one of the better mapmakers, Bernard Romans (ca. 1720–ca. 1784), which covered much of
West Florida, misplaced and misnamed a number of streams and native vil-

lages. Since his accuracy in areas he personally surveyed was impeccable, his mistakes likely arose from a reliance on hearsay, a necessary expedient when surveying wide and dangerous areas.[9] British colonial administrators, fully aware of the need for a cartographer to view the land firsthand so as to avoid disputes, authorized the superintendent of Indian Affairs for the Southern Department, John Stuart, to produce a general accurate map of the region. Stuart (1718–1779), a Scotsman from Inverness, began his colonial career in 1748 as a merchant in Charleston. He gained a place in the city's intellectual scene, becoming a member of the St. Andrew's Society and the Charleston Library Society, and, in 1762, largely due to his experience in the Anglo-Cherokee War, he was appointed the superintendent of Indian Affairs for the Southern Department of North America.[10] Stuart's experience with the many southern tribes impressed on him the importance of establishing accurate boundaries. Over a twelve-year period, he dispatched numerous cartographers across the southeast and employed a young, talented mapmaker, Joseph Purcell, to combine the surveys, including the boundary lines Stuart had negotiated with the southern Indians, into one general map of the district. The work produced a number of outstanding maps, notably a large map measuring six feet by six feet, now known as the Stuart-Purcell map, that includes roads, trails, mountain ranges, and settlements. Stuart's maps proved invaluable to government officials. The exercise also provided Stuart the opportunity to identify individuals who could look at the land with the eye of a naturalist, information he might have shared with Bartram.[11]

Stuart's refinement of the Proclamation Line did not solve the problem of New Orleans. British hopes for circumnavigating the town had focused on the Iberville River and its intersection with the Mississippi. Governor Johnstone thought it possible that boats could navigate down the Iberville, to the Amite River, through Lakes Maurepas and Pontchartrain, and then to the Gulf of Mexico. Subsequently, Johnstone ordered the construction of square-shaped Fort Bute, in honor of his patron, Lord Bute, at the intersection of the two rivers and next to the community of Manchac to defend this potentially strategic intersection. Johnstone directed that the Iberville's channel be cleared, and, later, in 1772 Thomas Hutchins (1730–1789), a British colonel who would become geographer of the United States, was charged with assessing the river's possible role in bypassing New Orleans. Hutchins had been here before, back in October of 1766, searching for the elusive bypass, and had registered his doubts about the Iberville as an alternative water route after observing its then dry riverbed.[12] Hutchins had gained a measure of fame since that first trip, his detailed descriptions of the area leading to his election to the American Philosophical Society on April 17, 1772, and his familiarity with the lower Mississippi region led to his reassignment to Pensacola as that fort's engineer.[13]

Hutchins did believe that the Iberville could serve as a shortcut between the Gulf and the Mississippi, albeit not as an all-water route. Subsequently, he proposed that a road be cut from Manchac to the fork of the Iberville and Amite rivers, a suggestion carried out in 1773.[14] This was the same road that Bartram would describe two years later, a "strait, spacious, and perfectly level [byway] under the shadow of à grand forest."[15] Had the Iberville proven viable for trade, Manchac would have become an essential port town for the British. As Hutchins envisioned it, Manchac "might be of consequence to the commerce of West-Florida; for it may with reason be supposed, that the inhabitants and traders who reside at Point Coupeé, . . . above and below the Natchez, . . . would rather trade at this place than at New Orleans, if they could have as good returns for their peltry and the produce of their country; for it makes a difference of ten days in their voyage, which is no inconsiderable saving of labour, money, and time."[16] Given the potential importance to trade, it is no wonder that the British refused to give up their dream of an Anglo passage to the Gulf.

Bartram on the Mississippi River

Bartram, making his way to Manchac using this all-British route, was likely unaware of Hutchins's efforts, although he probably was aware of Hutchins himself. He does not mention Hutchins in the *Travels*, and since Bartram's visit to Pensacola was unplanned and brief, it is possible that the two did not meet, although John Lorimer, the fort's physician and a noted naturalist, who had learned of Bartram's visit, had impressed on the Quaker the need to pay a visit to Governor Peter Chester. In late 1775, during the time of Bartram's visit, Pensacola was beginning to show the effects of the increasing neglect brought on by the Empire's preoccupation with the rebellious colonies in the north. Its stockades rotting, its garrison ill supplied, the fort at Pensacola seemed on the verge of oblivion—details Bartram does not mention in the *Travels*. Rather, he assesses the fortress in benign terms, describing it as a tetragon with salient angles at each corner. Bartram's description belies the fact that Britain lacked the resources needed to protect the settlers in her colony. Given the capital's remote situation, separated from most West Florida settlements by swamps, piney forests, and unsympathetic Choctaws, one planter complained that, in their time of need, the inhabitants of the region might as well look to the Tower of London for reinforcements.[17]

Bartram received from Governor Chester a permit for the purpose of "Collecting Rare and useful productions in Botany and Natural History." All "His Majesty's Servants and Subjects" were instructed by Chester to aid and assist Bartram as "encouragers of useful Discoveries."[18] The wording of the permit resembles that of the one Bartram received from East Florida's governor two years earlier, but there is a noticeable difference here. Although Bartram had left Philadelphia with apparently little idea of the precise shape of his journey, he did have numerous contacts on which he could draw, resources that allowed him to improvise as he went. His father's garden and fame had attracted the attention of persons from around the world, most particularly Scots. Dr. Alexander Garden, a Charleston intellectual, joined Dr. John Moultrie, Dr. Lionel Chalmers, John Stuart, and Henry Laurens as but a few of the educated Scotsmen who considered the elder Bartram a friend and who were eager to help his son.[19] They did aid William, but even their powerful reach weakened in West Florida. Bartram had to find a new cohort. And, as he usually did, he found his way.

He set off for the Mississippi River with letters of introduction to the gentlemen in the community of New Richmond (Baton Rouge). Passing from Lake Ponchartrain, to the Taensapaoa River, to Lake Maurepas, to the Amite River, to the Iberville River and its adjacent road, he finally arrived at Manchac. His circuitous journey accomplished, it was with palpable excitement that Bartram stood on the banks of the Mississippi River for the first time. He described the awe inspired by "the great sire of rivers," a river "that strikes us with ideas of magnificence, the altitude, and theatrical ascents of its pensile banks, the steady course of the mighty flood, the trees, high forests, even every particular object, as well as societies, bear the stamp of superiority and excellence."[20] Despite the innate difficulties created by Manchac's forced development as a port town, the small community had grown. Bartram describes large and commodious warehouses and a bustling merchant scene. In fact, Manchac was heavily used by British planters upriver, many of whom had settled at New Richmond, some fifteen miles upstream from the town. By chance, "one of these gentlemen" for whom he possessed a letter of introduction was in Manchac. That gentleman is identified as William Dunbar.[21]

The evidence that Bartram's host was Dunbar is not as strong as could be hoped. Nowhere in his *Travels* does Bartram identify Dunbar by name, referring to him only as "my friend."[22] And Dunbar does not mention the botanist in his surviving papers. Copious notes Dunbar made in his plantation journal would certainly have recorded the encounter, but the extant entries do not begin until 1776. Another individual who could have been the gentleman in question was Richard Carpenter, a fellow planter of Dunbar's and a Quaker. Carpenter shared Bartram's interest in plants and is credited with building the first Friends Meeting House in New Richmond, but in George Gauld's 1778 map of the area, a plantation belonging to "Carpenter" is too short a distance from Manchac to match the distances Bartram covered to reach his host's plantation.[23]

The sole document that points to Dunbar as Bartram's host appeared some fifty-three years after the visit. In his introduction to Alexander Wilson's masterpiece, *American Ornithology* (1828), George Ord produces a short biography of Wilson. Contained therein are some letters from Wilson to Bartram, whom the ornithologist considered a mentor. There is one letter, dated May 23, 1810, in which Wilson writes, "Mr. Dunbar, of Natchez, remembered you very well, and desired me to carry his good wishes to you."[24] Wilson knew Dunbar because the latter had invited him to stay at his house during Wilson's visit there in 1810, shortly before Dunbar's death. Wilson reported that he was "received with great hospitality and kindness," with a "neat bed-room" assigned to him.[25] We are certain of this visit because of a letter from Wilson to Dunbar that appears in Dunbar's papers, a letter in which Wilson thanks Dunbar for his kindness, remarking that "I never can forget the pleasure I enjoyed in the sweet Society of your charming family—nor the attention of your most excellent wife (pardon the familiarity of the phraze) to make my residence agreeable."[26]

Could Dunbar and Bartram have met at another time, in another place? It is possible. As mentioned earlier, Dunbar immigrated from England to Philadelphia in 1771. But Bartram was in the Cape Fear region of North Carolina at this time, in the midst of a near-disastrous experiment as a plantation owner.[27] Dunbar soon left Philadelphia after his arrival and traveled to Fort Pitt to trade with the local tribes. He then descended the Ohio and Mississippi rivers to search for a plantation and returned to Philadelphia in the spring of 1773. There he formed a partnership with a local merchant and American Philosophical Society member, John Ross, for the purpose of establishing an "agricultural adventure . . . upon the Mississippi."[28] It is possible that Dunbar and Bartram met when Dunbar was in Philadelphia in 1773. Bartram, after his experience in North Carolina, had returned to Philadelphia between the fall of 1772 and the early part of 1773 bruised but upbeat for he held in his hands the instructions from John Fothergill, requesting that William collect and ship him plants from Florida.[29] But Bartram wasted little time in his preparations and sailed to Charleston on March 20, 1773, to begin his journey, leaving little time for socializing. With Bartram busily preparing to leave and Dunbar trying to secure his partnership, their paths likely did not cross. John Ross's and the Bartrams' memberships in the American Philosophical Society would not have offered an opportunity to meet either, since William apparently never attended an APS meeting.[30]

Had they met in Philadelphia, Bartram and Dunbar would have found much in common. Bartram was older by about ten years, and the two men shared a deep love for nature, both having spent much of their youth collecting plants, animals, and stones—an activity they carried into adulthood. Unlike Bartram, Dunbar had benefited from an advanced education, having attended King's College in Aberdeen, Scotland, in the 1760s, during the height of the Scottish Enlightenment. But differences in education mattered little to Dunbar, and throughout his time in North America, he would continually seek out those who shared his interest in philosophy and natural history.

When Dunbar set up his 500-acre plantation in New Richmond in 1774, he began cultivating indigo, a popular crop in the lower Mississippi River valley. Indigo, a notoriously difficult crop to establish, as Bartram would readily agree, requires considerable capitalization for the vats and pots needed to refine the product, and Dunbar may have become discouraged early on or, perhaps, he recognized an even greater opportunity. In August 1775, he wrote his partner Ross and declared "that getting scantling [for barrel staves] for the French West India market is more profitable than Indigo making."[31] The quickening trade in the area meant an ever-increasing demand for containers and during the eighteenth century the container most everyone used was the barrel. Dunbar wrote to Ross that a slave could recapture his or her purchase price within one year solely by producing barrel staves. And Dunbar was not alone. The whole area was alive with the production of scantling. Bartram had reached West Florida just as the entire area committed to the wholesale felling of trees. To meet the increasing need for labor, the number of slaves brought into the area grew dramatically.

Back in 1766, when Thomas Hutchins had visited Point Coupée, just above New Richmond, he reported that "they are not strong Enough in Negroes to Attempt making Indigo, which is the only reason they don't."[32] But by 1773, the community contained some seven thousand slaves who grew tobacco, indigo, corn, and poultry, transforming the area into one of great wealth. Dunbar recognized the need for more labor, particularly if he were to succeed in the scantling market, and in October 1775, the month Bartram visited him, Dunbar wrote the firm of A & D Thompsons in Jamaica, asking them to send him "20 or 25 hearty young negroes, 1/3 or 1/4 only women."[33] With this kind of activity, Dunbar made frequent trips up and down the river and, as is evident in Bartram's narrative, was known by many of those who lived along the Mississippi.

A Hospitable Visit

Dunbar's name was most likely among the "recommendations" Bartram carried for the inhabitants of New Richmond. Dunbar was certainly known to Governor Chester, to whom he had applied for a land grant the year before. Dunbar might also have known of the Bartrams through his business relationship with John Ross in Philadelphia and Ross possibly recommended Dunbar to colleagues at the Philosophical Society. It is certainly easy to believe that members would have been asked about worthy individuals whom young William could visit during his peregrinations in West Florida.

In any event, the gentleman in Manchac extended Bartram "a friendly and polite invitation to accompany him on his return home" to New Richmond. Bartram accepted and early the next morning, the two set off in a "handsome convenient boat, rowed by three blacks." They were probably conveyed in a forty- to fifty-foot canoe or pirogue (dugout) powered by oars and sails. These pirogues, well suited for river travel, were the most popular type of boat during this period. In October, upriver travel was comparatively easy since the Mississippi typically crept at a sluggish three miles per hour, much slower than its average springtime rate of five miles per hour. By staying close to the banks, rowers could avoid the strongest pull of the current, although they did run the considerable risk of collapsing bluffs, an ever-present hazard on the Mississippi. Stopping at an Indian village, probably the Alibama Village identified on Gauld's map, Dunbar bought some baskets and earthenware. They continued their pull up the river and after traveling a reported fourteen miles, a much too high estimate given the distance between Manchac and New Richmond, they landed and spent the night at a large plantation with a "spacious garden" and "many useful as well as curious exoticks."[34]

The following day they continued their ascent, stopping along the way to visit several plantations before arriving at Dunbar's estate. Plantations along the river that are listed in George Gauld's map include those owned by Pollock, Williams, Flowers, Francis, Pousset, McIntosh, and Carpenter. Dunbar was friends with Flowers, Francis, and Pousset, with whom he formed a type of salon in which they dined together regularly and even engaged in activities such as microscopic observations.[35] Bartram described Dunbar's land as "a very delightful villa, with extensive plantations" of various crops. From the beginning, Dunbar had experimented with plants, looking for a reliable cash crop and to this end he tried growing—in addition to indigo—rice, tobacco, flax, corn, buckwheat, barley—even pineapples.[36] The two men lingered one or two days before setting off again, this time for Point Coupée. Before they reached the now-thriving community, Bartram requested that they stop along the way so that he could fulfill a promise. While he had been in Pensacola the month before, Bartram had met a planter and promoter named Montfort Browne and had agreed to explore some plains near Browne's 17,400-acre holding at the White Cliffs (near Port Gardner in present-day east Baton Rouge). On October 25, at White Cliffs, Dunbar and Bartram landed, secured horses, rode inland for almost eight miles, and emerged from the cane and forests into a sea of grass, "lying parallel with the river, surrounded and intersected with Cane brakes and high forests of stately trees; the soil black, extremely rich and productive." They saw the verdant *Magnolia grandiflora,* the *Liquadambar styraciflua* (sweet gum), *Tilia* (basswood or wafer ash), *Morus rubra* (red mulberry), and the *Laurus sassafras,* the latter's straight trunk prized for producing boards and scantling.[37]

The next day, they returned to the river and resumed their journey. At Point Coupée, they saw a place of great fertility and wealth, a place that ten years earlier had been barely developed. Now, each planter reportedly owned from twenty to one hundred slaves. They called on one of these planters, a French gentleman, whom Bartram described as "an ancient man and wealthy planter . . . his hair was of a silky white, yet his complexion was florid and constitution athletic." After a single day there, they returned to Dunbar's plantation. Bartram was forced to rest at this point due to the "severe disorder" in his eyes, a recurring problem for him since his visit in Pensacola the month before, the cause of which, unknown, has been attributed to everything from poison ivy to scarlet fever.[38]

During their time together, Bartram and Dunbar had shared a deep pleasure in discoveries, and discussions of the area's vast flora had quickened the young Scot's botanical interests. They had also shared the knowledge of the hardships in running a plantation. Dunbar's establishment appeared orderly, but such order was illusory. He dictated the systematic clearing of the land, directed his slaves to manufacture staves, and traveled to study the earth and the stars, but underneath the surface of this apparent order was the daily tension created by a captive population forced into backbreaking labor. Less than seven months after Bartram's visit, Dunbar discovered an apparent plot among his and his neighbors' slaves to kill their masters as they slept, a discovery that shook Dunbar to his core. Since Bartram knew firsthand the challenges in plantation life, perhaps this is why the Quaker's only comment regarding this captive population is his observation that the boat in which he was transported up the Mississippi was "rowed by three blacks," continuing a practice of not condemning slavery anywhere in the *Travels.*[39] This omission may have been due to his wish not to offend his many hosts combined with the peculiar institution's widespread practice in the southern colonies. During his trip up the Mississippi, he most likely saw more slaves in the field than anywhere else in his journey, making the total silence here all the more telling.

The timing of Bartram's visit provides other insights into the *Travels* as a whole. Had he arrived a year earlier, Bartram would have missed Dunbar entirely. Chance and fortune seemed ubiquitous in this new land. Their accidental rendezvous produced reciprocal effects: Bartram's enthusiasm most likely inspired Dunbar to look at the region with a newfound appreciation. Dunbar, still learning about his new home, could not offer the insights he gave Alexander Wilson thirty-five years later, since most of his life, up to this point in 1775, had been spent in the highlands of Scotland; a visitor like Bartram, who had grown up learning many of the plants that thrived in the lower Mississippi River Valley, would have had the botanical advantage.

In Dunbar, Bartram found a true "philosophic companion," the term Bartram used to describe another Scot, young John McIntosh, one of the Darien Scots whom Bartram had met in Georgia. Dunbar, unlike McIntosh, could speak easily on any topic, from the fluxions of Newton to the common-sense philosophy of Thomas Reid, and with this discourse the Scot encouraged Bartram, just as Bartram encouraged Dunbar. Bartram had discovered in the forests of West Florida a growing number of individuals who could not only speak to science, but could also provide the materials needed to explore nature.

Elected to the American Philosophical Society in 1799, Dunbar would become a regular correspondent with Thomas Jefferson, a frequent contributor to the *Transactions of the American Philosophical Society,* and a founder of a scientific society and a college. In 1805, he led an expedition into the Louisiana Purchase, the southern counterpart to the more famous trek of Lewis and Clark. Dunbar represented a growing network of philosophic-minded individuals who came to West Florida, turned their attention to Nature, and analyzed it for the world.

Notes

1. For examples of the use of slaves for transportation in West Florida, see William Bartram, *The Travels of William Bartram: Naturalist's Edition,* ed. Francis Harper (Athens: University of Georgia Press, 1998), 268, 272.

2. Ibid., 237.

3. Ibid., 1.

4. John Bartram to Peter Collinson, November 11, 1763, reproduced in William Darlington, *Memorials of John Bartram and Humphry Marshall* (New York: Hafner Publishing Company, 1967), 256.

5. Quoted in Isaac Joslin Cox, *The West Florida Controversy, 1798–1813* (Gloucester, Mass.: Peter Smith, 1967), 12. The 31st parallel had been used as a boundary in early Carolina grants and was considered a convenient designation.

6. Matthew Phelps, "Appendix to the Memoirs and Adventures of Captain Phelps," in *Memoirs and Adventures of Captain Matthew Phelps . . . Particularly Two Voyages from Connecticut to the River Mississippi, From December 1773 to October 1780* (Bennington, Vt.: Press of Anthony Haswell, 1802), 41–42.

7. Clinton Howard, "Colonial Natchez: The Early British Period," *Journal of Mississippi History* (July 1945): 166.

8. Quoted in Clinton Howard, *The British Development of West Florida, 1763–1769* (Berkeley and Los Angeles: University of California Press, 1947), 8, 9. For a

more recent study of British West Florida, see Robin F. A. Fabel, *The Economy of British West Florida, 1763–1783* (Tuscaloosa: The University of Alabama Press, 1988).

9. H. S. Halbert, "Bernard Romans' Map of 1772," in *Publications of the Mississippi Historical Society 6*, ed. Franklin L. Riley (Oxford, Miss.: Printed for the Society, 1902), 415–439.

10. John Richard Alden, *John Stuart and the Southern Colonial Frontier: A Study of Indian Relations, War, Trade, and Land Problems in the Southern Wilderness, 1754–1775* (1944; Reprint. New York: Gordian Press, 1966), 136, 159–171.

11. William P. Cumming, *British Maps of Colonial America* (Chicago: University of Chicago Press, 1974), 18–19; William P. Cumming and Louis De Vorsey Jr., *The Southeast in Early Maps*, 3rd ed. (Chapel Hill: University of North Carolina Press, 1998), 324–325; For more information on the Indian Boundary Line, see Louis De Vorsey Jr., *The Indian Boundary in the Southern Colonies, 1763–1775* (Chapel Hill: University of North Carolina Press, 1966).

12. Harry Gordon, "The Journal of Captain Harry Gordon," in *Travels in the American Colonies*, ed. Newton D. Mereness (New York: MacMillan Company, 1916), 481–482.

13. Dumas Malone, ed., "Thomas Hutchins," *Dictionary of American Biography*, vol. 9 (New York: Charles Scribner's Sons, 1932), 435–436. Anna Margaret Quattrocchi, "Thomas Hutchins, 1730–1789" (Ph.D. dissertation, University of Pittsburgh, 1944), 162–163. Brooke Hindle, *The Pursuit of Science in Revolutionary America, 1735–1789* (Chapel Hill, N.C.: Published for the Institute of Early American History and Culture, 1956), 179–80.

14. Quattrocchi, *Thomas Hutchins*, 143–149.

15. Bartram, *Travels*, ed. Harper, 270.

16. Thomas Hutchins, *An Historical Narrative and Topographical Description of Louisiana and West Florida* (1784; Reprint. Gainesville: University of Florida Press, 1968), 43.

17. Bartram, *Travels*, ed. Harper, 262–263. Peter Chester, an able administrator, had become governor of West Florida in 1770. Robin F. A. Fabel, "An Eighteenth Colony: Dreams for Mississippi on the Eve of the Revolution," *Journal of Southern History* 59 (November 1993): 663.

18. Bartram, *Travels*, ed. Harper, 406.

19. Edwin J. Cashin, *William Bartram and the American Revolution on the Southern Frontier* (Columbia: University of South Carolina Press, 2000), 6–7.

20. Bartram, *Travels*, ed. Harper, 271.

21. Ibid., 409. Francis Harper asserts unequivocally that Dunbar is the "gentleman." See also Cashin, *William Bartram and the American Revolution*, 194. A recent biography of Dunbar omits all mention of William Bartram. He is erroneously identified as "William Barton," the son of Benjamin Smith Barton and then only

as a link to Alexander Wilson. See Arthur H. DeRosier Jr., *William Dunbar: Scientific Pioneer of the Old Southwest* (Lexington: University Press of Kentucky, 2007), 78. I am grateful to Kathryn Braund for pointing out this mistake.

22. Bartram, *Travels,* ed. Harper, 272, 276. Bartram frequently does not identify his hosts.

23. George Gauld's map of 1778, "A Plan of the Coast of Part of West Florida and Louisiana including the River Mississippi from its entrances as high as the River Yazous," shows an "Alabama Village" on the east side of the river, just north of Manchac. Map reproduced in Margaret Fisher Dalrymple, ed., *The Merchant of Manchac: The Letterbooks of John Fitzpatrick, 1768–1790* (Baton Rouge: Louisiana State University Press, 1978), no page number. The map may be viewed online at http://memory.loc.gov/cgi-bin/map_item.pl. Gauld states that he identified the various properties along the river in the spring of 1774. Richard Carpenter was a Quaker who shared Bartram's interest in plants. See *Bartram Heritage: A Study of the Life of William Bartram by the Bartram Trail Conference* (Montgomery, Ala.: Bartram Trail Conference, 1979), 188. Bartram frequently misjudges distances in his writings but the passage of time and expected rate of travel make it unlikely that Carpenter was the host. Of course, it is possible that the property identified in Gauld's map is not Richard Carpenter's plantation.

24. Alexander Wilson, *American Ornithology: or, The natural history of birds of the United States. With a sketch of the author's life,* by George Ord. (New York: Harrison Hall; Philadelphia: Collins & Co., 1828), vol. 1, cli.

25. Ibid., cxlix.

26. William Dunbar, *Life, Letters, and Papers of William Dunbar of Elgin, Morayshire, Scotland, and Natchez, Mississippi. Pioneer Scientist of the Southern United States,* ed. Mrs. Dunbar Rowland (Jackson: Press of the Mississippi Historical Society, 1930), 205.

27. Bartram, *Travels,* ed. Harper, xix.

28. Benjamin Wailes, Extracts from the Letter Book of William Dunbar of the Forest from 18 June 1775 to 20 March 1802. Together with a Biographical Sketch, compiled by B.L.C. Wailes [uncertain]. William Dunbar, MMC-alpha, Library of Congress, MSS 92–498, 1–2. There is one entry in the Extracts for October 1775, written to merchants in Jamaica regarding the sale of slaves, an industry in which Dunbar was heavily involved during this time.

29. Bartram, *Travels,* ed. Harper, xix.

30. Ibid., xviii.

31. Wailes, *Extracts from the Letter Book of William Dunbar,* 13.

32. Gordon, "Journal of Captain Harry Gordon," 481–82.

33. Wailes, *Extracts from the Letter Book of William Dunbar,* 14.

34. Bartram, *Travels,* ed. Harper, 272.

35. Dunbar, *Life, Letters, and Papers,* 26, 39, 42.

36. Wailes, *Extracts from the Letter Book of William Dunbar,* 9–11.

37. Bartram, *Travels,* ed. Harper, 273.

38. Ibid., 274, 276, 407.

39. The suspected slave revolt is described in Dunbar, *Life, Letters, and Papers,* 26–28. Bartram, *Travels,* ed. Harper, 272.

II
Reading Bartram

5
William Bartram and the Forms of Natural History

Stephanie Volmer

Let me begin with a confession: I derive more consistent reading pleasure from Bartram's "Report to Dr. Fothergill" than from his *Travels*. No doubt part of my preference may be attributed to readerly idiosyncrasy, but it has prompted me to consider what the "Report" offers readers as compared to the *Travels*, and what the differences may mean with regard to the relationship between writing and the quest for natural knowledge. The question of how textual forms shape textual content is vital in the study of natural history because "natural history" serves as an umbrella category for a variety of textual forms, including letters, reports, natural histories, travels, observations, descriptions, journals, and promotional tracts, to name just a few. All natural history writing aims to describe the natural world, but not all of these textual forms accomplish the task in the same way, and so attending to the differences between them allows us to reach a more complex understanding of the culture of eighteenth-century natural history. I would suggest that in writing the "Report," William Bartram experimented with the conventions of textual forms just as he would do later—and more extravagantly—in writing the *Travels*. In the "Report," however, he stayed more obviously within the bounds of certain rhetorical conventions and, as a result, the "Report" has a formal coherence that provides specific reading pleasures.

The reading experience that prompted me to start thinking about these matters occurred a few years ago, when I realized that I needed to reread the *Travels* as part of my research on the Bartram family. By that time, the "Report"—which Bartram wrote for his patron Dr. Fothergill in London—had become widely available through the Library of America's edition of Bartram's writings. Since I had read the *Travels* before, I decided I would read the "Report" first before turning once again to the *Travels*. As I was reading the "Report,"

I was struck by a passage in which Bartram describes discovering a plant for which he had been searching.

The incident begins with Bartram explaining that he and his companions—who were on a surveying tour through northeastern Georgia—had set up camp on the banks of a branch of the Broad River. As evening approached, Bartram embarked on what he calls his "Botanical excursions," motivated in part by a desire to determine the source of a lovely and mysterious smell in the air. In the "Report," he writes, "Observing when descending the Hills to cross the Crick, a very agreeable fragrant smell like cloves defused about us in the air, the whole company being affected by it, I immediately concluded it must arise from some Vegitable, being bruised by the horses feet[.] I therefore designed to go in quest of it as soon as we came to camp." Bartram proceeds to describe his movements over the terrain, writing, "I cross't the Creek and began to assend the Hills, having attained a considerable hight, the Hills pretty steep, my feet suddenly slid from under me; I catch't hold of the sweet Calyconthus, that stretched out a friendly bow to my relief, however in the scuffle to save myself I discovered the lovely subject of my researches, by the figure of the leaf & Root took it to be a Species of Cariophylata, but as I could find no flower or part of fructification whereby to fix its tribe or family, I judged from the fragrance & clove like scent of the Root."[1] This is a brief but vivid description of a plant collector in the woods, and I thought it represented a nice example of the important role accident plays in the course of botanical investigations. Thus Bartram's evocative and energetic description of his fortuitous discovery stayed with me.

When I came upon the scene in *Travels,* however, I was surprised by how much the description had changed. In *Travels,* the account of the discovery of the aromatic plant is reduced. The passage, in its entirety, reads, "Before we left the waters of Broad River, having encamped in the evening on one of its considerable branches, and left my companions, to retire, as usual, on botanical researches, on ascending a steep rocky hill, I accidentally discovered a new species of caryophyllata (geum odoratissimum): on reaching to a shrub my foot slipped, and, in recovering myself, I tore up some of the plants, whose roots filled the air with animating scents of cloves and spicy perfumes."[2]

The most important difference between the two passages is that the sense of a traveler moving through the landscape has been diminished in *Travels.* For instance, the "Botanical excursions" and "quest" Bartram refers to in the "Report" have been compressed in the *Travels* into the phrase "botanical researches," thus reducing the rhetorical emphasis on movement conveyed by the words "excursion" and "quest." In addition, in the *Travels* Bartram is no longer "[questing]" for the source of the clovelike aroma. The smell has been eliminated as a motivation for his "researches," and in fact is only mentioned at the end of the short paragraph, almost as an afterthought, as though it were something he discerned *after* finding the plant, rather than something that inspired his quest. Also, notice how the role of the helpful shrub has changed. In the "Report," Bartram says that his foot "suddenly slid from under" him, prompting him to "catch't hold of the sweet Calyconthus, that stretched out a friendly bow to my relief." In the *Travels,* there is no specific mention of the Calyconthus, and the order of action has been reversed: it is now in "reaching to a shrub" that his foot slipped.

The idea of the accidental nature of the discovery is present in both versions, but the *Travels* eliminates many of the details of botanical exploration that dramatize the scene in the "Report," such as the fact that Bartram's feet "suddenly slid from under [him]" and that he discovers the source of the lovely aroma in, as he says, "the scuffle to save myself." Bartram's rhapsodic and anthropomorphic imagery in this scene disappears in *Travels,* such as his vision of the "sweet Calyconthus, that stretched out a friendly bow to my relief" and his description of the caryophyllata as "the lovely subject of my researches." In the "Report," then, as compared to the *Travels,* Bartram creates a sense of narrative and process as he describes his movement over a hilly landscape. He creates a sense of cause and effect as he describes a lovely smell on the air that motivates his movement. And he creates a sense of drama leading up to an unexpected discovery as he slips and slides in his quest. As a reader, I had a sense of a person moving through a particular landscape at a particular time— smelling the air, scrambling up rocky hills, and grasping at plants within reach. Taken together, the rhetorical differences between the two works highlight the immediacy of the "Report," in this description of a perhaps minor incident of botanical discovery.

There are a few reasons why the account in the "Report" might be, as its first editor, Francis Harper, said, "a far fresher document than the *Travels.*"[3] First, Bartram wrote it while he was still on his journey, and thus the events described occurred relatively close to the time of writing. The historical circumstances surrounding its production are a bit uncertain. We know that Bartram wrote the "Report" in two parts, and the best guess is that he sent part 1 to Dr. Fothergill in the autumn of 1774, probably from Florida, and that he sent part 2 to Dr. Fothergill in the spring of 1775 from Charleston.[4] The fact that Bartram wrote the "Report" *to* Dr. Fothergill suggests a second reason why the "Report" might have a greater sense of immediacy in some places than the *Travels.* Addressed to Dr. Fothergill, the "Report" in some ways formally resembles a letter and partakes of some of the features of the epistolary form.

First, it was written with a specific reader in mind. This feature is most evident at the beginning of part 2, which begins with a direct address. Bartram says, "Sir, being desirous of doing every thing that may tend towards the illustration of natural knowledge, I am glad of this opportunity by your aid & incouragement, of extending my reserches into Florida. I shall therefore with the highest sense of pleasure, for your particular amusement proceed, & indeavor to exhibit to your notice the natural productions of these countries as they offer to my view in the plain simple dress of Nature."[5] As Bartram says, he was writing the "Report" for Fothergill's "particular amusement," suggesting that he wrote with some awareness of being an "I" speaking to a "You." This dialogic impulse differs from the relationship between the author of *Travels* and his larger, more abstract audience, and it nurtured a sense of formal informality and contingency that facilitated Bartram's goals in writing the "Report."

The issue of audience highlights the fact that the "Report," like natural history letters, bridged the gap between public and private forms of writing in ways that the *Travels* did not. The "Report" was a private form written to a specific person, but, given the conventions of exchange within natural history networks, Bartram no doubt knew and perhaps hoped that it would circulate among other readers and possibly even be printed (as was the case with two of his father's travel journals[6]). The fact that the document could move fluidly between the public and private spheres allowed for a rhetorical flexibility and dynamism—apparent in eighteenth-century natural history letters more generally—that distinguishes the "Report" from the purpose of *Travels*, a book project designed to reach a broad public audience.[7]

The "Report" is linked to the letter form in that it too was written in direct relation to plant samples and other natural objects that Bartram had collected and prepared for Fothergill, as well as the numerous drawings and sketches Bartram produced for Fothergill during his trip. Fothergill, then, could examine these natural objects and drawings while reading the "Report."[8] Bartram's mode of writing and Fothergill's mode of reading thus dramatize the dynamic between text and object that was fundamental to natural investigations—a dynamic that was subordinated with the published *Travels*, which would have been read by many without the benefit of accompanying specimen sheets.

Letters held an important place in transatlantic natural history exchanges in this period, especially as Bartram's father, John, participated in those exchanges. For most of his life, William Bartram watched his father collecting botanical objects and making natural observations, and he often aided in those endeavors. William Bartram would also have been witness to the extensive epistolary work that John undertook in order to facilitate the work of botanical exchange with his English and European contacts. Reading and writing letters was fundamentally linked to John Bartram's natural history work, which involved collecting and sometimes transplanting botanical objects and shipping them across the Atlantic Ocean, as well as engaging in ongoing and extensive discussions about the beauties, uses, classification, and horticultural specificities of plants.[9] The reciprocity of the form—in which a letter is written with the expectation of receiving a response—cast a quality of fruitful contingency over the content, and this is one of the features of the form in play in Bartram's "Report." Indeed, what made letters uniquely valuable in eighteenth-century natural history endeavors is that they nurtured a continuous and collaborative exchange that produced natural knowledge as well as new efforts to articulate the impact of nature on the self.

William Bartram did not leave behind as vast a record of his epistolary labors as John Bartram did, and so we do not know a great deal about his style of letter writing before he began his famous journey in 1773.[10] However, given the culture of letter writing in which he was immersed, it is not a great leap to suggest that Bartram understood the unique importance of the letter form to natural history investigations, and the ways it accommodated a fluid movement between personal and empirical responses to the natural world. The "Report" illustrates this movement in self-conscious ways. For example, Bartram occasionally marks the passage of time by welcoming a new day, a rhetorical gesture he would use to great effect in the *Travels*. Two paragraphs before his accidental discovery of the caryophyllata, Bartram writes, "A pleasant morning attended by the feather'd inhabitants of these shady retreats with joyfull song invites us forth. [T]he elivated face of this Hilly country breathes an elastic pure air, inspireing health & activity, I arose & joyfully contributed My aid in the contemplation of the wonderfull Harmony & perfection in the lovely simplicity of Nature. . . . What a beautifull scenery is Vegitable Nature!"[11] The letter form encouraged a sense of open dialogue between reader and writer, and Bartram's sensibilities enabled him to adapt the familiarity cultivated by such rhetorical and formal flexibility in order to celebrate the beauties of nature and to describe his personal response to those beauties.

Bartram's primary goal and directive, of course, was to describe the natural history of the southern colonies, and the narrative of the "Report" is given shape not only by the conventions of the letter form but also by the conventions of the field journal or travel journal. A travel journal, unlike more loosely structured letters, is organized by movement over landscape and by the accumulation of observations about place. The uses of the travel journal for the purposes of natural history were fairly specific in the eighteenth-century transatlantic world. The role of the observer was disinterested and often almost invisible, as he described what Bartram and his fellow naturalists called the "soil and situation" of a particular region as well as its natural productions.

Dr. Fothergill explicitly asked Bartram to provide such information. In fact, his instructions to Bartram about the kind of writing Bartram should produce during his journey offer a useful backdrop to my interest in what Bartram intended the "Report" to accomplish as a piece of writing. In his letters, Fothergill told Bartram, "Write to me as often as opportunity offers. . . . Letters to me in London, by the post or packet will be sufficient.—. . . . It will be right to keep a little journal, marking the soil, situation, plants in general, remarkable animals, where found, and the several particulars relative to them as they cast up."[12] Fothergill also gave specific directions about what kinds of comments should accompany Bartram's botanical and zoological specimens and drawings. Fothergill's instructions make clear that Bartram's writing was part of his collecting and observing. As far as we know, Bartram did not write to Fothergill often and the "little journal" that Fothergill mentions (now lost) was most likely the source for the "Report." The "Report," then, was one of the first ways that Bartram reported natural history information to Fothergill, and he provided plenty of details about the "soil and situation" and natural productions he found on his journey. Indeed, one purpose of the "Report" was to convey a sense of place both through writing about that place and through collecting natural objects from that place.

One way Bartram records such objects in the "Report" is in an appended catalogue, which adheres to the flat descriptive rhetorical conventions of that form of natural history writing. The objects described in the catalogue are no longer connected to a figure moving across a landscape, and it is not always clear how the objects are connected to each other. But within the narrative of the "Report" itself, Bartram often fuses a mode of detached specificity in "marking the soil, situation, plants in general, remarkable animals" (as Fothergill put it) with more evocative language. For example, as you will recall, when Bartram describes his accidental discovery of the caryophyllata, he is in the process of recording his progress up a steep hill beside the river. He says that he reached the summit, from where he "had a very agreable prospect of the Plains below," before descending again to the riverbank. There, he writes, "a group of fine flowering Trees & Shrubs drew my attention." Flowering trees and shrubs were popular in England during the eighteenth century, and that phrase alone would have piqued Fothergill's interest.[13] In the ensuing list of trees and shrubs, Bartram ensures that Fothergill will take note:

> This noble assembly of vegitable could scercely be paralell'd in America, & would have been dificult for a Botanest on which to fix the preemenence. The Majestick Laurel Tree or Magnolia grandaflora towers above the chiefs of this vegitable Court, whose proud crest adornd with waving plumes of the most exquisite white flowers, attended by other beautifull tribes of this noble Family of Vegitables. The Rose Laurell Magnolea Glauca, almost equaling the first in magnitude & exceeded by none, in tallness & gracefull body, its piramedal head adorned with

leaves of a delicate asure green, thick seed with rose like blossoms of the most perfect whiteness. Magnolia Umbrella Tree whose horazontal branches, adornd with vast silkey leaves so uniformly disposed in form of an umbrella & crested by the finest flower, the whole presenting a most magnificent Canopy. Magnolia Altissima, Liriodendrum, Sugar maple, Pavia scarlet & white flowered, Azalia, Stewartia, Calyacanthus, & rose flower'd Chamerododendron & lesser Kelmia in the steep rockey Bank, bending with their heavy clustres of flowers toward the water.[14]

Bartram describes the terrain and establishes a sense of place for Dr. Fothergill in London. He fulfills the obligations of the field journal form, in that he provides information about the botanical productions in a natural situation and their manner of growth. But in its exuberance and descriptive excess, this is no mere catalogue. Bartram creates a visual scene for his reader. Even the last bit of the description, in which Bartram simply lists the trees, takes on lyric qualities coming as it does after such effusions of praise.

Bartram is experimenting with the descriptive potential of journal conventions, such as the catalogue and the role of "soil and situation," in order to demonstrate the impact of this botanical retreat on a specific traveler. Fothergill had of course instructed Bartram to describe such environmental specificities, both to convey a sense of place and to stimulate interest in the productions of that place. As he wrote to Bartram, "continue thy journey in such a manner as to visit the most likely places for plants at different seasons. Mark the places they grow in, whether in swamps, dry banks, under shade or in the open country. These circumstances will assist us in their culture here."[15] Yet in passages such as the catalogue of a "noble assembly of vegitable," Bartram expands the form in order to suggest that there are some aspects of nature that do not travel, that cannot be uprooted and reproduced in England. He takes a form whose primary purpose is to describe a place and, by making his personal response integral to that place through rhetorical description, he succeeds in highlighting the irreproducibility of that place.

The place of letter writing in natural history investigations was in transition by the last quarter of the eighteenth century, as the sciences became more specialized and professionalized. The conventions of journal writing were also in flux at that time. As the literary scholar Stuart Sherman has shown, journals and their generic hybrids were increasingly popular to the English reading public, but one of the challenges facing writers was how to balance the accumulation of detail with a narrative of movement, how to balance chronology with narrative interest, how to be both a self-reflective and a disinterested narrator.[16] Samuel Johnson, for instance, distinguished a journal—which he said was concerned with "regularity" and "minute exactness"—from history—which arranges facts according to their dependence on one another. Such questions, of course, take on special significance in relation to the natural history journal, and there are signs that in the "Report," William was exploring such matters, gesturing toward minute exactness even while arranging facts and events in such a way as to highlight the most significant or the most impressive. He remained within the formal expectations associated with a journal even while he inflected the writing with a quality of familiarity and contingency more common to the letter form.

One of my goals in studying the different textual forms of natural history is to complicate further the binary oppositions often associated with Bartram—Enlightenment versus Romantic, scientific versus aesthetic, didactic versus rhapsodic, colonial versus patriot. A sense of dynamism and process belying such oppositions appears in all of Bartram's natural history work. The dynamic process of travel and collection and transplantation was coextensive with the dynamic process of reading and writing and drawing. Dried specimens may seem detached and abstracted from their local environment, but recipients like Fothergill could restore them to that terrain through Bartram's prose descriptions. Bartram's writing—in his "Report" and the *Travels,* as well as on his drawings and specimen sheets—connected images and objects with their natural historical context. Whether he was writing a letter or a report or the *Travels,* he was moving constantly between reading, writing, collecting, observing—constantly comparing, constantly synthesizing, constantly selecting which features to highlight. In all of his descriptive efforts, Bartram searched for effective ways to render the experience of being in nature, both working within formal conventions and adapting those conventions to his own needs.[17]

What can a journal, as a piece of writing, accomplish? What can a letter accomplish? How do they differ as rhetorical performances, and what strengths does each form offer to a writer invested in describing the natural world? Teasing out the answers to such questions, I believe, opens up new possibilities for interpreting William Bartram's work and achievements. In the "Report," I would suggest that the letter form is in dialogue with the travel journal form in ways that capture both the spirit of the engaged mobile traveler and the engaging natural place. Many readers have described Bartram's talent for adopting and adapting various discursive styles in the *Travels,* including, for instance, the languages of taxonomic classification, the sublime, the picturesque, and natural history reportage. These gifts are certainly on display in the "Report." And yet the conventions of the letter and journal forms provide a rhetorical coherence to the narrative, which may account for the distinctive reading pleasures it offers.

Notes

1. William Bartram, Travels *and Other Writings,* selected by Thomas P. Slaughter (New York: Library of America, 1996), 447. Francis Harper, in his edition of *Travels,* identified the plant as "presumably avens (genus *Geum*)," William Bartram, *The Travels of William Bartram,* Naturalists's Edition, ed. Francis Harper (New Haven, Conn.: Yale University Press, 1958), 466.

2. Bartram, Travels *and Other Writings,* 59–60.

3. Francis Harper, Introduction to "Travels in Georgia and Florida: A Report to Dr. John Fothergill" by William Bartram, *Transactions of the American Philosophical Society,* New Series, vol. 33, Part 2 (Philadelphia: American Philosophical Society, 1943), 123. Other scholars have attended to some of the differences between the "Report" and *Travels.* For instance, Thomas Hallock points out that the "Report" is "surprisingly restrained in tone," combining "the genres of itinerarium, field notebook, and botanic report," and says that it "lacks the effusiveness and drama that characterizes the later book." *From the Fallen Tree: Frontier Narratives, Environmental Politics, and the Roots of a National Pastoral, 1749–1826* (Chapel Hill: University of North Carolina Press, 2003), 153. Nancy E. Hoffmann describes the prose as "terse" and says it shows "no philosophical meditations, few emotional expressions, little or no evocative language" of natural description, and "little reflective consciousness. . . . The movement of the prose is layered, not connected." "The Construction of William Bartram's Narrative Natural History: A Genetic Text of the Draft Manuscript for *Travels through North and South Carolina, Georgia, East and West Florida*" (Ph.D., diss., University of Pennsylvania, 1996), 6, 53. Thomas P. Slaughter says that Bartram "reverse[d] the reportorial style of his father, using the more private genre of personal correspondence for his discussion of productive potential [in the "Report"] and reserving his most romantic prose for the public audience of the *Travels.*" He claims that the "Report" is "irrepressibly visual" and "emotionally accessible," suggesting that even though it is stylistically close to John Bartram's published Florida journal, "adapting the tone of the philosophical reporter of size, distance, terrain, and 'useful' plant life," in fact William Bartram "is a more active, visible presence" in the writing. *The Natures of John and William Bartram* (New York: Alfred A. Knopf, 1996), 185, 187.

4. Bartram, Travels *and Other Writings,* 611.

5. Ibid., 480.

6. *Observations on the Inhabitants, Climate, Soil, Rivers, Productions, Animals, and Other Matters Worthy of Notice Made by Mr. John Bartram in His Travels from Pensilvania to Onondago, Oswego and the Lake Ontario in Canada, To which is annex'd, a curious Account of the Cataracts at Niagara by Mr. Peter Kalm, a Swedish Gentleman who travelled there* was published in London in 1751 without John Bartram's knowledge. A draft of Bartram's journal describing his exploration of

Florida was (most likely without Bartram's knowledge) appended to the second edition of William Stork's promotional tract, *An Account of East-Florida: A Journal kept by John Bartram of Philadelphia, Botanist to His Majesty for the Floridas; upon a Journey from St. Augustine up the River St. John's* (London: W. Nicoll, 1766).

7. See Nancy E. Hoffmann's invaluable research into the production of *Travels*: "The Construction of William Bartram's Narrative Natural History."

8. See Joseph Ewan, ed., *William Bartram: Botanical and Zoological Drawings, 1756–1788* (Philadelphia: Memoirs of the American Philosophical Society 74, 1968).

9. See Edmund Berkeley and Dorothy Smith Berkeley, eds., *The Correspondence of John Bartram, 1734–1777* (Gainesville: University Press of Florida, 1992). For recent critical work on John Bartram, see *America's Curious Botanist: A Tercentennial Reappraisal of John Bartram, 1699–1777*, ed. Nancy E. Hoffmann and John C. Van Horne (Philadelphia: Publications of the American Philosophical Society, 2004). For a recent scholarly study of eighteenth-century transatlantic natural history exchanges, see Susan Scott Parrish, *American Curiosity: Cultures of Natural History in the Colonial British Atlantic World* (Chapel Hill: University of North Carolina Press, 2006).

10. *William Bartram The Search for Nature's Design: Selected Art, Letters, & Unpublished Writings*, ed. Thomas Hallock and Nancy E. Hoffmann (Athens: University of Georgia Press, 2010), is an important contribution to the study of Bartram, publishing many of his letters and other previously unpublished writings.

11. Bartram, Travels *and Other Writings*, 446.

12. *Chain of Friendship: Selected Letters of Dr. John Fothergill of London, 1735–1780*, introduced by Betsy C. Corner and Christopher C. Booth (Cambridge, Mass.: Harvard University Press, 1971), 402.

13. See Mark Laird, *The Flowering of the Landscape Garden, English Pleasure Grounds, 1720–1800* (Philadelphia: University of Pennsylvania Press, 1999).

14. Bartram, Travels *and Other Writings*, 448–449.

15. *Chain of Friendship*, 402.

16. See Stuart Sherman, *Telling Time: Clocks, Diaries, and English Diurnal Form 1660–1785* (Chicago: University of Chicago Press, 1996).

17. Stephanie Volmer, "Planting a New World: Letters and Languages of Transatlantic Botanical Exchange, 1733–1777" (Ph.D. diss., Rutgers University, 2008).

6
Nature, Man, and God

The Introduction to Bartram's *Travels*

Burt Kornegay

Any attempt to explain William Bartram's basic beliefs about life in a short essay is doomed to incompleteness, if not to complete failure. Most writers about Bartram concentrate, as good writers tend to do, on specific topics. But it seems to me that on occasion, we should try to place all of these particular topics into context, should try to give an overview of William Bartram, to describe his sense of life, his fundamental assumptions about life—should try to explain his worldview—as a scholar might say; or, to put it in street talk, to tell where Bartram is "coming from." And that is what I will attempt here.

My authority for this is William Bartram himself. Those of you who have read his *Travels* know that Bartram begins his book with an "Introduction," a prefatory chapter that is meant to orient us and lead us into the book proper. Near the end of this chapter Bartram informs the reader that he has "passed through some remarks, which appeared of sufficient consequence to be offered to the public."[1] And it is in these "remarks of sufficient consequence" that Bartram tells us where he's coming from as a student of nature and man.

This is not to say that everything Bartram tells us is perfectly familiar and clear. And why would we expect it to be? Ways of thinking and views of life change over time, even from generation to generation; and more than ten world-changing generations have passed since Bartram wrote his introduction. At least—drawing on my own personal experience—when I first read the introduction, I found that some of Bartram's beliefs about nature differed markedly from mine and contained notions that seemed strange and antique. I also noticed that this was because my beliefs—and I think those of almost everyone interested in Bartram today—have been much more profoundly affected by the scientific way of looking at things than were Bartram's. And so, before turning to examine Bartram's "remarks of consequence" and the view of life they express, first let me try to point out what I think are some of the chief influences of modern science on our view of the world. That is, in a summary fashion, let me try to explain where *we* are coming from as students of nature and man. Doing this will give us the perspective we need to understand Bartram.

Our modern view of nature begins to emerge when we ask ourselves, what kind of world is it that science has revealed? I am not referring to the results of this or that experiment that students might conduct in a high-school biology class. Nor am I referring to the peculiarities of animal behavior that zoologists depict for us on public television specials (with a penchant, it seems to me, to show close-up shots of animals mating). I am referring to the view of the world we get when we look at pictures taken of our delicate-looking planet from a satellite orbiting in the black vacuum of space; the world we get an inkling of when we look through a telescope out into that spatial vastness without end. I am speaking about the sobering experience we have all known at some time or other when gazing out into the "billion-galaxied" universe as a whole that science presents to us, and we have wondered, "What does it all mean?"

Many of those who have pondered this important question and who have examined the facts of the case as presented by science have been troubled by the answer they found. Bertrand Russell, the well-known twentieth-century mathematician and philosopher, is one. Russell begins his famous essay "A Free Man's Worship" with the following story. Once upon a time (Russell tells us), Dr. Faustus, the learned man who, in his search for knowledge sold his soul to the Devil, was sitting in his study when the Devil came to tell him about creation. The Devil told Faustus that ages ago God (i.e., the Devil) had grown bored with the praises of the angels, since, after all, the angels had reason to praise him considering the blissful existence he had given them. God decided that it might be more amusing to obtain undeserved praise—to create a universe containing beings who worshiped him even though he made their existence miserable. So God got to work: "For countless ages the hot nebula whirled aimlessly through space. At length it began to take shape, the central mass threw off planets, the planets cooled, boiling seas and burning mountains heaved and tossed, from black masses of cloud hot sheets of rain deluged the barely solid crust. And now the first germ of life grew in the depths of the ocean."[2]

The Devil goes on to describe for Dr. Faustus the evolution of life on our planet and the eventual emergence of man, and he recounts how he afflicted man with a life of pain, sorrow, sin, sickness, accident, and death, yet at the same time infused man with "the cruel thirst for worship," so that, the more he tormented human beings, the more they begged his forgiveness for their sins and sang his praise, calling him "God." The Devil then ends his creation story by telling Faustus: "And God smiled; and when he saw that Man had become perfect in renunciation and worship, he sent another sun through the sky, which crashed into Man's sun; and all returned again into nebula. 'Yes,' he murmured, 'it was a good play; I will have it performed again.'"

Having begun his essay with this nightmarish creation story, Bertrand Russell then opens the essay proper by concluding: "Such, in outline, but even more purposeless, more void of meaning, is the world which Science presents for our belief . . . that Man is the product of causes which had no prevision of the end that they were achieving; that his origin, his growth, his hopes and fears, his loves and his beliefs, are but the outcome of accidental collocations of atoms; that . . . the whole temple of Man's achievement must inevitably be buried beneath the debris of a universe in ruins—all of these things, if not quite beyond dispute, are yet so nearly certain, that no philosophy which rejects them can hope to stand."

We may wish to take Russell's essay as a rather extreme statement of the modern worldview—and Bartram would have been horrified at it—but it does illustrate the profound effect of science on the modern mind. And in general we can say that the scientific view about the state of things does contain these key elements: that nature is an infinite process of atoms in motion and of vast forces at work, operating in independence of man and dwarfing him; and that man is but a minuscule part of nature and dependent on it—a nature that has no knowledge of him and no particular concern for his welfare.

I will not try to detail what I think are the pervasive and profound ways in which this view affects our civilization. But I will point out—speaking again from personal experience, since I make my living as a wilderness guide—that it even influences the nature of our outdoor recreational pursuits! We may head off to explore the wilderness, as William Bartram did more than two hundred years ago, but because of science's influence on us, we are likely to see and experience that wilderness in ways that would have been foreign to Bartram. Notice, to give one example, how the scientific view of nature comes to the fore in this selection from the classic outdoor guide book *Mountaineering:* "Mountains are turbulent places, full of swift violence, where humans are dwarfed by comparison. In the natural process of building and destruction, the entire mountain range is forever being reduced to sea level . . . Little insidious constant forces and tremendous crashing ones all work toward just one end, the leveling of the entire region . . . Time has no meaning here; neither has man. This is the ground the climber seeks for his sport, an arena of the elements, where destruction of a human is too minor an accomplishment to be worthy of note in the annals of nature. Through the labyrinth of these physical factors the mountaineer must thread his way."[3]

William Bartram would have found the theme of this text to be very strange.

First, he would have thought, why would anyone want to climb ice-shagged mountains just for the "sport" of it? Second, why would these writers say that in the mountains—or anywhere else on earth for that matter—man has no meaning? Bartram would have been puzzled by this latter statement because, as he clearly expressed in the "Introduction" to his *Travels*, he was a man who felt at home in the universe. In his view the world is literally the home and the domain of man; it is God-made for man, God-given to him. It is a splendid habitation created for human beings to live in, to study, to make use of, and to admire.

This belief is evident from the beginning of the introduction, when Bartram describes and praises the natural world: "This world, as a glorious apartment of the boundless palace of the sovereign Creator, is furnished with"— and he goes on to list some of the natural "furnishings" of the world. Notice that Bartram describes the world as an "apartment" in the "palace" of God, both terms being intimately associated with human life and both tending to humanize our world and universe. Even more important, Bartram tells us that our world is a "furnished" apartment, one prepared for human beings to inhabit.[4]

What a gulf between this description and that of Bertrand Russell, which describes the world as a spin-off from hot nebula whirling aimlessly in the void of space! No God in Russell's account; no purpose or meaning; no man either, except insofar as Russell stresses man's insignificance.

Unlike Russell (or the writers of *Mountaineering*), Bartram humanizes the world and makes it intimately familiar to us, and he does so not only with the kind of metaphoric descriptions just noted but in many other ways as well. This is evident, for instance, in the human-like qualities he sees in various species of plants. In the "Introduction," while giving a list of plants to be found in the temperate zone, he tells us that the magnolia possesses "dignity and magnificence," that the live oak is venerable, that the Turk's cap lily "represents pride and vanity," that the azalea and mountain laurel "exhibit a perfect show of mirth and gaiety."[5] Note how these are human attributes. When Bartram looks at a beautiful lily he sees that, just as with many beautiful people, it is a bit proud and vain.

Of course, if plants exhibit some human qualities, animals show even more. Midway through the introduction Bartram recounts his encounter with a very large spider during one of his trips to Florida: "As I was gathering specimens of flowers from the shrubs, I was greatly surprised at the sudden appearance of a remarkably large spider on a leaf. . . . At sight of me he boldly faced about, and raised himself up, as if ready to spring upon me." Bartram describes the spider, then says: "after I had recovered from the surprise, observing that the wary hunter had retired under cover, I drew near again, and presently discovered that I had surprised him on predatory attempts against the insect tribes."[6]

Bartram concludes by describing the spider's "predatory attempt" against an unwary bee. Notice how this story breaks down: First, Bartram appears, hunting flowers, then the spider appears, hunting bees on those flowers. Second, Bartram suddenly spies the spider, draws back and the spider, seeing Bartram, retreats too. Third, Bartram, recovering his composure, draws near again to observe the spider. The spider, recovering, reappears and continues his hunt, "at the same time keeping a wary eye upon me." Fourth, Bartram observes that "this cunning intrepid hunter conducted his subtil approaches [toward the bee] with the circumspection and perseverance of a Siminole when hunting a deer."[7]

Clearly, as Bartram describes it, this spider is more than a scientific collection of chemical processes and of genetically determined behavior. The spider responds to Bartram much in the same way that Bartram responds to it. And Bartram believes that he understands the spider in the same way that he understands an Indian stalking a deer.

As the spider episode shows, the world for Bartram, including its spiders, is a familiar place, human-like in many of its attributes and capable of being intimately known, just in the way that we human beings know each other—with an inside knowledge of what it means to be human. Now, in Bartram's view why is the world such an intelligible place? Because God made it for man and gave it to him to know.

That the world is "God-made" is evident from the apartment-palace metaphor noted earlier. But Bartram underscores this conviction throughout his "Introduction." For instance, he almost never refers to God simply as "God." No, God is "the great Creator," "the great Author," "the Almighty hand,"—all terms that stress that God is the maker of the world. And Bartram frequently depicts God as an architect, painter, writer, sculptor, and musical composer, as a supreme being who has "designed," "decorated," "enamelled," "embellished," and "furnished" the world. Early in the "Introduction" Bartram beckons to the reader: "Observe these green meadows how they are decorated; they seem enamelled with the beds of flowers."[8] In this one observation Bartram depicts the earth as the work of a god who is a landscape designer, a painter, and a gardener.

So the world is God-made. Equally important, it has been given by God to human beings not only as a place that they can intimately know, but as a place in which humans can find physical and spiritual nourishment. This is a recurrent theme. For instance, in the "Introduction," following a long list of the attributes of various species of plants, some remarkable for their beauty and fragrance, others for food, clothing, and medicine, Bartram exclaims: "Their valuable qualities and virtues excite love, gratitude, and adoration to the great Creator, who was pleased to endow them with such eminent qualities, and reveal them to us for our sustenance, amusement, and delight."[9]

Bartram points out still other plants that "astonish us by the figure and disposal of their vestiture, as if designed only to embellish and please the observer."[10] Why do flowers exist? One reason, Bartram tells us, is because God wants to please us with the sight of their beauty and with their fragrance.

So, nature is man's "furnished apartment," furnished by God. It is one more thing too: man's domain. In this view Bartram differs markedly from his modern scientific counterparts. In the scientific view, nature is not ordered into a hierarchy of worth or value: a man, so far as nature is concerned, has no more significance than a flower or a fly. And among the mountains, or so the author of *Mountaineering* assure us, puny man has no meaning at all. But for Bartram nature is hierarchical, and man stands at the apex of this hierarchy, the preeminent creature. Does this mean that the rest of nature—all that is below us on the scale of being—is worthless or good only insofar as we can exploit it for our benefit? Not at all. For Bartram everything in nature has God-given worth; nor is it right for us to treat nature abusively. For along with height, God has also given us responsibility. Or as Bartram wrote in *Travels:* "O Sovereign Lord! since it has pleased thee to endue man with power, and pre-eminence here on earth, and establish his dominion over all creatures, may we look up to thee, that our understanding may be so illuminated with wisdom, and our hearts warmed and animated with a due sense of charity, that we may be enabled to do thy will, and perform our duty towards those submitted to our service and protection, and be merciful to them, even as we hope for mercy. Thus may we be worthy of the dignity and superiority of the high and distinguished station in which thou has placed us here on earth."[11]

In brief, though Bartram believed that man's relationship to nature is hierarchical, it is not a hierarchy of tyrant to slave. Instead it is—or should be—a relationship guided by this model: do unto our fellow creatures as God has done to us. And since God, through his creation, has shown love, mercy, generosity to man, so man, in his keeping of God's creation, should show love, mercy, generosity to all things.

If we keep all that we have just said about Bartram in mind, we can see that when Bartram studied nature, it was at once a threefold act involving nature, man, and God. Bartram studied nature for nature's sake and to satisfy his curiosity about it; he studied nature to make useful contributions to his fellow man; and he studied nature to admire and worship the power and wisdom of God.

Now, having studied nature for many years, when Bartram introduces his

Travels with some "remarks of consequence," what, in his view, are the chief traits that he has discerned in nature? He identifies two and devotes most of the introduction to presenting the case for each. First, Bartram believes that nature is infinitely varied; but second (and seemingly contradictory at first glance) he also believes that all of nature is fundamentally uniform and one. In the first half of the introduction Bartram emphasizes "the infinite variety" to be found in nature. In the opening paragraphs he uses the words "variety" and "various" no fewer than six times to make this point. Take this sentence as an example: "Perhaps there is not any part of the creation . . . which exhibits a more glorious display of the Almighty hand, than the vegetable world. Such a variety of pleasing scenes, ever changing, throughout the seasons, arising from various causes and assigned each to the purpose and use determined."[12]

Bartram also underscores the variety to be found in nature by naming many species of plants and animals found there—thus giving rise to the long botanical lists that all readers of the *Travels* recognize. In the opening paragraphs, for instance, Bartram names no fewer than eighty-five species, genera, and families of plants, from exotic tropical flowers to wheat, from the clinging, dependent grape to "the beautiful Water Oak, whose vast hemispheric head, presents the likeness of a distant grove in the fields and savannas of Carolina."[13]

This theme of nature's variety also has a corresponding motif: each species not only has its very own attributes and functions but it also has just the right form to fulfill those functions. This is why in his introduction Bartram points out the perfect match of form and function in the tendrils of vines: "we see them invariably leaning, extending and like the fingers of the human hand, reaching to catch hold of what is nearest, just as if they had eyes to see with, and when their hold is fixed, to coil the tendril in a spiral form, by which artifice it becomes more elastic and effectual, than if it had remained in a direct line, for every revolution of the coil adds a portion of strength, and thus collected, they are enabled to dilate and contract as occasion or necessity requires."[14]

With this description of vines, however, Bartram, good writer that he is, kills two birds with one stone; or—that being an inappropriate metaphor to apply to this animal-loving naturalist—perhaps I should simply note that he does two things at once. On the one hand, he is pointing to yet another example of nature's remarkable variety; but on the other hand he is starting to present the second and seemingly contradictory of his two conclusions about nature: that nature is fundamentally uniform. For when Bartram says that we see vines, "like the fingers of the human hand, reaching to catch hold of what is nearest . . . just as if they had eyes to see with," notice that he is not only describing a unique plant but at the same time that he is likening that plant to something we rarely consider to have much in common with it, the human being. Bartram's aim here is more than just to entertain us with a clever simile. Bartram likens vines to humans because he believes (and is preparing to assert) that plants possess in common with humans and indeed with all of animate creation an essential quality. Or, as he broaches the subject: "The vital principle or efficient cause of motion and action, in the animal and vegetable system, perhaps may be more familiar than we generally apprehend."[15] And he goes on to argue that at heart what activates plants is the same inner impulse or faculty that prompts animals and humans too to move and to act. It is a secret, God-given impulse, and Bartram variously calls it "the vital principle," "the vivific principle of life," and "the intellectual system." In brief, according to Bartram all living things, from the simplest plants to the most complex animals, are fundamentally kindred in that they possess the same God-given "vital principle."[16] So when you see a Dutchman's pipe vine twining around a poplar branch, or a virginia creeper winding up an oak, Bartram would assure you that it does so in part because it *wants* to.

Bartram's belief in the essential unity of life prompts him to close his introduction by picking two arguments with those "philosophers" who stress dissimilarity among things. First he strongly disagrees with those who mark an essential difference between animals and man—with those who separate animals from man by, as he puts it, "an epithet which implies a mere mechanical impulse, which leads and impels them [animals] to necessary actions, without any premeditated design or contrivance: this we term instinct, which faculty we suppose to be inferior to reason in man."[17]

Bartram rejects the argument that animals are robotic creatures of instinct. He believes that animals possess parental and filial affections, express ardor for each other, can premeditate, be resolute, and engage in "consummate artifice in order to effect their purposes," just as human beings do. His encounter with the spider is one illustration of this. And it is to affirm his belief in the fundamental similarity between animals and man that he tells the poignant story of the shooting of a sow bear and its cub on the Mosquito River, in Florida. Bartram himself does not pull the trigger, but he does take part in the hunt with his river guide; and, once the guide shoots the sow bear, Bartram tells us that he himself was so moved by the bear cub's agony and childlike cries of grief for its slain mother that he damned the shooting as being "a cruel murder," charged himself with being an accessory to a crime, and tried, unsuccessfully, to prevail on the other man to spare the cub's life.[18]

The second argument Bartram picks is with almost all of his fellow Americans and Europeans: he does not agree with their "severe censure" of the American Indian, "that [Indians] are incapable of civilization."[19] Bartram argues that before we make this judgment, thus permanently separating the red man from the white and relegating them to a subhuman status, we ought to send sympathetic, educated observers to live with the Indians and to study their ways. One of the things those observers would learn, Bartram implies, is that at heart the red man is not so different from the white.

In summary, if we divide people into those who see distinctions between things and those who see fundamental unity and likeness, Bartram was one of the latter. For Bartram, all of animate creation is united by possession of the secret vital principle from God, and the many tribes or species in existence—though remarkably varied and distinct in form and function—are more alike than not. Nature offers to the casual observer unlimited variety and change; but the close observer will see and intuit fundamental unity there. In short, Bartram was what we call a "vitalist"—one who believes that the origin and phenomena of life are due to a vital principle as distinct from a purely chemical or physical force.

And now, rounding back to where we began, with Bartram and modern science, I will be bold to state that the world made more sense to William Bartram than it does to many twentieth-century scientists. I know there are scientists reading this who will ask, "What's this? What's this?" So let me quickly explain what I mean by the word *sense*. It is clear that the factual details and the intricate physical processes of nature make more empirical sense to us today than they did to Bartram. And, to give just a few examples, Bartram was wholly ignorant of DNA, photosynthesis, plate tectonics, and many other important, recently discovered facts about nature.

But the *sense* I am referring to when I say that the world made more sense to Bartram is of a different order. The world made philosophic and religious sense to Bartram; he understood the whole of it, knew its origin, its destiny. For him it was a purposeful and meaningful universe, one in which human beings had their rightful, important place. Bartram understood the whys and wherefores of existence. And it is just this all-important, embracing knowledge that is increasingly perplexing to modern man and of which many people now admit a profound ignorance.

Notes

1. William Bartram, *The Travels of William Bartram,* Naturalists's Edition, ed. Francis Harper (New Haven, Conn.: Yale University Press, 1958), lx.

2. "A Free Man's Worship" was first published in 1903. For an on-line version of the essay, see *Modern History Sourcebook* at http://www.fordham.edu/halsall/mod/1917russell-worship.html.

3. Harvey Manning, *Mountaineering: The Freedom of the Hills* (Seattle, Wash.: Mountaineers Books, 1967), 291.

4. Bartram, *Travels,* ed. Harper, li.

5. Ibid., lii–liii.

6. Ibid., lviii–lix.

7. Ibid., lix.

8. Ibid., liii.

9. Ibid., liii.

10. Ibid., liii.

11. Ibid., 65.

12. Ibid., li.

13. Ibid., lii.

14. Ibid., liv–lv.

15. Ibid., lv.

16. Ibid. A full assessment of Bartram's belief in vitalism and its relationship to the idea in the eighteenth century is lacking.

17. Ibid., lvi.

18. Ibid., lvii.

19. Ibid., lx.

7
Before Bartram

Artist-Naturalist Mark Catesby

Arlene Fradkin and Mallory McCane O'Connor

Introduction

Sixty-two years before William Bartram's southern tour, Mark Catesby embarked on his own journey of discovery. Catesby made two extended visits to England's American colonies. During his first trip (1712–1719), Catesby was a casual observer, exploring the natural history of the colonies and gathering some plants to send back to his friends in England. For the second trip (1722–1726), however, Catesby came as a commissioned scientific researcher and painter with the expressed purpose of observing, collecting plant and animal specimens, and visually documenting the native flora and fauna in the southern colonies. His efforts resulted in 263 watercolors and drawings, which, along with field notes and hundreds of preserved specimens, constituted one of the earliest and certainly one of the most comprehensive systematic studies of the flora and fauna of southeastern North America.[1]

Catesby's illustrations and notes were the basis for his monumental publication, *The Natural History of Carolina, Florida and the Bahama Islands.*[2] William Bartram later used Catesby's work as a reference in his report to his primary patron, John Fothergill. Published from 1729 to 1747, Catesby's two-volume work earned him membership in the venerated Royal Society of London and a respected place in the history of natural science. Cromwell Mortimer, secretary of the Royal Society, praised Catesby's publication as "the most magnificent work I know since the Art of printing has been discovered."[3] The Swedish naturalist Carl Linnaeus used the book to develop his revolutionary classification of species.[4] Thomas Jefferson avidly sought a copy of the *Natural History.* John and William Bartram pored over Catesby's magnum opus before embarking on their own travels in the Southeast.[5]

In this chapter, our objective is to draw parallels between William Bartram and his predecessor, Mark Catesby, and to establish a historical and cultural context for understanding and appreciating their work. We concentrate on five aspects of their monumental achievements: (1) the men themselves and the context in which they worked; (2) the route of their travels in the Southeast; (3) their mentors, patrons, and assistants; (4) the techniques and materials they used to realize their goals; and (5) Bartram's and Catesby's legacies in light of today's environmental issues and concerns. Here, we will address these issues in comparing Bartram's and Catesby's magnificent accomplishments.[6]

Background and Fieldwork

Mark Catesby (1682–1749) was born in England in 1682 and raised in the town of Sudbury in Suffolk, East Anglia, a rural section of eastern England. Catesby was the youngest son and the fourth of five surviving children of Elizabeth Jekyll and John Catesby, a prosperous lawyer and politician. Catesby probably received an informal education in gardening from his maternal uncle, Nicholas Jekyll, who maintained a botanical garden, and additional training in natural history from Jekyll's friend, the eminent English naturalist John Ray, who lived nearby. Through his uncle, Catesby also became acquainted with the apothecary, physician, and botanist Samuel Dale, who would become a lifelong mentor and friend and would eventually introduce Catesby to London's community of botanists, horticulturists, and gardeners.[7]

Although William Bartram had formal schooling, he learned botany from his father, who instilled in him, at a very young age, an intense love of the wilderness and the wonders of nature. William also was encouraged by his father's friends, Benjamin Franklin, Cadwallader Colden, and John Gardner. In addition, William was inspired by his tutor, Charles Thomson, later secretary of the Continental Congress, who introduced him to William Hogarth's *Analysis of Beauty* and Edmund Burke's aesthetics of the sublime and gave him "a way of seeing nature that John [Bartram] never possessed."[8]

William was less than a year old when, in November 1739, his father, John Bartram, began a correspondence with Mark Catesby that would last for many years. At the time, Catesby was engaged in the production of his monumental publication and had been depending upon their mutual friend, Peter Collinson—an English Quaker textile merchant and avid collector of exotic plants—as a go-between. Catesby decided that direct correspondence with John Bartram to request plant specimens and information would be more satisfactory and proposed that, in exchange for providing plant and animal specimens, he would send John sections of his book as they were published from year to year. Bartram responded with a letter accepting the proposal and added, "I am exceedingly pleased with thy proposals, and shall do what I can, conveniently, to comply with them. I have a great value for thy books, and esteem them as an excellent performance, and an ornament for the finest library in the world.'"9

Thus, William grew up in a household where botany was a topic of lively conversation and where letters frequently arrived from the most esteemed naturalists of the day—Carl Linnaeus, Peter Collinson, Johann Friedrich Gronovius, Benjamin Franklin, and others. Francis Harper, in the introduction to his annotated version of Bartram's *Travels*, writes, "there was no more likely source of William's inspiration than Catesby's *Natural History*, which had been presented to John Bartram by the author himself. As a boy he [William] must have felt an urge to emulate Catesby in preparing colored plates."10

Although John Bartram never received Catesby's book in its entirety, he did receive examples to provide William with a source for study. William also had the opportunity to see Catesby's work when he and his father visited John's circle of friends who owned copies of the *Natural History*. By the time he was fourteen, William was already making skillful drawings of birds and other nature subjects. When John, who called William "my little botanist," sent several examples of William's work to his colleague Peter Collinson in England, the English collector responded with "'a little token . . . for Billy whose pretty performances please me much'"—high praise indeed from such a renowned source.11

In comparing the work of young William with that of his model, Catesby, William's father is quick to point out that William's "performances" were more true-to-life. In a letter to Peter Collinson dated 1753, John commented that during a trip to the Jersey side of the Delaware River "'my son [William] spied a large rattle snake quoiled up. . . . I wished my son had brought his box of paints with him . . . to have drawn him in his greatest beauty for he was a yellow one such as Catesby drew, but I believe he drew him dead, but we could not make him offer to bite so we mercifully let him go without harm.'"12

As artists, both Bartram and Catesby were largely self-taught. Bartram left a detailed journal and other numerous writings. On the contrary, Catesby left no journal. Most of what we know about Catesby is from his published works and his correspondence. Bartram and Catesby traveled extensively throughout parts of the southern colonies, each making two extended trips. Catesby got his first glimpse of the American colonies in 1712 when he accompanied his sister Elizabeth to Williamsburg, Virginia, where he stayed with her and her husband, Dr. William Cocke, a successful physician turned politician. Catesby remained in the Williamsburg area for seven years, casually observing and admiring the local flora and fauna and visiting with the gentlemen planters, such as William Byrd II. As he explored the plantation fields and wilderness, he collected some plant specimens, which he sent back home to his friends in England, particularly Samuel Dale, and did a number of drawings of the plants and animals he saw. He also traveled to Jamaica where he perused the natural resources of the West Indies.[13]

By the time Catesby returned to England in 1719, he was known in the scientific community as "that curious Botanist" for his abilities as a botanical collector. A group of scientifically minded men—including South Carolina's newly appointed royal governor Colonel Francis Nicholson; the eminent botanist William Sherard; and the physician, naturalist, and later founder of the British Museum, Sir Hans Sloane—pledged funds to sponsor Catesby's second trip to North America. Catesby was to conduct a systematic study of the colonial Southeast. Eventually, the circle of Catesby's supporters and advisers widened to include colonists in North America, such as John Bartram, as well as experts on the European continent.[14]

Bartram first experienced the southern colonies in 1765–1766, when he accompanied his father on one of his collecting expeditions. After having sailed from Philadelphia to Charleston, South Carolina, they traveled overland through Georgia and northeast Florida, where they explored the St. Johns River. The Bartrams casually observed the natural history of the areas they explored, and William helped his father collect plants and executed some drawings. For his second journey, which lasted four years, 1773–1777, Bartram embarked on his own expedition and was commissioned by his chief patron, Dr. John Fothergill. His assignment was to conduct an extensive expedition of the southern colonies, collect specimens, make drawings of the plants he encountered, and send plant specimens and drawings to Fothergill. He retraced the route previously taken by him and his father a decade earlier and traveled through North and South Carolina, Georgia, and East Florida. In addition, he ventured west over the Appalachian Mountains into Cherokee country, traveled through what is now Alabama, Mississippi, and Louisiana, visited the Creek and Choctaw Indians, and sailed along the Gulf of Mexico and up the lower Mississippi River.[15]

In their travels, both men were interested in new plants and animals and diligently recorded the species they encountered. But Bartram was always looking to discover new species previously unknown to science and thus never named before. Catesby was looking to *discover* New World species not known in the Old World, that is, those *new* to European naturalists. Of modest means, both Bartram and Catesby relied on the funds supplied by their patrons. To meet the expectations of their sponsors, Bartram and Catesby sent back natural history specimens and notes of their observations. Peter Collinson, a critical middleman and patron for William's father, John Bartram, and for Mark Catesby, was responsible for finding William two sponsors: Dr. John Fothergill, also a Quaker gardener, and Margaret Cavendish Bentinck, the Duchess of Portland, a most important benefactor who had commissioned art prior to William's southern journey.[16]

In 1722, Catesby embarked for Charleston, South Carolina, also Bartram's base. Whereas Bartram was thirty-four years old when he embarked on his second expedition, Catesby was forty years of age, a late bloomer, when he began his adventure. For the next four years, Catesby plunged into the colonial wilderness, collecting specimens, taking notes, and drawing and painting the plants and animals he encountered. Catesby was aided in his work by a variety of informants and helpers including colonial governors and well-to-do planters as well as Native American guides who led him into the hinterland and African American slaves who advised him on folk uses of native plants. Bartram also traveled accompanied by traders, Native American guides, and planters' servants.[17]

Both Bartram and Catesby did their fieldwork under trying circumstances. Tramping through the southern wilderness, they daily faced a variety of obstacles. Bartram wrote of encountering alligators, which he greatly feared, enduring biting mosquitoes, being entrenched in southern rainstorms, sleeping under live oak trees when no pioneer cabins were available, carrying all his supplies and collection equipment on a single horse, and suffering from an eye ailment. Catesby mentioned poisonous snakes (he feared rattlesnakes), a mysterious mouth infection, inclement weather conditions, and a chronic lack of supplies necessary to conduct his work.[18]

Their sponsors were demanding, constantly requesting more specimens. Bartram's patron, Dr. Fothergill, became annoyed at the delay in receiving shipments and also expressed disappointment in content of the shipments. Catesby's patrons also complained about the delayed shipments. Dried plants molded. Animal specimens, packed into wide-mouthed jars filled with rum as a preservative, rotted when thirsty sailors raided the shipment and drank the spirits. William's specimens fared somewhat better in shipment, thanks to John Bartram's ingenious methods of packing seeds and plants to withstand the rigors of ocean travel.[19]

Bartram's and Catesby's writings reflect great respect for and genuine interest in Native American culture. During Catesby's travels, Indians assisted the naturalist and helped him survive the rigors of his adventures. Catesby wrote, "To the Hospitality and Assistance of these Friendly *Indians*, I am much indebted, for I not only subsisted on what they shot, but their First Care was to erect a Bark Hut, at the Approach of Rain to keep me and my Cargo from Wet."[20] Catesby's descriptions of the Indians he encountered were adapted from the accounts written by his predecessor, John Lawson, British surveyor-general of North Carolina, who was killed by Tuscarora Indians in 1711. Bartram wrote his own detailed observations of the Indians he met in his travels. Although John Bartram regarded the Native Americans as "ignoble savages"—John's father had been killed in an Indian attack—William, according to Thomas Slaughter, saw them as descendants of "'the ancients,' bearers of wisdom that civilized people had lost." He attempted to observe without judgment and to report on Indian culture and customs as objectively as possible. The Creek mico Cowkeeper gave Bartram the nickname of *Puc Puggy*, or Flower Hunter. Like other artist-naturalists who came after them, such as George Catlin and John James Audubon, both Catesby and especially Bartram were pioneering anthropologists.[21]

Subsequent to their travels, Bartram and Catesby earned international recognition during their lifetimes. Bartram, one of the most highly respected naturalists in America, served as an unofficial teacher and adviser to many aspiring naturalists. He generously shared his knowledge of nature with others and became the "sage" of natural history in America. Distinguished political dignitaries and international scientists also visited Bartram and the Kingsessing garden. Catesby too was also sought out for his great understanding of natural history. Both became members of honorary societies. Catesby was elected fellow of the Royal Society of London in 1733. Bartram was made a member of the prestigious American Philosophical Society in 1768 and was elected to the newly formed Academy of Natural Sciences of Philadelphia in 1812.[22]

Travel Routes

Both Bartram and Catesby were keen observers of nature. Yet neither of them kept accurate records of the chronology and route of their travels. Bartram was careless in his recording of dates and distances and his travel reports contain many errors. He traveled throughout the Southeast, including Florida and the interior portions of the region, and visited the Cherokee, Creek, and Choctaw Indians. But he never ventured offshore to the Caribbean islands.[23]

Even though Catesby's book was titled *The Natural History of Carolina, Florida and the Bahama Islands,* the geographical range given in the title exceeds that of his actual journey. He ventured into parts of South Carolina and Georgia but never made it as far south as Florida. Catesby's own words can reconcile this apparent disparity. He wrote, "After my Continuance almost three Years in *Carolina* and the adjacent parts (which the *Spaniards* call *Florida,* particularly that Province lately honour'd with the name of *Georgia*) I went to *Providence,* one of the *Bahama* Islands."[24] In fact, John and William Bartram, inspired by Catesby's work, completed the promise of Catesby's title and explored north Florida during their travels in the Southeast several decades later. But because Catesby's distances were rough estimates, they were not able to actually retrace Catesby's travels even in the Carolinas and Georgia. Catesby also attempted a trip to the interior to the mountainous Cherokee country but, for some unknown reason, had to turn back and never reached his destination.[25]

Catesby's correspondence with his patrons back in England, particularly his major benefactor and promoter, William Sherard, provides most of our knowledge of his travel route. Unfortunately, his notes and letters tell us little about where he found particular specimens or where he did his illustrations. Furthermore, most of the species he described ranged widely in the New World, thereby increasing the difficulty of pinpointing his travel itinerary.[26]

Catesby, like Bartram, spent a considerable amount of time in Charleston. From there, he made trips inland into the South Carolina uplands, or Piedmont, especially to Fort Moore, a frontier garrison located opposite the future site of Augusta, Georgia. He also mentioned having surgery for an infected mouth and surviving a hurricane in fall 1722. Early the following year, Catesby traveled up the Ashley River, staying at the home of Alexander Skene, "across from the old town of Dorchester." In March 1724, he departed Charleston to visit the "Cherikees who lived in the Apalathean Mountains about 400 miles from hence." Apparently, he never made it that far inland as he was back in Charleston within less than a month and spent the summer exploring the Piedmont area and the coastal plain. In January 1725, Catesby left for the Bahamas, where he visited the islands of New Providence, Eleuthera, Andros, and Abaco. He returned to England in 1726.[27]

Interestingly, after their second expedition in the southern colonies, both men returned home—Bartram to Philadelphia and Catesby to England— and neither of them ever came back to the Southeast. They remained in their hometowns for the rest of their lives, tending plants, drawing natural history illustrations, and preparing their field notes for their major publications.

Manuscript Production

The processes involved in producing Bartram's *Travels* and Catesby's *Natural History* have interesting histories. Bartram was instructed by Fothergill to keep a field journal during his expedition. He sent reports to his patron expecting that they might be published as a scientific work. These vanished in Fothergill's files or were somehow lost and it was almost a century later before two manuscript volumes of reports were found which covered the first two seasons of fieldwork. Bartram returned home from his travels in early 1777 as the American Revolution was just beginning. The outbreak of the Revolution cut off the possibility of further contact with his British patron, Fothergill, who died in 1780, while the war was still going on. Nevertheless, Bartram drew upon his field notes for writing his *Travels,* which was published in 1791. During this time Bartram supported himself by helping oversee the seed business at the family nursery. The Fothergill reports remained in manuscript form until 1943 when Francis Harper published a carefully annotated edition.[28]

Although Bartram seems to have made the decision to publish long after his journey, Catesby became determined to publish a comprehensive natural history of America halfway through his travels. This decision is demonstrated by his resistance to sending his drawings to his supporters, wishing instead, "to keep my Drawings intire that I may get them Graved, in order to give A genll History of the Birds And other Animals, which to distribute Seperately would wholly Frustrate that designe, And be of little value to those who would have so small fragments of the whole."[29]

Upon his return to London in 1726, Catesby sought financial backing for his planned book. Because he was no longer collecting specimens, the stipend from his patrons was terminated. To support himself, Catesby worked as an horticulturist while he began the monumental task of organizing his field notes and preparing his sketches and watercolors for publication. Lacking the funds to employ a professional engraver to reproduce his designs and wishing to maintain control over the printing of his images, Catesby learned how to etch his own copper plates by taking lessons from the French painter and printmaker Joseph Goupy. He also planned to hand-color most of the illustrations himself.[30]

Both Bartram and Catesby sold their books by subscription. Bartram's publisher sought subscribers for his forthcoming *Travels,* which included President George Washington, Vice President John Adams, and Secretary of State Thomas Jefferson. In 1729, Catesby issued a one-page prospectus for his *Natural History.* The album was to be produced in ten installments, each part consisting of twenty hand-colored etched plates accompanied by descriptive texts. He planned to issue an installment every four months. The serial nature of the project meant that each subscriber was responsible for having the volumes bound. Consequently, no extant sets of plates are exactly alike.[31]

Catesby's subscribers included a broad range of people: Englishmen, Continentals, and Americans; royals, aristocrats, gentlemen, merchants, and working men; scientists, physicians, apothecaries, gardeners, collectors, booksellers, and speculators in colonial enterprise. By pledging to purchase the book in advance of publication, subscribers assured the capital necessary to complete the project. Collinson loaned Catesby a substantial amount of money at the outset to help meet the production costs.[32]

For both Bartram and Catesby, there was a long delay between the completion of their travels and the publication of their respective books. Bartram's *Travels* was published in 1791, about fourteen years after his return. Catesby returned home in 1726, but his book was not finished till 1747. The publication of Catesby's *Natural History*, in fact, took eighteen years to complete (1729–1747), including the addition of an eleventh part that was issued as an appendix.[33]

Techniques

During Bartram's youth, the American colonies had almost no professional artists and no schools that included training in fine art. The Columbian Academy, founded by Charles Willson Peale in Philadelphia, was a short-lived experiment that soon disappeared, and it was not until the first decade of the nineteenth century that the Pennsylvania Academy of Fine Arts—the first successful art school in America—was formed. Of necessity, Bartram was self-taught. Two artists had special influence—the daughter of John Bartram's friend Cadwallader Colden, Jane, and the Swedish portrait painter Gustavus Hesselius. Of the two, Jane may have attracted the fourteen-year-old Billy's attention, but it was more likely Hesselius who provided the best artistic advice. Young William gave Jane a gift of several of his own works after spending a day at the Colden home while on a trip with his father in 1753. According to Thomas Slaughter in *The Natures of John and William Bartram*, the "Switzer gentleman" referred to by John in a letter to Peter Collinson might well have been the painter Gustavus Hesselius who visited the Bartram's Philadelphia home and who gave Billy a gift of paints and paper. Slaughter hypothesizes that "maybe Billy watched the adult artist at work; perhaps the man gave some lessons, or at least pointers, to the promising boy."[34]

William's early work was imitative of Catesby and George Edwards, Catesby's protégé and a noted English naturalist. Shortly after John sent William's drawings to Collinson in 1753, Collinson, in turn, showed these to Edwards. By May 1753, William was corresponding regularly with Edwards and sending him dried birds from Pennsylvania. In return, Edwards sent him European books on natural history. William continued to send Edwards specimens and pictures of birds while he drew plants and other organisms for Collinson. Edwards encouraged William to pursue ornithological illustrations in America. Eventually, Bartram developed his own style.[35]

Joseph Ewan, the editor of a book of William Bartram's drawings published by the American Philosophical Society in 1968, divides Bartram's artistic evolution into three periods. During the first period (1753–1770), his work, according to the Bartram Trail Conference's *Heritage Report*, expressed youthful awkwardness but possessed "a certain primitive charm."[36] This was the period when Bartram was strongly influenced by the works of Catesby and George Edwards, and Bartram's "Magnolia Warbler" might well have been derived from Catesby's "Small Bittern." In the second phase (1770–1788), Bartram's works were far more skillful and painterly. During this period, Bartram executed some of his most famous works, including the well-known drawing of the *"Franklinia alatamaha"* and the American lotus (see Figure 7.1). The *Bartram Heritage* report noted that Bartram's "compositions fill the pages with bold confidence. His flowing lines and pleasing colors create visual impressions as sophisticated as any natural history paintings produced in America prior to John James Audubon."[37] Georg Dionysius Ehret, a German-born botanical illustrator residing in England, may have influenced Bartram's work at this time. Finally, during the third period (1788–1803), Bartram developed a more "controlled and accurate illustrative style" that shared the objectivity demonstrated by his contemporaries and protégés Alexander Wilson and Titian Ramsey Peale and was common for scientific illustrations.[38]

The 263 original watercolors and drawings produced by Catesby were the working models from which he composed the illustrated plates for his *Natural History*. From these originals, he produced 220 folio-sized hand-colored etched plates for the book. Most likely, Catesby reduced the number of illustrations because of the high costs involved as well as the enormous amount of time required to produce the plates. In many cases, he took images from different originals and juxtaposed them on the same plate. In other instances, certain images in the originals were not used in the published etchings.[39]

Catesby combined drawings of individual animals and plants together in the same plate, thereby showing environmental associations. He often pictured birds with the plants on which they feed and frequent. Bartram also showed subjects in their natural environment. Like Catesby, Bartram was foreshadowing the importance of the ecosystem concept. As reflected in their artwork and writings, both men shifted away from the categorical conception of the universe and the hierarchical ordering of Creation that were prevalent in seventeenth- and eighteenth-century classifications of nature. In turn, they moved toward a more complex environmental view of the universe, defining elements of nature as interdependent, rather than separate, entities. Moreover, they viewed humans as equals with other components of nature and as part of a wholly integrated universe.[40]

In addition to the 220 illustrations, Catesby's two-volume work included detailed descriptions for every species depicted in the etched plates, title pages, dedications to Queen Caroline (vol. I) and Princess Augusta (vol. II), a map, a list of subscribers, preface, and indexes. Furthermore, he gave a brief account of the history, climate, geology, topography, natural resources, and agricultural products of Carolina and the Bahamas. His descriptions of the Indians he encountered were largely borrowed from accounts written by John Lawson, whom he acknowledged in his book. The text of the *Natural History* was

Tab. 1.

7.1. William Bartram's colocasia, the American lotus or water chinquapin (*Nelumbo lutea* Willd.), with Venus flytrap (*Dionaea muscipula* J.Ellis [Droseraceae]), and great blue heron (*Ardea herodias* Linnaeus), (1767). (Courtesy The Natural History Museum, London).

printed in English and French, thereby anticipating continental European audiences.[41]

Bartram's *Travels* is divided into four major sections. The first three sections detail his adventures during his travels while the fourth section provides his observations on the Indians he encountered in his journey and descriptions and interpretations of various aspects of their cultures. Throughout the book, Bartram pursues two themes—the wondrous fertility and variety to be found in nature and the dignity and worthiness of the Indians.

Bartram produced numerous illustrations of the flora and fauna that he observed and initially hoped that *Travels* would include more images than were eventually published, including six hand-colored flowers that were designed for a larger format than the publication could accommodate. The frontispiece of *Travels* is Bartram's portrait of Mico Chlucco the Long Warrior, or King of the Seminoles, a detailed rendering of the Indian leader portraying him in his ceremonial finery. On the reverse side of the original pen-and-ink drawing of the mico, Bartram noted that there "should be twelve feathers in the Eagle's Tail or ensigne," a correction that was acknowledged in the published version of the image.[42]

Most of Bartram's illustrations, done originally in pen and ink, made corrections difficult. The drawings are also very meticulous, although they sometimes take as much "poetic license" as does Bartram's vivid narrative. Thomas Slaughter goes so far as to label them "surrealistic" since they combine "William's various ways of seeing into an extraordinary vision from the South, from his past, from nowhere to represent everything that he knows, that he saw, that's still alive in his head."[43] He uses as an example Bartram's colocasia, in which the enormous blossoms of the American lotus tower over a crane that is "all out of proportion to the gigantic plants . . . A dragonfly perches on a flower, which is perhaps the next meal of the Venus flytrap in the lower left corner; next in nature's consuming plan is the crane, which stalks a small fish that, in turn, is searching for plant life to eat."[44] We are drawn into Bartram's intense, almost voyeuristic observations. His art and his writing reveal to us the extent of the complexity and oneness of the natural world. Clearly, his work demonstrates a synthetic view of the world integrating nature and humans within a wholly unified cosmos.

Catesby rendered his subjects as simple flat images. Although he attributed this technique to his lack of training as an artist, he also considered this advantageous to his work as he was more concerned with accuracy than with aesthetics.

Whenever possible, Catesby drew his subjects directly from life. For his plant drawings, he claimed that he did these in the field from freshly gathered specimens. It is very likely, however, that he drew some plants later on when he was back in England, using specimens he had gathered on his expeditions. In drawing plants, he depicted some at different stages of development (seed, bud, flower, nut, fruit) within the same image.[45]

For his animal drawings, where specimens were harder to obtain and preserve, Catesby's source materials varied, and the accuracy of his illustrations varied accordingly. Although he again claimed that he drew them "while alive," it is more likely that, like Audubon, he did kill some of his models before painting them.[46]

Although Catesby was a botanist at heart, birds predominated in his art. In the *Natural History*, he wrote that he drew more birds than any other animal as he believed them to be the most numerous and most beautiful of living creatures. He remarked on the ease of drawing reptiles and amphibians because they can be kept alive for long periods of time without food. Indeed, his frogs are considered by modern zoologists to be unusually accurate, with details such as the eardrums and feet very carefully depicted. Drawing fish, however, proved more difficult because they change color when taken out of water. Thus, Catesby resorted to using a succession of models in order to capture the true color of his fish subjects.[47]

With larger animals, such as the buffalo, where Catesby found his field sketches inadequate, he used and adapted illustrations done by other artists. He had access to a set of natural history illustrations from the collection of Sir Hans Sloane. Sloane's collection provided Catesby not only with alternative sources of images but also with the opportunity to interact with other artist-naturalists. These individuals included George Edwards, who contributed a drawing to Catesby's book, and Georg Dionysius Ehret, who provided Catesby with twelve plant images and who actually etched two of the plates in the *Natural History*. These were the same artists who influenced William Bartram.[48]

Catesby also consulted published books. Of these, the most outstanding was one by Dr. Martin Lister, Royal Society founder and a recognized natural history authority. Lister's book, a four-volume treatise published in 1692, contained more than one thousand copper plate engravings. The artists of the colored plates and original drawings were Lister's daughters, Susanna and Anne, great-grandnieces of the well-known gardener and herbalist John Parkinson. Viewing these remarkable images, Catesby must have recognized the challenge before him as he saw his own work through the printing process.[49]

History of Original Artworks

Currently housed in repositories, the artworks of both naturalists have been conserved and are kept in optimal conditions. There are three known repositories of Bartram's original artwork. The largest collection of Bartram's originals—fifty-nine drawings and paintings, which were executed for John Fothergill—was purchased by England's great botanist Sir Joseph Banks after Fothergill's death in 1780. In 1827, the Banks collection, which included the two manuscript journals Bartram had sent to Fothergill, was transferred to the British Museum in accordance with Banks's will. These illustrations, as well as some early sketches from the Collinson collection and a few later ones made for Robert Barclay, were later transferred to the Natural History Museum in London. Today, they are kept in a bound album at the Botanical Library of the museum. This collection consists of sixty-eight drawings, of which seventeen are watercolors, six are incomplete watercolors, and the remaining forty-five are rendered in pen and ink. They have been reproduced in *William Bartram: Botanical and Zoological Drawings, 1756–1788.*

A second group of Bartram's artwork was originally Peter Collinson's collection. These were purchased from Collinson's estate in 1834 by Aylmer B. Lambert, a celebrated antiquarian and botanist. Following Lambert's death, the collection was purchased by Edward Smith Stanley, the thirteenth Earl of Derby. This collection—consisting of twenty-eight drawings of birds, twelve of trees in flower and fruit executed for Collinson before Bartram's first trip to Florida (1765–1766) and several later works—is now in the library of the eighteenth Earl of Derby at Knowsley Hall in Merseyside, northwest England.

A third collection of Bartram's drawings remained in North America and were originally owned by the botanist Benjamin Smith Barton and William Hamilton. These include several illustrations made on the 1773–1777 expedition, or at Bartram's home shortly thereafter, and others drawn for illustrating Barton's book, *Elements of Botany.* These drawings, which mostly date to Bartram's third stylistic period, are now housed at the American Philosophical Society in Philadelphia.[50]

Nearly twenty years after Catesby's death in 1749, his 263 original watercolors were purchased in 1768 for 120 English pounds by England's George III, a natural history buff, who obtained them from a London bookseller named Thomas Cadell. Bound in three volumes, the watercolors were housed in the king's large famous library in Buckingham House, now Buckingham Palace, where they were shelved in the natural history section.[51]

In 1823, King George IV donated most of his father's library to the British Museum. The Catesby volumes and some other treasures, however, were held back and subsequently were moved to the newly established Royal Library set up at Windsor Castle by King William IV in 1833. Since then, the Catesby volumes remained on the shelf, virtually untouched. Because the volumes remained closed for over two centuries, the watercolors were protected from exposure to light and thus remained in excellent condition. However, because they were bound, the watercolors were subject to rubbing from the pages of the books and therefore were in need of conservation. In 1994, a Japanese benefactor, Mrs. Hiroko Usami, gave a generous gift for the conservation of the watercolors. The paintings were removed from their mounts, cleaned, conserved, and remounted separately. Subsequently, fifty-two of the original watercolors were organized into an exhibition, which traveled to several venues in the United States and to the Queen's Gallery in London in 1997–1998.[52]

Because of the great interest in their artwork, as well as the need to preserve and protect the collections, Alecto Historical Editions, United Kingdom, prepared facsimiles of Bartram's 68 original illustrations at the Natural History Museum and of Catesby's 263 original watercolors at Windsor Castle. These prints were produced by a process called *stochastic lithography*. A new advance in printing technology, stochastic lithography uses a system of computer-controlled microdots distributed in accordance with the tonal values of the original. Consequently, the facsimiles are almost indistinguishable from the originals. The quality of the facsimiles is further enhanced by the use of a special mold-made paper, conservator-approved and acid-free, which is virtually identical to that used by Bartram and Catesby.[53]

Legacy

William Bartram and Mark Catesby were pioneers in the field of scientific illustration in a time when science and art overlapped. Their *Travels* and *Natural History*, respectively, were models of the spirit of scientific inquiry and reporting prevalent during their time and were certainly among the greatest achievements of eighteenth-century art and science.

These early artist-naturalists have left an incredibly rich legacy. Through their artwork and written accounts, these "nature reporters" have provided detailed documentation on American landscapes that have since been drastically altered. Their works were among the earliest attempts at a natural history of what is today the southeast United States and the Caribbean. Both individuals strove for accurate and comprehensive reporting and endeavored to explain and interpret for their readers the natural history of the new and exotic regions that they explored firsthand. As scientists, they focused on data gathering and recording. As artists, they sought to render faithful observations of the natural world.

The Swedish naturalist Carl Linnaeus drew heavily on Catesby's *Natural History* in creating his scientific classification and nomenclature of plants and animals and, moreover, retained Catesby's own Latin designations for 75 North American and 3 Bahamian bird species. Bartram, whose writings postdated

7.2. *Rana maxima Americana Aquatica,* the bullfrog; *Helleborine:* the lady's slipper of Pensilvania, from Mark Catesby's, *The Natural History of Carolina, Florida and the Bahama Islands: Containing the Figures of Birds, Beasts, Fishes, Serpents, Insects, and Plants* (1754) Vol. II, pp. 72-T 72 (Image courtesy of the University of Wisconsin Digital Collections).

Linnaeus's revolutionary work, included in his *Travels* a catalogue of 215 species of birds of eastern North America, the most complete and accurate ornithological listing compiled up to that time and a basis for future compilations. He also proposed 123 new binomial designations for American flora and fauna. Moreover, a number of Bartram's original images are of species previously unknown to science when he illustrated them.[54]

Interestingly enough, several species were named in honor of these artist-naturalists. For Bartram, the upland plover was called Bartram's plover (*Bartramia longicauda*).[55] Three species were named after Catesby: the bullfrog, *Rana catesbeiana;* Catesby's lily, *Lilium catesbaei;* and Catesby's lily-thorn, *Catesbaea spinosa*[56] (see Figure 7.2).

Both naturalists were very active in the transatlantic trafficking of plant specimens. The eighteenth century was a dynamic period in the history of British and American gardens, with plants being shared by collectors on both sides of the Atlantic. Both men had close associations with botanical collectors and their gardens in England and in America, and they played a major role in the establishment, stocking, maintenance, and perpetuation of garden culture. Gardens served as living laboratories for experiments in naturalizing plants, studios for artistic illustrations, and venues for the distribution of seeds and plants locally and internationally. This is still apparent as living descendants of plants they introduced can be found growing in English and American gardens today.

Bartram and Catesby also made significant contributions to zoology. In addition to including the catalogue of birds in his *Travels*, Bartram provided detailed accounts of animals. Of particular note were his descriptions of amphibians and reptiles in the Southeast. His *Travels* and personal contacts inspired and trained several young naturalists including the noted ornithologist Alexander Wilson.[57]

Both Bartram and Catesby had a great interest in animal behavior and made some interesting observations. In investigating the migratory habits of birds, Catesby rejected the prevailing explanation for seasonal variation in bird populations that birds hibernate in caves or beneath ponds. Rather, he espoused the view that birds do not hibernate but instead fly to warmer climes when the weather turned too cold for them. Catesby's explanation of bird migration is one of his most distinctive contributions to natural history. He read his paper, "Of Birds of Passage," subsequently published in the Royal Society's *Philosophical Transactions* in 1747.[58]

Bartram's descriptions of Southeast Indian tribes are among the best Indian studies of that time period. As a Quaker, Bartram believed in the worth of all creation, regarding Indians and whites as equals, and followed the Quaker tradition of tolerance and pacifism. In addition, he valued Indian knowledge regarding the natural world.[59]

The importance of Catesby's *Natural History* as an illustrated guide to American species led to the work being republished several times after Catesby's death. Two more English editions were published: a second edition in 1754 by Catesby's protégé, the ornithologist George Edwards, who revised and reissued the original publication; and a third edition in 1771 by Benjamin White, who reissued Edwards's edition and included a catalogue of the Linnaean names assigned to Catesby's plants and animals. In addition, several pirated European editions of the *Natural History* were published in German, Latin, Dutch, and French. Catesby's *Hortus Britanno-Americanus* was finished shortly before his death in 1749 but was not published until 1763. In this book, Catesby focused on the practical uses of American flora and promoted the introduction and domestication of these exotics into English gardens.[60]

Bartram's *Travels* was first published in Philadelphia and subsequently in London and then other parts of Europe. *Travels* received a respectful but tepid reception in America. *Travels* fared much better in Europe where, translated into Dutch, German, and French within a decade, a total of nine foreign editions were printed. In addition, Bartram's *Observations on the Creek and Cherokee Indians* was published posthumously in 1853 and is a rich source of ethnological information, still a valuable reference for anthropologists today.[61]

Bartram and Catesby produced a magnificent record of what the environment was like in the southern colonies in the 1700s. Both *Travels* and *Natural History* had a great impact on their European readers. Paradoxically, Catesby's love of the New World landscape helped contribute to the eventual changes that took place. Addressing a European audience, Catesby interpreted the New World for residents of the Old and thus stimulated an interest in colonization, thereby drawing more Europeans to America. Even by the American Revolution, the wilderness had begun to disappear. Bartram addresses some of the changes he noted even in the ten years since he visited the southeast region with his father. Some of the species Catesby painted and described, such as the passenger pigeon and the Carolina parakeet, are now extinct. Many are endangered. In fact, the ivory-billed woodpecker is now almost gone. Only a few, if any, survive in isolated parts of Louisiana and Florida. Likewise, the *Franklinia* shrub that Bartram discovered in Georgia does not occur in the wild today. Bartram's and Catesby's illustrations captured a world that no longer exists, and that is itself a monumental legacy.[62]

In his book *Romantic Natural Histories* Ashton Nichols writes, "Romantic natural histories link 'animated nature' with what Samuel Taylor Coleridge will call 'the one Life within us and abroad.'"[63] Nichols, like other literary critics, points out William Bartram's impact on the Romantic poets. He notes, "ever since John Livingston Lowes chronicled every detail that might have fostered Coleridge's eidetic imagination, we have appreciated the way that Bartram's roaring alligators, unfolding tropical blossoms, and lush Floridian landscape played on the minds of poets in the chilly mists of the Lake District. . . . His detailed, flowing, and sometimes startled prose reminds us of the way that verbal pictures of the vastness, strangeness, and natural beauty of America have stimulated European imagination over the past two centuries."[64]

Catesby considered his images of the flora and fauna of the southern wilderness more important than his written descriptions of them. His paintings are simply beautiful and charming works of art. But Catesby's illustrations are so much more than observation and depiction. His plants and animals are not static portrayals but rather are captured in motion,[65] doing what they ordinarily do, full of life and vitality. The bluejay, with its tail cocked, screams down from its perch on a branch of the *Smilax* plant. The ground squirrel, or chipmunk, holds a nut in its front paws while standing on its hind legs.

Catesby displays a sense of wonder and delight in the natural world. A green tree frog, perched on a skunk cabbage, has its mouth open and tongue extending toward an unsuspecting spider. Catesby was precise as well as witty, and his whimsical nature and sense of humor shine through many of his illustrations. A buffalo, dwarfed by a locust, scratches itself against a broken trunk of the tree.

For both Bartram and Catesby, the natural world was their subject. They portrayed the colonial American landscape as they saw it: fascinating, beautiful, and alluring. They captured their enthusiasm and awe on canvas and in words. Indeed, their greatest gift has been in directing subsequent generations to find that pleasure and awe in nature.

Notes

1. George Frederick Frick and Raymond Phineas Stearns, *Mark Catesby: The Colonial Audubon* (Urbana: University of Illinois Press, 1961), 11–17, 22–34, 37, 45.

2. Mark Catesby, *The Natural History of Carolina, Florida and the Bahama Islands,* 2 vols. (London: Printed for the author, 1731–1743 [1729–1747]). The dates 1731 and 1743 are the publication dates that appear on the title pages of the first and second volumes of *Natural History,* respectively. The publication of *Natural History,* however, actually began before and ended after these dates. The first part was issued in 1729, and the Appendix was completed in 1747.

3. Frick and Stearns, *Mark Catesby,* 38–39; Amy R. W. Meyers, "'The Perfecting of Natural History': Mark Catesby's Drawings of American Flora and Fauna in the Royal Library, Windsor Castle," in *Mark Catesby's Natural History of America: The Watercolors from the Royal Library, Windsor Castle,* ed. Henrietta McBurney (London: Merrell Holberton, 1997), 11 (quotation).

4. Alan Feduccia, ed., *Catesby's Birds of Colonial America* (Chapel Hill: University of North Carolina Press, 1985), 11–13; Frick and Stearns, *Mark Catesby,* 58–59, 65, 70, 76–85; Richard A. Howard and George W. Staples, "The Modern Names for Catesby's Plants," *Journal of the Arnold Arboretum* 64 (1983): 511–546; Henrietta McBurney, *Mark Catesby's Natural History of America: The Watercolors from the Royal Library, Windsor Castle* (London: Merrell Holberton, 1997), 37; Robert L. Wilbur, "Identification of the Plants Illustrated and Described in Catesby's *Natural History of the Carolinas, Florida and the Bahamas,*" *SIDA, Contributions to Botany* 14 (1990): 29–48.

5. Frick and Stearns, *Mark Catesby,* 106; David Scofield Wilson, *In the Presence of Nature* (Amherst: University of Massachusetts Press, 1978), 139; David Brigham, "Mark Catesby and the Patronage of Natural History," in *Empire's Nature: Mark Catesby's New World Vision,* ed. Amy R. W. Meyers and Margaret Beck Pritchard (Chapel Hill: University of North Carolina Press, 1998), 121–122; Catesby, *Natural History,* II, 72, Appendix, 4, 15, 17; Frick and Stearns, *Mark Catesby,* 90–91, 106; Thomas P. Slaughter, *The Natures of John and William Bartram* (New York: Random House, 1996), 50.

6. Arlene Fradkin and Mallory McCane O'Connor, eds., *Opening the Door to a New World: Mark Catesby's Travels in La Florida, 1722–1726,* exhibition catalogue, Schmidt Center Gallery, Florida Atlantic University (Boca Raton: Florida

Atlantic University, 2001). We have based our overview of Catesby's life and work on a series of essays that were included in this catalogue produced to accompany the exhibition. Contributing humanities scholars included David R. Brigham, director of Collections and Exhibitions, Worcester Art Museum, Worcester, Massachusetts; Henrietta McBurney, deputy curator of the Print Room, the Royal Library, Windsor Castle, Great Britain; Charlotte M. Porter, curator and professor of History, Florida Museum of Natural History, University of Florida, Gainesville; Donna Waller, associate professor of History and Political Science, Santa Fe Community College, Gainesville, Florida; and Joseph L. Aufmuth, Geographic Information Systems (GIS) coordinator, George A. Smathers Libraries, University of Florida, Gainesville.

7. Frick and Stearns, *Mark Catesby,* 3–5, 8–10; Amy R. W. Meyers and Margaret Beck Pritchard, "Introduction: Toward an Understanding of Catesby," in *Empire's Nature: Mark Catesby's New World Vision,* eds. Amy R. W. Meyers and Margaret Beck Pritchard (Chapel Hill: University of North Carolina Press, 1998), 2.

8. Slaughter, *The Natures of John and William Bartram,* 123, 118 (quotation), 196.

9. Ibid., 249; Edmund Berkeley and Dorothy Smith Berkeley, *The Life and Travels of John Bartram: From Lake Ontario to the River St. John* (Tallahassee: University Presses of Florida, 1982), 69–70 (quotation).

10. William Bartram, *The Travels of William Bartram, Naturalists's Edition,* ed. Francis Harper (New Haven, Conn.: Yale University Press, 1958), xxi.

11. Quoted in Slaughter, *The Natures of John and William Bartram,* 111, 112.

12. Ibid., 113.

13. Frick and Stearns, *Mark Catesby,* x, 11–16, 45, 50; Slaughter, *The Natures of John and William Bartram,* 115, 117, 258, 259; Catesby, *Natural History,* I, v, 48, 67, 70.

14. Frick and Stearns, *Mark Catesby,* 14–19, 42–43; Charlotte M. Porter, "Mark Catesby's Audience and Patrons," in *Opening the Door,* ed. Fradkin and O'Connor, 12–13.

15. Slaughter, *The Natures of John and William Bartram;* Bartram, *Travels,* ed. Harper, xviii; Gregory A. Waselkov and Kathryn E. Holland Braund, eds., *William Bartram on the Southeastern Indians* (Lincoln: University of Nebraska Press, 1995), 11.

16. Catesby, *Natural History,* I, v–vi, viii; Berkeley and Berkeley, *The Life and Travels of John Bartram,* 275; Slaughter, *The Natures of John and William Bartram,* 169.

17. Frick and Stearns, *Mark Catesby,* 22–34, 50; Catesby, *Natural History,* I, vi, viii–ix, 31, 35, 43; David R. Brigham, "Mark Catesby: The Man and His Work," in *Opening the Door,* 8; Joseph Kastner, *A World of Naturalists* (Great Britain: John Murray, 1978), 99, 105; Slaughter, *The Natures of John and William Bartram,* 200.

18. Wayne Hanley, *Natural History in America: From Mark Catesby to Rachel Carson* (New York: Quadrangle/The New York Times Book Co., 1977), 25; Frick and Stearns, *Mark Catesby*, 26.

19. Berkeley and Berkeley, *The Life and Travels of John Bartram*, 288; Frick and Stearns, *Mark Catesby*, 23, 25–26, 28; Kastner, *A World of Naturalists*, 83.

20. Catesby, *Natural History*, I, viii–ix.

21. Catesby, *Natural History*, II, vii–xvi; Frick and Stearns, Mark Catesby, 18; Waselkov and Braund, *William Bartram on the Southeastern Indians*, 1, 15; Slaughter, *The Natures of John and William Bartram*, 211 (quotation); Robert Elman, *First in the Field: America's Pioneering Naturalists* (New York: Mason/Charter, 1977), 15.

22. Bartram, *Travels*, ed. Harper, xxviii–xxxv; Bartram, *William Bartram on the Southeastern Indians*, ed. Waselkov and Braund, 19–23; Frick and Stearns, *Mark Catesby*, 38–39.

23. Kastner, *A World of Naturalists*, 86; Bartram, *William Bartram on the Southeastern Indians*, ed. Waselkov and Braund, 11.

24. Catesby, *Natural History*, I, x.

25. Amy R. Weinstein Meyers, "Sketches from the Wilderness: Changing Conceptions of Nature in American Natural History Illustration: 1680–1880," 2 vols. (Ph.D. diss., Yale University, 1985), I, 126–127; Porter, "Mark Catesby's Audience and Patrons," 13; Frick and Stearns, *Mark Catesby*, 28–29.

26. Joseph L. Aufmuth, "Mark Catesby's Travels in La Florida 1722–1726: A Present-Day Mapping Retrospective," in *Opening the Door*, 10.

27. Frick and Stearns, *Mark Catesby*, 23–24 (quotation), 28–29, 33; Catesby, *Natural History*, I, x.

28. Bartram, *Travels*, ed. Harper, xx; Bartram, *William Bartram on the Southeastern Indians*, ed. Waselkov and Braund, 10, 19; Kastner, *A World of Naturalists*, 109; Slaughter, *The Natures of John and William Bartram*, 185; William Bartram, *Travels in Georgia and Florida, 1773–74: A Report to Dr. John Fothergill*, annotated by Francis Harper, *Transactions of the American Philosophical Society*, new series, vol. 33, part 2 (Philadelphia: 1943).

29. Frick and Stearns, *Mark Catesby*, 28; Meyers, "'The Perfecting of Natural History,'" 15.

30. Frick and Stearns, *Mark Catesby*, 35, 37; Catesby, *Natural History*, I, xi; Meyers, "'The Perfecting of Natural History,'" 17; Meyers and Pritchard, "Introduction," 14.

31. Kastner, *A World of Naturalists*, 110; David R. Brigham, "Mark Catesby and the Patronage of Natural History in the First Half of the Eighteenth Century," in *Empire's Nature*, 110–111; Brigham, "Mark Catesby: The Man and His Work," 8; Frick and Stearns, *Mark Catesby*, 37; Meyers, "'The Perfecting of Natural History,'" 17; Brigham, "Mark Catesby and the Patronage of Natural History," 92.

32. Brigham, "Mark Catesby and the Patronage of Natural History," 113; Brigham, "Mark Catesby: The Man and His Work," 8; Frick and Stearns, *Mark Catesby,* 36, 50–51.

33. Brigham, "Mark Catesby and the Patronage of Natural History," 111; Brigham, "Mark Catesby: The Man and His Work," 8.

34. Slaughter, *The Natures of John and William Bartram,* 115; Berkeley and Berkeley, *The Life and Travels of John Bartram,* 149.

35. Elman, *First in the Field,* 33–34; Slaughter, *The Natures of John and William Bartram,* 112, 114, 121.

36. Bartram Trail Conference, *Bartram Heritage: A Study of the Life of William Bartram by the Bartram Trail Conference, including the Report to the Heritage, Conservation and Recreation Service, U.S. Department of the Interior* (Montgomery, Ala.: Bartram Trail Conference, 1979), 45.

37. Bartram Trail Conference, *Bartram Heritage,* 48.

38. Ibid., 48 (quotation); Joseph Ewan, ed., *William Bartram: Botanical and Zoological Drawings, 1756–1788* (Philadelphia: American Philosophical Society, 1968).

39. Meyers, "'The Perfecting of Natural History,'" 11; Henrietta McBurney, "Mark Catesby's Techniques as a Draftsman and Printmaker," in *Opening the Door to a New World,* ed. Fradkin and O'Connor, 16; McBurney, *Mark Catesby's Natural History,* 37; Meyers and Pritchard, "Introduction," 9.

40. Catesby, *Natural History,* I, xi; Frick and Stearns, *Mark Catesby,* 60; McBurney, *Mark Catesby's Natural History,* 37; Meyers, *Sketches from the Wilderness,* 142, 178.

41. Brigham, "Mark Catesby and the Patronage of Natural History," 91–93; Brigham, "Mark Catesby: The Man and His Work," 8; Catesby, *Natural History,* II, vii–xvi; Meyers and Pritchard, "Introduction," 14–15.

42. Slaughter, *The Natures of John and William Bartram,* 240; see Bartram, *William Bartram on the Southeastern Indians,* ed. Waselkov and Braund, 67.

43. Slaughter, *The Natures of John and William Bartram,* 231.

44. Ibid.

45. Catesby, *Natural History,* I, xi; McBurney, "Mark Catesby's Techniques," 16; Frick and Stearns, *Mark Catesby,* 67.

46. Catesby, *Natural History,* I, xi (quotation); McBurney, "Mark Catesby's Techniques," 17.

47. Catesby, *Natural History,* I, ix, xi; McBurney, *Mark Catesby's Natural History,* 95; McBurney, "Mark Catesby's Techniques," 17.

48. Catesby, *Natural History,* Appendix, plate 20; McBurney, *Mark Catesby's Natural History,* 33, 115, 116, 120; McBurney, "Mark Catesby's Techniques," 17; Meyers, "'The Perfecting of Natural History,'" 25. The drawing contributed by George Edwards was the Razor-billed Black-bird of Jamaica, RL 26068, which Catesby

etched for his *Natural History*. Catesby, *Natural History*, Appendix, plate 3; McBurney, *Mark Catesby's Natural History*, 68; McBurney, "Mark Catesby's Techniques," 17. The two plates etched by Georg Dionysius Ehret were *Magnolia altissima:* The Laurel Tree of Carolina, Catesby, *Natural History*, II, plate 61, and The Mangrove Grape Tree, Catesby, *Natural History*, II, plate 96. Frick and Stearns, *Mark Catesby*, 66; McBurney, "Mark Catesby's Techniques," 17; Wilson, *In the Presence of Nature*, 153.

49. Porter, "Mark Catesby's Audience and Patrons," 13; Martin Lister, *Historiae Sive Synopsis Methodicae Conchyliorum* (London: 1685–1692).

50. Ewan, *William Bartram: Botanical and Zoological Drawings, 1756–1788*, 31–33.

51. Oliver Everett, "Preface," in *Mark Catesby's Natural History*, 7; McBurney, *Mark Catesby's Natural History*, 29–31.

52. McBurney, *Mark Catesby's Natural History*, 31; Everett, "Preface," 7; Meyers and Pritchard, "Introduction," 24.

53. Alecto Historical Editions, *Prospectus for the Facsimile Edition of the Original & Unpublished Watercolour Drawings for the Natural History of Carolina, Florida and the Bahama Islands by Mark Catesby* (London: Alecto Historical Editions, 1998); Meyers and Pritchard, "Introduction," 25.

54. Frick and Stearns, *Mark Catesby*, 83; David Scofield Wilson, *In the Presence of Nature* (Amherst: University of Massachusetts Press, 1978); Feduccia, *Catesby's Birds of Colonial America*, 11–13; Frick and Stearns, *Mark Catesby*, 58–59, 65, 70, 76–85; Howard and Staples, "The Modern Names for Catesby's Plants"; McBurney, *Mark Catesby's Natural History*, 37; Wilbur, "Identification of the Plants"; Elman, *First in the Field*, 46.

55. Elman, *First in the Field*, 42.

56. The bullfrog, the largest frog in North America, was named by the English naturalist George Shaw to honor Catesby's work. Frick and Stearns, *Mark Catesby*, 81. The red lily was renamed "Catesby's lily" by the eighteenth-century botanist Thomas Walter. McBurney, *Mark Catesby's Natural History*, 102. The lilythorn was named by the eighteenth-century naturalist Johann Friedrich Gronovius in honor of Catesby. Catesby, *Natural History*, II, 100; Frick and Stearns, *Mark Catesby*, 42, 65.

57. Therese O'Malley, "Mark Catesby and the Culture of Gardens," in *Empire's Nature*, 147–183; Frick and Stearns, *Mark Catesby*, 67–68; Elman, *First in the Field*, 42; Bartram, *Travels*, ed. Harper, xxxi–xxxii.

58. Frick and Stearns, *Mark Catesby*, 43–44, 63–64.

59. Bartram, *William Bartram on the Southeastern Indians*, ed. Waselkov and Braund, 204.

60. Frick and Stearns, *Mark Catesby*, 100–103, 109–110; Mark Catesby, *The Natural History of Carolina, Florida and the Bahama Islands . . .* 2 vols., 2nd ed., re-

vised by George Edwards (London: 1754); Mark Catesby, *The Natural History of Carolina, Florida and the Bahama Islands . . .* 2 vols. 3rd ed., revised by George Edwards (London: 1771). Frick and Stearns, *Mark Catesby,* 68–69, 102–103, 110.

61. Bartram, *Travels,* ed. Harper, xxii–xxviii; William Bartram, "Observations on the Creek and Cherokee Indians, 1789, with Prefatory and Supplementary Notes by E. G. Squier," *Transactions of the American Ethnological Society,* vol. 3, part 1, 1–81 (New York: 1853).

62. Donna Waller, "Mark Catesby's Legacy," in *Opening the Door,* ed. Fradkin and O'Connor, 21. The passenger pigeon numbered three to five billion when the first Europeans arrived in North America. In the late 1870s, the population of this species began to quickly decline. The last bird died in captivity in 1914 at the Cincinnati Zoological Garden. A. W. Schorger, *The Passenger Pigeon: Its Natural History and Extinction* (Norman: University of Oklahoma Press, 1973). The Carolina parakeet also became extinct by the early 1900s. The last bird was reported in 1920 in Florida. Roger Tory Peterson, *A Field Guide to the Birds: A Completely New Guide to All the Birds of Eastern and Central North America,* 4th ed. (Boston: Houghton Mifflin, 1980), 178; National Geographic, *Field Guide to the Birds of North America,* 4th ed. (Washington, D.C.: National Geographic, 2002), 284; Elman, *First in the Field,* 38.

63. Elman, *First in the Field,* 38; Ashton Nichols, ed., *Romantic Natural Histories: William Wordsworth, Charles Darwin, and Others* (Boston: Houghton Mifflin, 2004), 1.

64. Ibid., 187–188.

65. Frick and Stearns, *Mark Catesby,* 61–62; McBurney, *Mark Catesby's Natural History,* 37.

III
Uncovering Bartram: New Discoveries

8

The Bartrams, Clarence B. Moore, and Mount Royal

Early Archaeology on the St. Johns River, Florida

Jerald T. Milanich

When John and William Bartram first traveled the St. Johns River in 1765 and 1766, nearly all of east Florida was wilderness, home to Seminole Indians with rare outposts of Anglos. The indigenous Timucua, whose ancestors had lived on the St. Johns River for centuries, were gone, victims of European colonization. The Seminoles, relatives of Creek and other Indians, had began to move into Florida and to establish towns beginning about 1750.

Among the many things the Bartrams noted were archaeological sites, some of which may have been villages occupied by Timucuan-speaking Indians less than a century earlier. Other sites visited by the Bartrams had much great antiquity.

One archaeological site visited by the Bartrams was Mount Royal, one of Florida's two most famous archaeological monuments (the other is the Crystal River site on the Gulf coast). Mount Royal (Florida archaeological site 8Pu35, where 8 is for Florida, the eighth state alphabetically—prior to Alaska and Hawaii; Pu for Putnam County; and 35 as the thirty-fifth site recorded in the county), is adjacent to Fruitland Cove on the east side of the St. Johns River just north of Lake George in what today is western Putnam County, Florida. The site was occupied by Indians over hundreds, perhaps thousands, of years, though it is best known for the large sand mound that is at the head of a long causeway delineated by two parallel sand ridges, both features thought to date about AD 1200.

Though reduced in size, the mound still exists and can be visited by the public (take Fort Gates Ferry Road off State Road 309, then Mount Royal Avenue and follow the signs). The causeway and ridges have been badly eroded and can only be seen in older aerial photographs (Figure 8.1).

John and William Bartram were at the site in early 1766 while Florida was a British colony. John wrote:

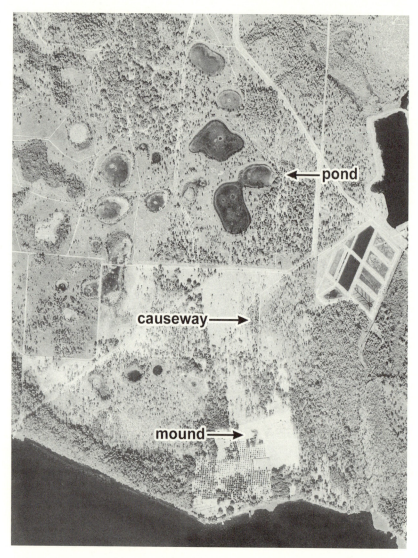

8.1. Aerial photograph of the Mount Royal site showing the mound and a portion of the causeway. The causeway extended to the small pond on the right almost directly north. That pond and the one on the left probably formed a single, oblong pond when the Bartrams were at Mount Royal. The small black dots south of the mound are orange trees (United States Department of Agriculture, print CYZ-1C-157, flown January 17, 1943, Map and Imagery Library, University of Florida, George A. Smathers Libraries).

About noon we landed at Mount-Royal, and went to an Indian tumulus, which was about 100 yards in diameter, nearly round, and nearly 20 feet high, found some bones scattered on it, it must be very ancient, as live-oaks are growing upon it three foot in diameter; what a prodigious multitude of Indians must have labored to raise it? to what height, we can't say, as it must have settled much in such a number of years, and it is surprizing where they brought the sand from, and how, as they had nothing but baskets and bowls to carry it in; there seems to be a little hollow near the adjacent level on one side, though not likely to raise such a tumulus the 50th part of what it is, but directly north from the tumulus is a fine straight avenue about 60 yards broad, all the surface of which has been taken off, and thrown on each side, which makes a bank of about a rood wide and a foot high more or less, as the unevenness of the ground required, for the avenue is as level as a floor from bank to bank, and continues so for about three quarters of a mile to a pond of about 100 yards broad and 150 yards long N. and S. seemed to be an oblong square, and its banks 4 foot perpendicular, gradually sloping every way to the water, the depth of which we could not say, but do not imagine it deep, as the grass grows all over it; by its regularity it seems to be artificial; if so, perhaps the sand was carried from hence to raise the tumulus, as the one directly faces the other at each end of the avenue; on the south side of the tumulus I found a very large rattle-snake sunning himself, I suppose this to be his winter-quarters; here had formerly been a large Indian town; I suppose there is 50 acres of planting ground cleared and of a middling soil, a good part of which is mixed with small shells; no doubt this large tumulus was their burying-place or sepulchre: Whether the Florida Indians buried the bones after the flesh was rotted off them, as the present Southern Indians do, I can't say.[1]

William returned to Mount Royal alone in 1774 and wrote his own description of the site:

At about fifty yards distance from the landing place, stands a magnificent Indian mount. About fifteen years ago I visited this place, at which time there were no settlements of white people, but all appeared wild and savage; yet in that uncultivated state it possessed an almost inexpressible air of grandeur. . . . But what greatly contributed towards completing the magnificence of the scene, was a noble Indian highway, which led from the great mount, on a straight line, three quarters of a mile, first through a point or wing of the orange grove, and continuing thence through an awful forest of live oaks, it was terminated by palms and laurel magnolias, on the verge of an oblong artificial lake, which was on the edge of an extensive green level savanna. This grand highway was about fifty yards wide, sunk a little below the common level, and the earth thrown up on each side, making a bank of about two feet high.[2]

A short distance upriver (south) from Mount Royal, William Bartram stopped at a second archaeological site, one much less well known. Exploring Drayton Island in the northern end of Lake George, he described what he saw:

The Island appears . . . to have been once the chosen residence of an Indian prince, there being to this day evident remains of a large town of the Aborigines. It was situated on an eminence near the banks of the lake, and commanded a comprehensive and charming prospect of the waters, islands, east and west shores of the lake, the capes, the bay, and Mount Royal. . . . On the site of this ancient town, stands a very pompous Indians mount, or conical pyramid of earth, from which runs in a straight line a grand avenue or Indian highway, through a magnificent grove of magnolias, live oaks, palms, and orange trees. . . . This island appears to have been well inhabited, as is very evident, from the quantities of fragments of Indian earthen ware, bones of animals and other remains, particularly in the shelly heights and ridges all over the island.[3]

Like the causeway at Mount Royal, Bartram's "grand avenue" on Drayton Island (part of archaeological site 8Pu43) can be seen in aerial photographs.[4]

These were not the only archaeological sites along the St. Johns River on which the Bartrams camped. Some they did not realize were sites, locales like the "little promontory, at the turning of the river . . . containing about three acres of high ground" that was "one entire orange grove" where William Bartram camped in 1774 and where he had his famed alligator encounters.[5] The high ground on the river was a shell midden. Two days later he camped on another shell midden ("a high perpendicular bluff") on which he observed a number of (above ground?) human burials of people he referred to as Yamassee Indians, calling the burials "the monuments of ancients."[6] Though he does not say so, William Bartram's identification of the burials as colonial-period Indians probably was based on European objects buried with the people. Most likely, the site had been associated with Creek or other Indians, relatives of the Seminoles. At other sites, Bartram recognized broken Indian pottery and other refuse.

The nineteenth-century archaeologist Jeffries Wyman, Harvard Peabody Museum curator, was acquainted with the Bartrams and relied on their eighteenth-century narratives for information. Using the Bartrams' accounts for reference, Wyman revisited the "little promontory, at the turning of the river," in 1867, describing it as a large freshwater shell midden on the left bank of the river just north of Lake Dexter in Lake County (site 8La24). He named the site Bartram's Mound or Little Orange Mound.[7] Wyman was unable to relocate the "high perpendicular bluff" upriver, certainly a second shell midden.[8]

Another archaeologist who followed the Bartrams was Clarence B. Moore of Philadelphia. In the 1890s, Moore, like Wyman, traveled on the St. Johns River itself, though he couched himself in luxury aboard steamboats outfitted for the task. One hundred twenty years after William Bartram's lone trek, Moore returned to Mount Royal and carried out excavations in the "mount."

Moore was well aware of the writings of John and William Bartram, quoting both in his Mount Royal reports. He also read Ephraim Squier and Edwin Davis's 1848 book *Ancient Monuments of the Mississippi Valley*, which contains a quote regarding Mount Royal taken from William Bartram's at-the-time-unpublished manuscript "relating to the history, religion, manners, institutions, etc., of the tribes which composed the Creek confederacy."[9] Moore reproduced the quote in one of his Mount Royal reports and commented on it: "'The vast mounds upon the St. John's, Alachua, and Musquito Rivers,' he [William Bartram] writes, 'differ from those among the Cherokees, with respect to their adjuncts and appendages, particularly in respect to the great highway or avenue, sunk below the common level of the earth, extending from them, and terminating either in a vast savanna or natural plain, or an artificial pond or lake. A remarkable example occurs at Mt. Royal, from whence opens a glorious view of Lake George and its environs.' He [Bartram] goes on to describe by the aid of a little sketch the highway and mound, making the latter 40 feet in perpendicular height."[10]

Among the other sites revisited by Moore is Bartram's Mound or Little Orange Mound, mentioned by Wyman. Moore also might have found Bartram's second bluff site, which he calls Orange Mound (site 8Or1). This appears to be the same Orange Mound visited about 1873 by "old Cone," an alligator hunter, who, perhaps like Bartram, found European artifacts there.[11]

Good observers though they were, the Bartrams were not infallible. Moore wryly noted that John Bartram's estimate of the height of the Mount Royal mound at 20 feet was much more correct than William's 40 feet: "His father, years before, by an estimate half that amount, had come nearer the truth."[12] Moore measured the height of the Mount Royal mound at 16 feet with a circumference of 555 feet.

Elsewhere William Bartram stated that the mound was 20 yards high, though as Francis Harper notes, Bartram often wrote "yards" when he meant "feet."[13] If he did mean 20 feet, then both he and his father provided a measurement close to the mound's true height. I suspect that William Bartram also meant feet and not yards in his above quoted description of the "grand highway" at Mount Royal. The width of that earthwork is nearer 50 feet than 50 yards.

John Bartram was aware that the oyster shell middens found on the northeast Florida coast were refuse left by early American Indians, but nowhere in his diary or William's narrative is it explicitly stated that the freshwater shell middens of the St. Johns River were cultural constructions.[14] In the late eighteenth century people did not realize that the snail and mussel shell middens represented hundreds, even thousands of years of refuse accumulation, the remains of meals eaten by Precolumbian Florida Indians. Many observers believed the shells were natural accumulations. Jeffries Wyman, writing a century after the Bartrams, first concluded that "the [St. Johns River] shell heaps are the work of man," an observation echoed by Clarence Moore.[15]

Another of William Bartram's St. Johns area archaeological observations merits mention: "the largest Indian Mount I have Yet seen in Florida, having a long wide Causey leading from it into the Pine Forest, lake as to Mt. Royal."[16] As Harper notes, this locale was by Lake Beresford and the "mount" was possibly the Stark's Grove mound on the southeastern shore of the lake in Volusia County (site 8Vo39).[17] But by no means is it as large as Mount Royal or other mounds along the river.[18] Nor has anyone yet identified a causeway or earthwork in that immediate area.

The Bartrams also observed colonial Spanish sites, for instance on Fort George Island and at Rollestown.[19] The former, in Duval County, included old fields and the remains of buildings associated with what is now known to have been the Franciscan mission of San Juan del Puerto (site 8Du53) founded to serve Timucua Indians about 1595. Carolinian militia led by Colonel James Moore destroyed the mission in a 1702 attack, part of the same military advance that devastated all the Spanish missions between Amelia Island and St. Augustine and then laid siege to that colonial capitol.[20] The site near Rollestown in modern-day Putnam County (8Pu64) on the west bank of the St. Johns River possibly was the location of the Indian town called "Antonico" by the Spaniards.[21]

The writings of both John and William Bartram contain frequent mention of orange trees along the St. Johns River. The conventional wisdom is that such stands of trees mark places where Creek Indians moving into Florida after 1750 established settlements (soon emerging as Seminole Indians). But that explanation becomes less likely when one considers the numerous places where orange trees were found. It may instead be that Timucua and other Indians spread orange trees throughout the St. Johns drainage during the Spanish colonial period. Archaeologists still have much to learn from John and William Bartram.

Let us turn now to Mount Royal, the most famous archaeological monument in Florida associated with the Bartrams. What do the post-Bartram investigations of Clarence Moore and other archaeologists tell us about the site and the people who lived there and built the earthworks?

Moore at Mount Royal

Though never formally trained as an archaeologist, Clarence B. Moore (1852–1936) is a major figure in the archaeology of the Southeast United States. Between 1891 and 1918 he investigated literally hundreds of Indian sites across the region. His earliest work was in Florida on the St. Johns River. In 1891, then near forty years of age and self-financed, Moore traveled up the river on a steamboat, scouting and excavating shell midden sites along its banks. The results of those early investigations were published between 1892 and 1894 in eight articles in the *American Naturalist* and one in the *American Antiquarian and Oriental Journal*. His interest in the archaeology of the St. Johns may have developed when he was young and his family wintered at a resort near Green Cove Springs.[22]

Mount Royal was among the very first mounds Moore excavated after he abandoned shell middens and began to concentrate on mounds. He was at the site March 31 to April 17, 1893, and February 20 to March 14, 1894, during which times he and his field crew (twenty-one men the first year and more than thirty the second) worked a total of thirty-nine days. Many of the artifacts he recovered are in the Smithsonian Institution's National Museum of the American Indian. His field notes and some correspondence, formerly in the Huntington Free Library in the Bronx, New York, are now in the Division of Rare and Manuscript Collections, Cornell University Library, as part of the Clarence Bloomfield Moore Collection (#9181).[23]

Moore produced two reports on Mount Royal, one for each field season. They are included, respectively, in his monographs *Certain Sand Mounds of the St. Johns River, Florida, Part I* and *Part II*, both published in 1894 in the series *Journal of the Academy of Natural Sciences of Philadelphia*. Moore's well-illustrated and informative reports on Mount Royal brought instant recognition to the site, which is oft-cited in modern overviews of southeastern United States archaeology.[24]

In 1893 Mount Royal was owned by David Wright of Auburn, New York, who, according to Moore, had "kept it [the mound] intact, carefully guarding it against depredations of unsystematic relic hunters." Prior to Moore's work the mound "knew no explorer other than the gopher [*Gopherus polyphemus*], the salamander, and the scarlet snake."[25] At the time he worked at Mount Royal the site was under cultivation and Moore could not discern the junction of the causeway/linear earthwork with the mound.

Moore, who said the mound at Mount Royal was "the St. Johns's largest," wrote a description of the site, providing measurements for the sand mound and the causeway leading from it to the pond about a half mile away. He noted the causeway was "a depression twelve to twenty yards in width at different points, between embankments of sand with an average height of 2.5 feet, and 12 feet in breadth." Also mentioned is an adjacent freshwater shell midden, probably the one near the river.

Moore's excavations focused entirely on the large high mound and a second, nearby (500 yards away) smaller mound, though almost nothing was found in the latter: "Its height was 3 feet 2 inches, its circumference 195 feet. . . . No skeletons were met with, nor relics of any sort, with the exception of two fragmentary arrow points of chert."[26] In his first report Moore described the large mound as having two strata. A lower layer of yellow sand "with pockets and local layers of white sand," over which was a layer of sand mixed with powdered hematite that reached a maximum depth of 7 feet. The hematite gave the layer a "crushed strawberry" color; where the hematite was denser, the stratum had a "brick-red" color. Artifacts, including whole pottery vessels, often were found where the hematite was most dense, though artifacts also were found in the yellow sand stratum. Under the mound on the old surface on which the mound was deposited Moore found charcoal, suggesting the ground surface was ritually cleaned by burning before the yellow sand was deposited.

Throughout both mound strata Moore's field crews also found fragments of badly preserved human bones. In many instances the acidic nature of the soil had left literally only the enamel from teeth or small deposits of powdery bone. Consequently, no information was recovered about the nature of interments (e.g., primary or secondary) or the biology of the people buried in the mound.

However, a variety of artifacts, some well preserved, were recovered. For instance, Moore commented on the very large number of whelk shells in the mound (fashioned from *Busycon carica*, the knobbed whelk, a marine gastropod). These were not drinking cups, such as those found in other mounds in Florida, and most had their beaks (pointed ends) intentionally broken off. One wonders if they were used as shell trumpets or if they represented a valued raw material brought to Mount Royal from the Atlantic coast.

Many of the shells were found in caches in the upper reddish stratum, with as many as 136 in one cache. All total, 1,307 *Busycon* shells were found in Moore's main excavation trench. Stone points, including one deposit of 53 small arrow points, were recovered. Illustrated in Moore's reports, some appear not to be native to Florida and resemble a type of point found in the Mississippi River Valley between AD 1050 and 1300.[27] Other stone artifacts included polished celts, chisel-shaped implements, and two maces, nearly all made of greenstone or a similar stone not native to Florida and probably mined in the Appalachian Mountains. Such items suggest the Mount Royal people were in direct or indirect contact with peoples living well beyond Florida. Moore also excavated stone plummets, mica, stone beads, iron pyrite, pieces of galena, a quartz crystal, and sharks teeth, some from fossil species.

Throughout the mound, often next to human remains, there were shell beads, most small but some manufactured from the columellae of *Busycon* shells. There also were beads made from freshwater pearls.

The pottery and the copper artifacts excavated by Moore from the Mount Royal mound continue to draw the attention of modern scholars. The pottery vessels, nearly all made with a distinctive chalky paste typical of ceramics made in the St. Johns River region (the chalkiness comes from freshwater sponge spicules in the clay), come in a variety of unique shapes and sizes. Some are cone-shaped and are more funnels than vessels; others are shaped like gourd dippers. Moore also found miniature vessels, one vessel with two hemispherical cups, an hourglass-shaped ceramic object, and a wedge-shaped vessel (see Fig. 8.2).

The assemblage of ceramics from the large mound suggests the various vessels were used for other than everyday cooking and serving food. Moore noted that some of the pottery vessels had perforations made in their bottoms before the vessels were fired, further evidence that some of the ceramics were never meant to be normal containers. The array of ceramic vessels and objects may have been used in the ritual brewing and serving of sacred teas such as the Black Drink, brewed from the leaves of the Yaupon holly (*Ilex vomitoria*).[28]

As spectacular as the ceramics are the copper artifacts excavated by Moore from the mound. Southeastern Indians valued the metal highly, and chiefs and other high-ranking individuals wore ornaments and artifacts fashioned from the metal. Typically nuggets of copper, usually mined from deposits in the Appalachian Mountains, were hammered flat to form small sheets about two inches square. Larger pieces were made by overlapping small ones and securing them with small copper rivets. The larger sheets were then fashioned into a wide array of ornaments. One spectacular two-piece copper plate from Mount Royal measured ten and one-half inches square and probably was worn on the chest of a chief. Moore described the object: "Beneath the upper plate was a layer of reeds . . . bound together by closely woven vegetable fibre. On one side . . . the reeds were replaced by twisted vegetable fibre of equal length

8.2. Ceramic tubes or funnels, a dipper, and a double
bowl from Mount Royal; the upper left tube or fun-
nel is 2 ⅞ inches long (from Moore, "Certain Sand
Mounds, Part II," Plate XVII).

and diameter. Behind this layer was a backing of bark about 0.25 of an inch in
thickness. Next came another copper plate bent over on itself. . . . Behind [this
plate] were fragments of wood one inch in thickness."[29] Four forked eyes were
inscribed on the upper plate (see Fig. 8.3). The forked eye motif is associated
with the Southeastern Ceremonial Complex, an assemblage of artifacts and
iconography found mainly at Mississippian period (post AD 1000) mound sites
in the interior of the Southeast. Those paraphernalia and symbols reflect social and religious beliefs of the Southeastern Indians; some are tied to ancestor
cults, others to agricultural fertility, and still others to warrior chiefs.[30]

In addition to the plates, there were rolled and tubular copper beads, discs,
pins or hair ornaments, ear spools, a number of small round and rectangular
flat ornaments (many with bosses), a small "serpent effigy," and many pieces

8.3. Painting of the copper plate with forked eye motifs excavated by Moore; 10½ inches square (from Moore, "Certain Sand Mounds, Part I," Plate I).

of scrap copper (see Fig. 8.4). There also were artifacts fashioned of wood or stone that had been covered with copper.

Moore observed that some of the copper ornaments resembled those worn by the Timucua Indians depicted in Theodore de Bry's late-sixteenth-century engravings.[31] A few of the copper ornaments had string attachments made from vegetable fibers. The fibers were preserved by metallic salts from the copper. Moore also noted copper objects apparently wrapped in bark. The large quantity of copper found at Mount Royal suggests the people who lived there were a wealthy community with ties to trading networks that reached well beyond central Florida.

Moore observed that stamped pottery—a ceramic type called St. Johns Check Stamped—was found throughout the mound (see Fig. 8.5). Today we know that St. Johns Check Stamped pottery dates from circa AD 750 into the very early colonial period. Moore additionally remarked: "Among the hun-

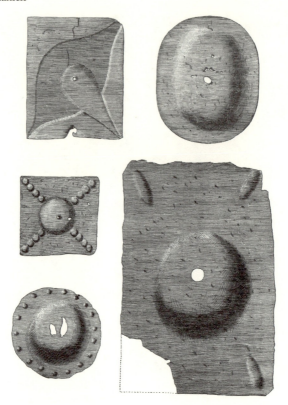

8.4. Copper objects from Mount Royal; the lower
right specimen is 4½ inches long. The lower right
specimen and the lower left object are from Moore,
"Certain Sand Mounds, Part II," Figures 7, 9, pp. 140
and 141; the other three are from Moore, "Certain
Sand Mounds, Part I," Figures 14–16, p. 31.

dreds of objects taken from the great mound was not one bead of glass nor im-
plement of iron, nor was any object met with obviously of European manufacture, or of necessity connecting the mound with a period subsequent to the
arrival of the whites."[32] He correctly placed the mound prior to the colonial
period and the intrusion of Europeans into east Florida. These are astute conclusions and they were key in helping modern archaeologists to place Mount
Royal's large mound in the cultural chronology of the St. Johns area.

Upon finishing his second season of excavations at the site, Moore wrote:
"the mound was restored, that so great and historical a land mark should not
pass from sight."[33] Like the Bartrams before him, Moore felt the grandeur of
Mount Royal.

8.5. St. Johns Check Stamped Bowl from Mount Royal; 6½ inches in diameter (from Moore, "Certain Sand Mounds, Part II," Plate XIX, 2).

Research in the Modern Era

In the late 1940s, using Moore's information as well as that of other earlier visitors and his own reconnaissances, the University of Florida archaeologist John M. Goggin recorded the Mount Royal site in the Florida archaeological site file, a file of all known sites in the state, which presently is kept by the Florida Division of Historical Resources. He also visited the site on multiple occasions, collecting pottery from the surface of the village area.

In 1952, Goggin again relied on Moore's Mount Royal reports in his synthesis *Space and Time Perspective in Northern St. Johns Archaeology, Florida,* noting the mound dated to what he called the St. Johns IIb period, today known to be from about AD 1050 to the time of Spanish contact. Goggin realized that the people living at the site in the late Precolumbian period were ancestors of Timucua Indians. Other archaeologists have subsequently used Goggin's conclusions and data in writing about the archaeology of the St. Johns River region.[34]

In 1983, 1994, and 1995, the archaeologist B. Calvin Jones of the Florida Division of Historical Resource's Bureau of Archaeological Research returned to Mount Royal to carry out the first excavations since those of Clarence Moore in 1894. Jones died before completing his report, a task subsequently taken on by Louis Tesar of the Bureau.[35] In an interview about his work recorded before his death, Jones opined, "Mount Royal is one of the most fascinating places of all the sites I've ever worked. . . . The aura that it gives off from people having lived there is absolutely marvelous."[36]

Jones's excavations produced new knowledge about three aspects of the site. First, he determined that the spatial distribution of village middens was much more extensive than previously known. Mount Royal is a very large site.

Second, Jones found evidence that a portion of the Mount Royal midden near the St. Johns River had been occupied as early as circa 2000–1000 BC. Last, Jones archaeologically documented the presence at Mount Royal of a Spanish Franciscan mission, one whose presence was hinted at by the ceramic collections made by John Goggin. Those collections included significant amounts of mission-period (seventeenth-century) Indian and Spanish ceramics.[37] The Bartrams had indeed found a treasure.

Interpreting Mount Royal

Like other sites along the St. Johns River, especially those in the central portion of the drainage, Mount Royal was first home to American Indians as early as four thousand years ago during what archaeologists call the Orange period.[38] Orange period shell middens, marked by fired-clay pottery tempered with vegetable fibers, including palmetto and Spanish moss, also are found on the coast of east Florida.

By 500 BC and probably several hundred years earlier, the St. Johns culture, with its distinctive, chalky pottery, developed throughout east and central Florida, including the coastal marshes and lagoon from Brevard County north to Amelia Island, the St. Johns River from west of Cocoa Beach north to Jacksonville, the Oklawaha River in Marion County, and the many lakes in Orange, Lake, and Seminole counties.[39] The St. Johns people lived close to wetlands where the shellfish and fish that sustained them were easily available. They also hunted and collected animals and plants collected from nearby forests and they grew squashes.

The period of the St. Johns culture is divided into sub-periods based on changing styles of their pottery vessels, which waxed and waned over time. Dating 500 BC to AD 750, St. Johns I sites typically are shell middens found along the St. Johns and Oklawaha rivers and the coastal lagoon. Some middens lie atop older ones, forming heaps of shell whose size is impressive.

Individual St. Johns I period villages probably consisted of several family lineages or clans. When a village grew too large to be supported by local resources, one or more lineages moved to another location to found a new village. Sometimes one lineage became more important than the others and it took a leadership role in the village. Its "big man" or leader acted as a village chief.

The St. Johns region was not isolated from the ideas, events, and peoples found elsewhere in Florida and the Southeast. Trade was widespread and archaeological evidence points toward contact with other cultures in Florida and the Southeast.

During St. Johns II times, which began about AD 750, a significant Indian population lived at Mt. Royal. Sites of that period always contain St. Johns

Check Stamped pottery, the type Clarence B. Moore said was "in use at the inception of the mound."[40]

Many archaeologists believe that St. Johns II people in the St. Johns River Valley from Lake George northward grew maize (Indian corn), along with squashes, gourds, and tobacco. Maize, however, was the most important agricultural crop. The Indians harvested the cobs and either stored them in cribs for later use or they husked and shelled them, grinding the kernels into meal that was eaten in a porridge or gruel, often mixed with meats or other foods. Corn meal also was baked into cakes, predecessor of modern cornbread.

Though the Mount Royal people and their ancestors were farmers, agriculture was never as important as it was in the eastern panhandle of Florida and the interior Southeast. The sandy soils of much of the St. Johns region do not have great natural fertility. Intensive maize agriculture requires soils whose fertility is replenished when fields lie fallow or annual floods deposit new nutrients, situations that occur in northwest Florida and the river valleys of the interior Southeast, but not in the St. Johns region.

In the later St. Johns II period, after AD 1050, more complex political structures developed, including chiefdoms and confederations of chiefdoms. Each chiefdom consisted of a main village whose chief also ruled other nearby villages and their chiefs. Confederations resulted when more powerful chiefs used diplomacy and military force or its threat to create alliances, increasing their domination over larger areas.

In several localities the power of a few chiefs and their families reached even greater heights. Main villages became major centers of political and religious life and other communal activities. Large mounds were built and served as bases for temples or chief's houses and as burial repositories for chiefs and their relatives, monuments to their importance.

Mount Royal appears to be one such important village center. Perhaps for several hundred years beginning about AD 1050 or shortly after it was *the* major mound center in the region. Its geographical location allowed the town's villagers to maximize agricultural production even while having access to the productive wetlands of Lake George and the St. Johns River. From the town Mount Royal's chiefs and elite families controlled trade that used the St. Johns River as a water highway connecting north and south Florida. Such trade brought to Mount Royal the copper and other exotic raw materials and artifacts found in the mound, items of wealth and status. We do not have any radiocarbon dates to pinpoint the dates of Mount Royal's political and economic heyday, but artifacts from the mound and comparisons with other sites suggest it was between about AD 1050 and 1300.

By no means did Mt. Royal's importance fade away after AD 1300, when people continued to live there. In 1565 French colonists from Fort Caroline (east of Jacksonville on the St. Johns River) visited the town whose Timucuan

Indian name was Enacape. The French stopped at Enacape on their way north after traveling south on the St. Johns River to another Timucua town, Edelano. Edelano, said to be on an island, is certainly the site William Bartram visited on Drayton Island at the north end of Lake George, just south of Mount Royal. The French described the town of Edelano as having an earthwork/causeway that was about 300 paces long and 50 paces wide.[41] Later in 1565, René de Laudonnière, leader of the Fort Caroline colony, sent a second expedition up the St. Johns River to take corn from Enacape to feed his starving French colonists back at Fort Caroline.[42]

In 1566, shortly after ousting the French from Fort Caroline and founding St. Augustine, the new Spanish governor of La Florida, Pedro Menéndez de Avilés, led three Spanish brigantines up the St. Johns River and into Lake George before sailing farther south into the territory of the Mayaca Indians.[43] On the trip Menéndez handed out gifts to many Timucuan chiefs along the river. Although it is not mentioned specifically, the Spanish expedition could well have stopped at Enacape. The next year a second Spanish expedition traveled the St. Johns River, also reaching Lake George.

Spanish Franciscan missionary friars traveled to Enacape in the 1590s. The town was near the southern end of the *Agua Dulce,* or Fresh Water, mission district, a name given by the Spaniards to the middle portion of the St. Johns River. By that time diseases already had devastated the Timucua Indian population in the vicinity of St. Augustine and the nearby St. Johns River. However, Enacape and the Timucuan towns further south on the St. Johns River, relatively isolated for thirty years, still retained a significant native population. At Mount Royal, a major town accessible by river, the friars and Spanish officials established mission San Antonio de Enacape in 1595.[44] B. Calvin Jones uncovered portions of that mission during his Mount Royal excavations.[45]

San Antonio, sometimes referred to as San Antonio de Anacabila (Anacabila is a Timucua Indian word), was among the earliest Franciscan missions in Spanish Florida. It continued to administer to Timucua Indians until sometime after 1656 when the villagers were moved north to mission San Diego de Salamototo. At that town, the Spaniards conscripted the Indians to ferry passengers by canoe across the St. Johns River. The *camino real,* the main Spanish road leading west from St. Augustine across northern Florida, intersected the east bank of the St. Johns at San Diego. The site of San Diego is near modern-day Orangedale, Florida, across (east) the river from Green Cove Springs.[46]

Another early name (1602) for Mount Royal was Nyaautina.[47] "Utina" is a Timucuan Indian term for "chief," or "power" or "lands controlled by a chief," while "nya" or "nia" means female. Thus, in 1602, early in the mission period, Mount Royal most likely was under the control of a female chief. Spanish documents mention female chiefs at other colonial-period Timucuan towns.[48]

In the 1680s San Antonio de Enacape was reoccupied by Yamassee Indians resettled from Franciscan missions on the Georgia coast. Raids by Carolinian-backed Indians and even English pirates had caused the Spaniards to abandon their missions on the coast.

The new Native American residents of San Antonio de Enacape, like their Timucuan neighbors in northern Florida, could not maintain their population in the face of diseases and the harsh rigors of colonization. Most likely the mission was abandoned in the very early eighteenth century and the Indians who survived moved to refuge villages close to St. Augustine, seeking succor near the Spaniards.

~

Today the large Mount Royal mound, restored in the early 1970s by the Northeast Florida Anthropological Society (supported by a grant from the Florida Division of Historical Resources) is a monument to the many generations of Native Americans who once lived at Enacape. It also is significant for its association with John and William Bartram and Clarence B. Moore, and it remains a major source of information on the St. Johns culture of late-Precolumbian times. Archaeologists continue to use data collected from the site by Clarence Moore, B. Calvin Jones, and other archaeologists to better understand our native American heritage.[49]

In 1973 Mount Royal was nominated for listing in the National Register of Historic Places and subsequently was placed on that registry. Presently the state of Florida owns about 1.1 acres of the site, including the big mound. The causeway and middens are privately owned, though the present landowner has been more than cooperative in preserving large portions of the site and allowing archaeological investigations. There is still much to learn from Mount Royal (and from John and William Bartram and Clarence B. Moore).

Notes

1. John Bartram, "Diary of a Journey through the Carolinas, Georgia, and Florida, from July 1, 1765 to April 10, 1766," edited and annotated by Francis Harper, *Transactions of the American Philosophical Society,* new series, vol. 33, part 1 (Philadelphia: APS, 1942), 45.

2. Mark Van Doren, ed., *Travels of William Bartram* (New York: Dover Publications, 1928), 101–102.

3. Van Doren, ed., *Travels of William Bartram,* 104.

4. Virgil R. Beasley III, "Location of Edelano, a Timucua Village Encountered by the French Huguenots: 1564–1565" (paper presented at the 54th annual meeting of the Southeastern Archaeological Conference, Baton Rouge, Louisiana, November 5–8, 1997).

5. Van Doren, ed., *Travels of William Bartram,* 113–124.

6. Ibid., 130.

7. Jeffries Wyman, "Fresh-water Shell Mounds of the St. John's River, Florida," *Memoirs of the Peabody Academy of Science* 1:4 (Salem, Mass.: Peabody Academy of Science, 1875), 35–36.

8. John M. Goggin, *Space and Time Perspective in Northern St. Johns Archeology, Florida,* Yale University Publications in Anthropology 47 (New Haven, Conn.: Yale University Press, 1952), 90–91.

9. William Bartram, *William Bartram on the Southeastern Indians,* ed. Gregory A. Waselkov and Kathryn E. Holland Braund (Lincoln: University of Nebraska Press, 1995).

10. Clarence B. Moore, "Certain Sand Mounds of the St. John's River, Florida, Part I," *Journal of the Academy of Natural Sciences of Philadelphia* 10 (1894): 18.

11. Jerald T. Milanich, ed., *Frolicking Bears, Wet Vultures, and Other Oddities: A New York City Journalist in Nineteenth-Century Florida,* Florida History and Culture Series (Gainesville: University Press of Florida, 2005), 113–114.

12. John Bartram, "Diary," 185; Moore, "Certain Sand Mounds, Part I," 18.

13. The 20 yard estimate is in William Bartram's report to Fothergill. See William Bartram, "Travels in Georgia and Florida, 1773–74: A Report to Dr. John Fothergill," edited and annotated by Francis Harper, *Transactions of the American Philosophical Society,* new series, vol. 33, part 2 (Philadelphia: APS, 1942), 150, 185.

14. John Bartram, "Diary," 47.

15. Wyman, "Fresh-water Shell Mounds," 86; Clarence B. Moore, "Certain Shell Heaps of the St. John's River, Florida, Hitherto Unexplored (Second Paper)," *American Naturalist* 27 (1893): 116–117.

16. John Bartram, "Diary," 154.

17. For more on the St. Johns River sites and correlations among Moore and other archaeologists, see Jeffrey M. Mitchem, "Introduction: Clarence B. Moore's Research in East Florida, 1873–1896," in *East Florida Expeditions of Clarence Bloomfield Moore,* ed. Jeffrey M. Mitchem (Tuscaloosa: The University of Alabama Press, 1999).

18. John Bartram, "Diary," 187.

19. Ibid., 48, 74–75. See also Goggin, *Space and Time Perspective in Northern St. Johns Archeology.*

20. Charles W. Arnade, *Siege of St. Augustine in 1702,* University of Florida Monographs 3 (Gainesville: University of Florida Press, 1959).

21. John E. Worth, *Resistance and Destruction,* vol. 2 of *Timucuan Chiefdoms of Spanish Florida,* Ripley P. Bullen Series (Gainesville: University Press of Florida, 1998), 187.

22. For biographical information on Moore and his archaeological endeavors, see Lawrence E. Aten and Jerald T. Milanich, "Clarence Bloomfield Moore: A Philadelphia Archaeologist in the Southeastern United States," in *Philadelphia*

and the Development of Americanist Archaeology, ed. Don D. Fowler and David R. Wilcox (Tuscaloosa: The University of Alabama Press, 2003).

23. Mary B. Davis, *Field Notes of Clarence B. Moore's Southeast Archaeological Expeditions, 1891–1918: A Guide to the Microfilm Edition* (Bronx, N.Y.: Huntington Free Library, 1987).

24. Both reports have been reprinted. See Jerald T. Milanich, ed., *Famous Florida Sites: Mount Royal and Crystal River,* Southeastern Classics in Archaeology, Anthropology, and History (Gainesville: University Press of Florida, 1999), 29–77; Mitchem, "Introduction Clarence B. Moore's Research in East Florida," 1–52. Excerpts from the original reports also were reprinted in 1895 in the popular magazine, *Archaeologist* 3, nos. 1, 2, 4, and 5.

25. Moore, "Certain Sand Mounds, Part I," 128.

26. Ibid., 35.

27. Milanich, ed., *Famous Florida Sites,* 11.

28. Charles M. Hudson, ed., *Black Drink: A Native American Tea* (Athens: University of Georgia Press, 1979).

29. Moore, "Certain Sand Mounds, Part I," 32.

30. For more on the complex and Mississippian religion, see James A. Brown, "Mississippian Period," in *Ancient Art of the American Woodland Indians* (New York: Harry N. Abrams, 1985), 93–140; Patricia Galloway, ed. *Southeastern Ceremonial Complex: Artifacts and Analysis: The Cottonlandia Conference* (Lincoln: University of Nebraska Press, 1989); Charles M. Hudson, *Elements of Southeastern Indian Religion,* Iconography of Religion, fasc. 1 (Leiden, Netherlands: E. J. Brill, 1984); and Vernon James Knight Jr., "Institutional Organization of Mississippian Religion," *American Antiquity* 51 (October 1986): 675–687.

31. Stefan Lorant, ed., *New World, the First Pictures of America Made by John White and Jacques Le Moyne and Engraved by Theodore de Bry, with Contemporary Narrative of the Huguenot Settlement in Florida, 1562–1565 and the Virginia Colony, 1585–1590* (New York: Duell, Sloan & Pearce, 1946).

32. Moore, "Certain Sand Mounds, Part I," 35.

33. Clarence B. Moore, "Certain Sand Mounds of the St. John's River, Florida, Part II," *Journal of the Academy of Natural Sciences of Philadelphia* 10 (1894): 137.

34. For examples, see Jerald T. Milanich, *Archaeology of Precolumbian Florida* (Gainesville: University Press of Florida, 1994), and James J. Miller, *An Environmental History of Northeast Florida* (Gainesville: University Press of Florida, 1998).

35. B. Calvin Jones and Louis D. Tesar, *1985–1995 Survey, Salvage and Mitigation of Archaeological Resources within the Mount Royal Site (8PU35) Village Area, Putnam County, Florida* (Tallahassee: Florida Bureau of Archaeological Research, 2001).

36. B. Calvin Jones, with transcriptions by Louis D. Tesar and Jonathan Lam-

mers, "B. Calvin Jones: Comments and Commentary, Video-Taped Interview Excerpts," *Florida Anthropologist* 51 (1998): 86.

37. John M. Goggin, *Spanish Majolica in the New World: Types of the Sixteenth to Eighteenth Centuries,* Yale University Publications in Anthropology 72 (New Haven, Conn.: Yale University Press, 1968), 70.

38. Milanich, *Archaeology of Precolumbian Florida,* 87–95.

39. Ibid., 243–248, 254–274.

40. Moore, "Certain Sand Mounds, Part I," 27.

41. Quinn, ed., "La Caroline," in *Major Spanish Searches,* 347.

42. Ibid., 507–508.

43. John H. Hann, "Summary Guide to Spanish Florida Missions and Visitas with Churches in the Sixteenth and Seventeenth Centuries," *Americas* 46 (April 1990): 439–440; Worth, *Timucuan Chiefdoms,* 187–188. Spaniards called Lake George the Lake of San Antonio.

44. Jones and Tesar, *1985–1995 Survey, Salvage and Mitigation of Archaeological Resources.*

45. Worth, *Timucuan Chiefdoms,* 166.

46. Ibid., 188.

47. Ibid., 188.

48. Milanich, *Timucua* (Cambridge, Mass.: Blackwell Publishers, 1996), 157; Ruth Trocolli, "Elite Status and Gender: Women Leaders in Chiefdom Societies of the Southeastern U.S." (Ph.D. diss., University of Florida, 2006), 77–117.

49. For example, see Keith H. Ashley, "Interaction, Population Movement, and Political Economy: The Changing Social Landscape of Northeastern Florida (A.D. 900–1500)" (Ph.D. diss., University of Florida, 2003).

9
Where Bartram Sat

Historic Creek Indian Architecture in the Eighteenth Century

Craig T. Sheldon Jr.

Introduction

In the last half of the eighteenth century, William Bartram, the noted naturalist from Philadelphia, traveled throughout the southern English colonies, observing and recording local flora, fauna, geography, and the culture of the indigenous Cherokee, Creek, Seminole, and other Indian groups. He was impressed with the architecture of the indigenous groups, particularly their elaborate public structures. None of the structures or other parts of the built environment survived the humid southeastern climate or the Indian removal in the nineteenth century. For over 150 years, his accounts, together with those of James Adair, David Taitt, Benjamin Hawkins, Bernard Romans, Henry Timberlake, and other European visitors have been used by scholars in reconstructing eighteenth-century Southeastern Indian culture and architecture. Until recently, the accuracy of any particular architectural observations or descriptions could only be measured by comparison with similar contemporary accounts. Now, archaeological investigations of historic Indian sites in Alabama, Florida, Georgia, and Tennessee have added data that can correct and augment historic accounts. Hopefully, by combining subsurface dimensional and feature information from archaeology with the above-ground riches of historical descriptions, a fuller understanding of Southeastern historic Indian architecture will emerge.[1]

In this chapter, Bartram's written descriptions and drawings of the structures and towns of the Creeks of central Alabama and Georgia are compared to structures and community features revealed in archaeological investigations of historical Indian sites in the Chattahoochee valley and the lower Tallapoosa and Coosa river valleys of central Alabama and Georgia.[2] Many sites with historic Creek occupations have been recorded in this region, but few have been tested and still fewer have been excavated to the extent necessary to reveal architectural and community features. Investigations in the lower Tallapoosa and Coosa river valleys at Cussita and Yuchi (visited by Bartram in 1775) near Columbus, Georgia, and at Tuckabatchee, Otassee (visited by Bartram in 1775–1776), Hickory Ground, Hoithlewaulee, and Fusihatchee have produced copious data on indigenous and imported material, diet, architecture, and community plans (Figure 9.1).[3]

Presently, historic Creek architecture is exposed in archaeological excavations as patterns of postholes, sunken house floors, raised clay hearths, burned clay daub or wall plaster, borrow pits for clay, and subfloor pits and graves. Features on the floors of the houses, such as clay hearths, were destroyed by nineteenth- and twentieth-century plowing. For most of their structures, the Creeks relied upon an earthfast construction technique in which wall and support posts were erected in postholes spaced at intervals. Common structural elements in both domestic houses and large public structures were unhewn logs and saplings, often selected for convenient forks and natural shapes, split river cane woven between into wall sections, local red or yellow clays used for wall plaster and hearths, and large sections of bark used for roofs.

Most historic Creek structures are best understood in terms of two cross-cutting persistent architectural divisions: winter-summer and public-domestic. The existence of distinctive house types for summer or winter occupancy was first noted by Spanish expeditions in the sixteenth century. Archaeological investigations have uncovered large semisubterranean circular or rounded "winter" houses adjacent to rectangular or "summer" houses at protohistoric Creek sites in Georgia and Alabama. By the end of the seventeenth century, "winter" style houses were no longer built, leaving only variations of the rectangular "summer" houses, which persisted as the year-round dwellings of the historic Creeks until removal in the 1830s.

Public buildings and ceremonial areas at the center of each Creek town or *talwa* stood in contrast to the surrounding zone of domestic houses. Also built in "winter" and "summer" forms, the public structures were elaborations of the domestic houses. The large eighteenth-century winter council houses or "rotundas," so carefully described by Bartram at the Upper Creek town of Otassee, were enlarged versions of the former domestic "winter" structures. The four structures enclosing the ceremonial square grounds used during warmer months were modifications of the common rectangular "summer" houses.[4]

Bartram spent about twenty-four days in the territory of the Upper and Lower Creeks, traveling from near Augusta, Georgia, to Mobile in July 1775 and returning from Mobile to the Georgia coast in December 1775 and January 1776. Leaving the Savannah River near Augusta in June 1775, Bartram traveled with two companies of traders across central Georgia. By mid-July, they arrived at the Chattahoochee River and the beginning of occupied Creek country. Bartram spent a week at Yuchi Town (1RU63) in Russell County and

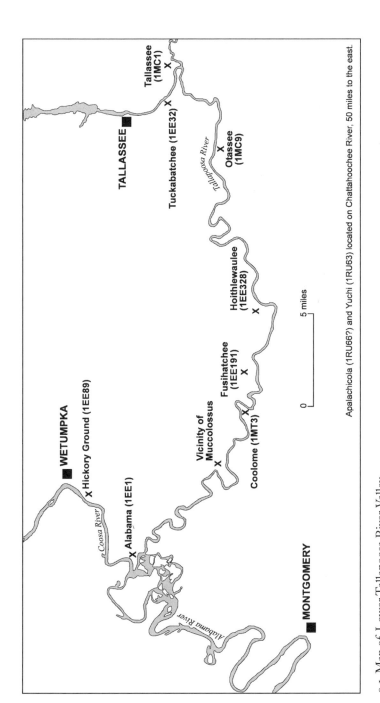

9.1. Map of Lower Tallapoosa River Valley.

at Apalachicola Town (Site #IEE66) and described domestic houses and pre-historic mounds and terraces. Leaving the Chattahoochee, Bartram traveled west to Tallassee (1TP1) in Tallapoosa County on the lower Tallapoosa River. Moving along the left side of the river, he passed Otassee (1MC3) in Macon County and moved on to Old Coolome Town (1MT3) in Montgomery County. By the time of Bartram's visit, most of the inhabitants of Coolome had moved to the northern or right bank of the Tallapoosa River to a presently unknown location in Elmore County. Left behind on the southern bank were a prehistoric mound, "two or three Indian habitations," and the stores of James Germany, the principal trader. In New Coolome, Bartram described compounds of four domestic houses arranged into squares. From Coolome, Bartram traveled southwestwards to Mobile, where he arrived at the end of July 1775.[5]

By the end of November 1776, Bartram left Mobile and returned to the Upper Creek country. Arriving on the banks of the Tallapoosa River near the town of Savannuca (present location unknown), Bartram spent the night and in the morning, crossed the river to the town of Muccolossus where he described the houses, stores, and compounds of the principal trader. He traveled to the junction of the Coosa and Tallapoosa rivers to visit Alabama or as the town was also known, Taskeegee (1EE1). Here he attended an all-night dance in the public square and saw the remains of the French Fort Toulouse, abandoned in 1763. After short visits to Coolome and Tuckabatchee (1EE32), Bartram traveled to Otassee (1MC3) where he spent nearly a week awaiting the departure of a trading caravan to Augusta. Here, he presents his most elaborate accounts of a Creek community, including descriptions of the rotunda, square ground, artificial ponds, ceremonies using tobacco and cassine tea, and the ritual, political, and daily activities associated with a town. On January 3, 1775, Bartram left Otassee and by the middle of January he was in Savannah.[6]

In his *Travels* and "Observations," Bartram identified ten elements of built environment in the eighteenth-century Creek towns he visited on the Tallapoosa and Chattahoochee rivers: settlements divided into residential and public areas, domestic houses, complexes of two, three, or four houses, arbors, rotundas or council houses, public square grounds, chunkey or ball yards, borrow pits or ponds, groves of *Ilex vomitoria*, and compounds of European traders. Many but not all of the structures and community arrangements described by Bartram are generally confirmed in observations by other European visitors.[7]

Creek Town Plans

Although they varied in size and arrangements, most eighteenth-century Creek towns appear to conform to Bartram's well-known illustration of a community with a ceremonial and public center of rotunda, square ground, and chunky yard surrounded by a residential zone of carefully arranged clusters of houses separated by dashed lines which probably represent wooden fences (Figure 9.2). Drawn from memory, and probably not based upon a specific town, Bartram's plan was idealized to some extent. Large-scale archaeological excavations at the Fusihatchee and Hickory Ground sites indicate that Bartram's sketch is a good approximation of an eighteenth-century Creek town (Figure 9.3). The drawing is most accurate in the arrangement of buildings in the public center, but less so in the surrounding residential area, where the domestic houses are more randomly oriented.[8]

Domestic Houses

By the late eighteenth century, rectangular earthfast houses were the most common type of structure built by the Creeks. At Yuchi Town in Russell County, Alabama, on the central Chattahoochee River in July 1776, Bartram wrote: "it is the largest, most compact and best situated Indian town I ever saw; the habitations are large and neatly built; the walls of the houses are constructed of a wooden frame, then lathed and plastered inside and out with a reddish well tempered clay or mortar which gives them the appearance of red brick walls; and these houses are neatly covered or roofed with Cypress bark or shingles of that tree."[9]

Several days later, at the Upper Creek Town of Coolome on the lower Tallapoosa River in Montgomery County, Alabama, he remarks: "their houses are neat commodious buildings, a wooden frame with plastered walls and roofed with Cypress bark or shingles; every habitation consists of four oblong square houses, of one story, of the same form and dimensions, and so situated as to form an exact square, encompassing an area or court yard of about a quarter of an acre of ground, leaving an entrance into it at each corner."[10]

Bartram's descriptions of ordinary Creek houses are similar to the contemporary accounts of other eighteenth-century visitors such as Wight, Swan, and Adair who provide additional details on dimensions, construction techniques, raised wooden beds, and doors.[11] His accounts of compounds of two or more houses and of the functionally different "cook," "provisions," or "skins" houses, however, are unique (see Figure 9.2):

> The habitations of the Muscogulges or Upper Crick towns . . . consist of Little Squares, or four oblong square houses, encompassing a square area, exactly on the plan of the <u>Publick Square</u>,—every Family however have not four of these Houses—some 3,—some 2,—and some but one, according to their circumstances, of largeness of their family, &c.— but they are situated so as to admit of four building when conveniency

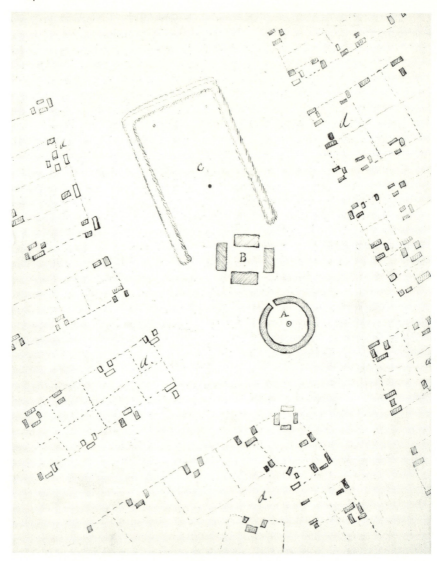

9.2. Bartram's "Plan of the Muscogulge or Upper Creek Town" (Copy by Edwin H. Davis, courtesy of the National Anthropological Archives, Smithsonian Institution).

or necessity require it—Wealthy citizens, having large Families, generally have Four Houses; and they have a particular use for each of these buildings—One serves for a <u>Cook Room & Winter Lodging House</u>—another for a Summer Lodging House & Hall for Receiving Visiters—and a 3d for a Granary, or Provision House, &c:—This is commonly two Stories high and divided into two apartments transversely—the lower

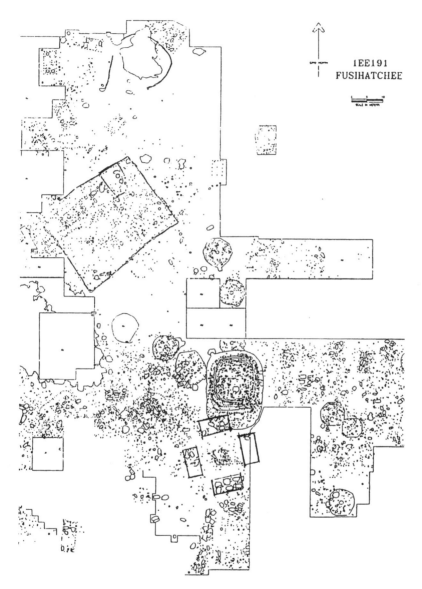

9.3. Central area of archaeological excavations at Fusihatchee (1EE191), Elmore County, Alabama.

story of one end being a potatoe house & for keeping such other roots & fruits as require to be kept close or defended from cold in Winter— The chamber over it is the Corn Crib—The other end of this building, both lower & upper stories are open on 3 sides—The lower story serves for a shed for their saddles, packsaddles & geers & other Lumber; the loft over it is a very spacious airy pleasant Pavilion—where the Chief of the Family reposes in the hot seasons & receives his Guests, &ca.— And the Fourth House which (compleats the Square) is a Skin House or Ware-house, if the proprieter is a wealthy man, and engaged in Trade or Traffick—where he keeps his Deer Skins, Furs & Merchandize & treats with his Customers—Smaller or less Wealthy Families, make one, two or 3 houses serve all these purposes as well as they can.[12]

He describes a very similar elaborate compound belonging to the Boatswain, a leader at Apalachicola on the central Chattahoochee River (Figure 9.4):

There were Three oblong uniform Frame Buildings, and a Fourth Four Square fronting the principal House or Common Hall, after this manner, encompassing an area: the Hall was his Lodging House, &c—large & commodious—The two wings were,—one, a Cook House, & the other Skin Houses, or Ware Houses—and the large Square One was a vast Open Pavillion supporting a canopy, or cedar roof, by two rows of columns, one within the other—Between each range of pillars was a Platform, or what the Traders call Cabins,—a sort of sopha raised about two feet above the common ground & ascended by two steps—This was covered by checquered mats woven of splints of canes dyed of different colors. The middle was a four square stage, or platform, raised nine inches or a foot, higher than the cabins, and was covered with chequered mats of the same curious manufacture.[13]

Rectangular patterns of postholes, identified as eighteenth-century Creek houses, have been found at the archaeological sites of Cussita on the Chattahoochee River and at Tuckabatchee, Hoithlewaulee, Fusihatchee, and Hickory Ground in central Alabama.[14] At Fusihatchee, forty-two archaeological examples of eighteenth-century rectangular houses varied in form and dimension, but generally corresponded to the houses described by Bartram at Yuchi and Coolome. The typical house at Fusihatchee was formed by lines of upright posts enclosing a rectangular area averaging 12.1 by 22.7 feet (Figure 9.5). The three- to four-inch diameter posts were spaced about 3.3 feet apart. Based on Bartram's account, the spaces between the posts were filled with wattle and red clay daub. Each structure had three to five posts at the ends and five to seven

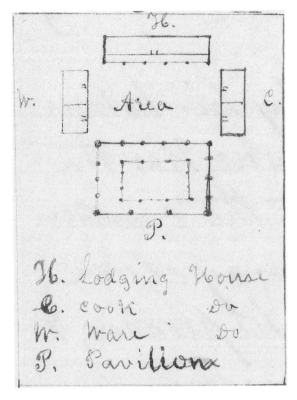

9.4. Bartram's drawing of the Apalachicola Headman's House (Copy by Edwin H. Davis, courtesy of
the National Anthropological Archives, Smithsonian
Institution).

posts on the sides. One to two interior posts supported ridge poles of gabled
roofs with cypress bark coverings. Paired wall posts on the center of one side
marked the doorways described by Caleb Swan. Low circular clay hearths were
probably located in the center of the earthen floor of each structure, but both
hearth and floor were destroyed by plowing in the nineteenth century. At one
or both of the ends of the houses, two rows of three small posts spanned the
width of the structure. These were the "forked stick" supports for the wooden
bed frames observed by Wight in 1771. Each frame was covered with split
canes, deer and bear skins, and blankets and averaged 5.3 feet in width. When
Bartram stayed in a Creek house, he would have slept on such a bed.[15]

In the earthen floor under the beds and along the back wall of the forty-
two houses at Fusihatchee were one or more storage pits. These square flat-
bottomed pits averaged 2.7 feet across by 3.3 feet in depth. Given their secure

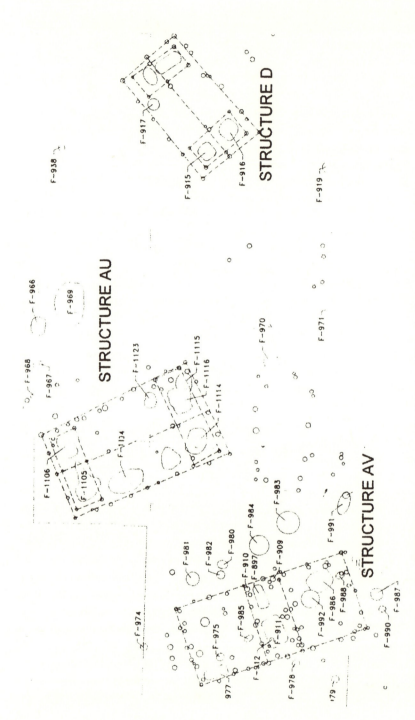

9.5. North-central area of archaeological excavations at Fusihatchee (1EE191), Elmore County, Alabama.

locations under beds, their dimensions, and an average soil temperature of 23 degrees centigrade at three feet below the surface, it is very likely that such pits served to preserve perishable food stored in covered pottery jars or baskets. After serving for food storage, many of the pits were subsequently used for disposal of animal bones, hearth ashes, and other debris.

At Fusihatchee, Hickory Ground, and Hoithlewaulee, almost all of the interments of men, women, and children were under beds and along interior back walls of domestic houses. At Fusihatchee alone, thirty-four houses contained 124 human burials. Placed in rectangular pits, often lined with bark or a blanket, individuals lay on their backs or sides, with the legs drawn up in a semi-flexed ("sitting") position. The majority were accompanied by various cultural objects, placed there as personal belongings or as offerings by relatives and friends. Most individuals wore personal ornaments of trade silver earrings and bracelets and necklaces of glass beads. Other items in the graves ranged from a simple pottery bowl to elaborate collections of flintlock muskets, iron axes, knives and hoes, brass kettles, saddles and horse gear and other items, mostly of European manufacture.[16] Bartram's description bears a close resemblance to other extant descriptions of eighteenth-century Creek burials and the archaeological record: "The Muscogulges bury their deceased in the earth. They dig a four-square deep pit under the cabin or couch which the deceased lay on, in his house, lining the grave with Cypress bark, where they place the corpse in a sitting posture, as if it were alive; depositing with him his gun, tomahawk, pipe, and such other matters as he had the greatest value for in his life time."[17]

In the archaeological excavations at Cussita, Fusihatchee, and Hickory Ground, most domestic structures stood singly or in loose clusters, but none exhibited the precise geometric arrangements of the town plan of Bartram, who probably drew his map from memory and may have "tidied-up" actual looser arrangements (see Figure 9.2). One possible domestic compound with three structures of possibly different functions was found north of the trader's compound at Fusihatchee (see Figure 9.5). Structure D on the east side was a typical Creek house, 11.8 by 20.5 feet, with two large storage pits beneath the beds at the southwest end and two adult burials under the northeast beds. Forty-two feet west was one of the largest rectangular buildings (Structure AU) found at Fusihatchee. It measured 16.6 by 29.5 feet and was oriented northwest-southeast. Under the large beds at both ends and along the back wall were eight large storage pits suggesting that the structure was used to store provisions. Twenty feet further to the west, in a parallel but staggered arrangement, was another rectangular building (Structure AV), measuring 12.7 by 28.1 feet, but of entirely different construction. Interior posts divided the building into rooms: two at each end (11.6 by 12.7 feet) and a narrow hall-like room (5.7 by 12.7 feet) in the center. This arrangement best corresponds with Bartram's description of the "Granary, or Provision House" with two lower rooms and two second-story rooms. Under the floor of the southeastern room were two large pits perhaps for the storage of "potatoe[s] . . . other roots & fruits." In one corner of the northwest room was the interment of an adult male (Feature 977) accompanied by an English-style glass bottle, an iron snuff box, and gun spalls. In the entryway or center room, there were two adult burials. On the east near the door, an adult female (Feature 897) was buried with an iron axe. On the west end of this room was Feature 911, the burial of an adult male and one of the most elaborate burials at Fusihatchee. The individual was accompanied by a riding saddle, bits and horse tack, a broken high-grade English musket, two brass kettles, straight razors, iron knives, silver ornaments, and glass beads. Possibly such an individual was a "Chief of the Family" as mentioned in Bartram's description of a domestic compound.[18]

Arbors

One of the most common types of structures on southeastern historic Indian sites, but barely mentioned by Bartram other than as elaborated forms of "pavilions" were the arbors. Arbors were formed by erecting two parallel rows of three to six tall posts each. Across the natural forks of the upper ends, were lain saplings and above these, boughs with green leaves. At Fusihatchee, the typical arrangement covered a rectangular area 10.5 by 14.0 feet. Arbors were temporary shelters erected near the houses, providing shade for various outside activities such as hide processing. Passing through central Georgia and Alabama in July 1775, Bartram would have almost certainly rested under arbors during his visits to Creek communities.[19]

Ceremonial Centers

Bartram reserved his most-detailed descriptions and drawings for the elaborate public structures at the center of large Creek towns. He described two types of ceremonial complexes. His "A View of the Antient Chunky Yard" shows the winter council house or rotunda on a "circular eminence" or mound at one end of the embanked chunky yard and the square ground on a "four square eminence" at the other end (Figure 9.6). He clearly distinguishes between the underlying older mounds, now recognized as prehistoric Mississippian Period mounds, and the contemporary eighteenth-century council structures. Although five of the historic Creek town sites in the lower Tallapoosa River valley (Tuckabatchee, Otassee, Old Coolome, Old Muccolossus, and

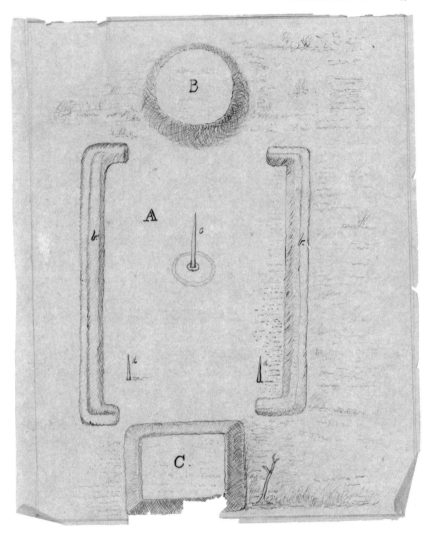

9.6. Bartram's "A View of the Antient Chunky Yard." (Copy by Edwin H. Davis, courtesy of the National Anthropological Archives, Smithsonian Institution)

Taskeegee) have prehistoric mounds near their centers, none has been sufficiently excavated to reveal historic structures on the summits of the mounds.[20]

In the second type of ceremonial center, shown in Bartram's "The Chunky Yard, Publick Square & Rotunda, of the Modern Crick Town" (Figure 9.7), the basic structural components are present but no longer built on mounds: "In the lately built, or New Towns of the Cricks, they dont raise the ground or foundation whereon their <u>Rotunda</u>, or <u>Publick Square</u> stands. But the Yard

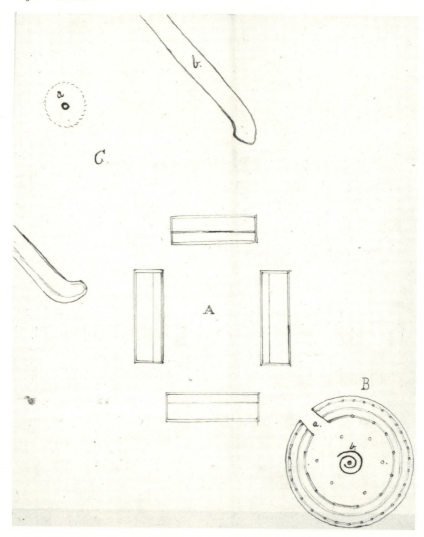

9.7. Bartram's "Plan or arrangement of the Chunky Yard, Publick Square & Rotunda, of the Modern Crick Towns." (Copy by Edwin H. Davis, courtesy of the National Anthropological Archives, Smithsonian Institution).

is in appearance nearly the same; & these Publick building stand in the same order and position and they retain the Obelisk & Slave Posts."[21]

Only three historic Upper Creek sites have yielded archaeological remains of public architecture. Recently at Hickory Ground (1EE89) on the lower Coosa River, the remains of two rotundas and a square ground were found. At the site of Otassee on the lower Tallapoosa River, amateur excavations in 1936 uncovered part of a rotunda, perhaps the one described by Bartram in his 1775–

1776 visit. Nine miles downstream at the site of Fusihatchee, extensive excavations exposed a central complex of public buildings and open areas. The ceremonial core that persisted in the same location throughout the seventeenth and eighteenth centuries was surrounded by a zone of domestic houses (see Figure 9.3). A large oblong area with no structures or other features represented the chunky yard. Arranged along its northern side were six rotunda council houses, four of which successively overlapped in a complex at the eastern end. An intact square ground and other individual square ground structures were located at the east end of the chunky yard and south of the rotunda complex. The overall ceremonial complexes at Fusihatchee and Hickory Ground are close approximations of Bartram's plan of a "Modern Crick Town."[22]

Public Squares or Square Grounds

The "Publick Square" or square ground was the summer or fair-weather center for most public ceremonial and political activities in a Creek community. In *Travels,* Bartram wrote:

> The great or public square generally stands alone, in the centre and highest part of the town: it consists of four-square or cubical buildings, or houses of one story, uniform, and of the same dimensions, so situated as to form an exact tetragon, encompassing an area of half an acre of ground, more or less, according to the strength or largest of the town or will of the inhabitants: there is a passage or avenue at each corner of equal width: each building is constructed of a wooden frame fixed strong in the earth, the walls filled in, and neatly plaistered with clay mortar; close on three sides, that is the back and two ends, except within two feet of the wall plate or eves, which is left open for the purpose of a window and to admit a free passage of the air: the front or side next to the area is quite open like a piazza. One of these buildings which is properly the council house . . . This building is somewhat different from the other three: it is closely shut up on three sides, that is, the back and two ends, and besides, a partition wall longitudinally from end to end divides it into two apartments, the back part totally dark, only three small arched apertures or holes opening into it from the front apartment or piazza, and little larger than just to admit a man to crawl in upon his hands and knees. This secluded place appears to me to be designed as a sanctuary dedicated to religion or rather priest craft. . . . The piazza or front of this building, is equally divided into three apartments, by two transverse walls or partitions, about breast high, each having three orders or ranges of seats or cabins stepping one above and behind the other which accommodate the senate and audience, in the like order as observed in the rotunda.

The other three buildings that compose the square are likewise furnished with three ranges of cabins or sophas, and serve for a banqueting-house, to shelter and accommodate the audience and spectators at all times, particularly at feasts or public entertainments, where all classes of citizens resort day and night in the summer or moderate season.[23]

Bartram also provided a drawing of a square ground, including an elevation view of the "principal" structure with its three divisions and enclosed back compartment (Figure 9.8). This drawing clearly shows that square ground structures had gable roofs of poles and bark, not the simpler shed style or arbor style roofs adopted in the nineteenth century after removal of the Creeks to Oklahoma.[24]

At Fusihatchee, a public square ground partially overlapped the southern edge of the earliest of the seventeenth-century rotundas (Figure 9.9). It was composed of four wooden rectangular structures measuring 12.3 by 30.3 feet arranged around a central courtyard 46 feet across. Gaps of 14 feet lay between the corners of adjacent structures in the square. Agricultural plowing had destroyed the central hearth in the courtyard. Wall post placement in the structure closely agrees with Bartram's description. Regularly spaced posts extended along the sides and back while four large posts defined the open front facing the courtyard. In the interior, scattered posts, mostly along the center line, held up the tiered benches. Two lines of posts supported the transverse partitions that divided each structure into the "three cabins or sophas" described by Bartram and others. Numerous replacement or prop postholes suggest that some efforts were made to extend the life of the structures. The four structures were very close in appearance, dimensions, and internal layout; none could be singled out from the other three as having the back apartment of the "council house proper."[25]

Throughout the history of Fusihatchee and other Creek communities, there were probably several square grounds at different times. The Fusihatchee square ground predates Bartram's visit to the Upper Creek country by many years. Under the floors of the four structures, 26 interments of adolescent and adult males and females date from the late seventeenth to the late eighteenth centuries. Burial under the floors of square ground structures was probably infrequent in the later eighteenth century as the practice was not recorded by any historic visitor.[26]

Rotundas

Bartram was also impressed with the large Creek rotundas or winter council houses that stood adjacent to the square grounds. He observed: "It is a vast

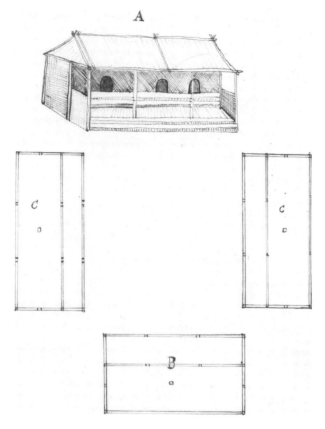

9.8. Bartram's "The Principal, or *Council House*." (Copy by
Edwin H. Davis, courtesy of the National Anthropological
Archives, Smithsonian Institution).

conical building or circular dome capable of accommodating many hundred
people; constructed and furnished within, exactly in the same manner as those
of the Cherokees already described, but much larger than any I had seen of
them."[27]

Earlier in his *Travels*, he had described the council house at the Cherokee
town of Cowe in what is now Tennessee:

The council or town-house is a large rotunda capable of accommodating several hundred people. . . . The rotunda is constructed after the following manner: they first fix in the ground a circular range of posts or
trunks of trees, about six feet high, at equal distances, which are notched
at top, to receive into them from one to another, a range of beams or wall

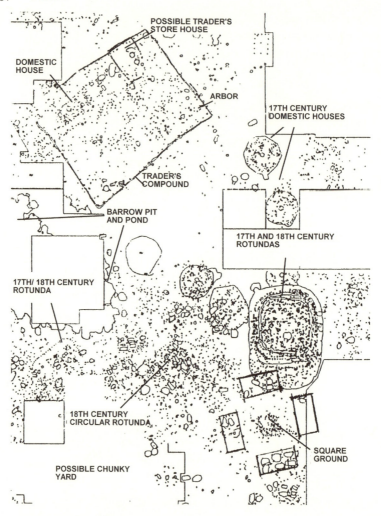

9.9. Excavated rotundas, square ground, and trader's compound at Fusi-hatchee (1EE191), Elmore County, Alabama.

plates; within this is another circular order of very large and strong pillars, above twelve feet high, notched in like manner at top, to receive another range of wall plates; and within this is yet another or third range of stronger and higher pillars, but fewer in number, and standing at a greater distance from each other; and lastly, in the centre stands a very strong pillar, which forms the pinnacle of the building, and to which the rafters centre at top; these rafters are strengthened and bound together by cross beams and laths, which sustain the roof or covering, which is a layer of bark neatly placed, and tight enough to exclude the rain, and sometimes they cast a thin superficies of earth over all. There is but one large door, which serves at the same time to admit light from without and the smoak to escape. . . . All around the inside of the building, betwixt the second range of pillars and the wall, is a range of cabins or sophas, consisting of two or three steps, one above or behind the other, in theatrical order, where the assembly sit or lean down; these sophas are covered with mats or carpets.[28]

At Otassee, Bartram also described complex traditional seating arrangements for leaders, warriors, and visitors on the raised benches. On the large central hearth, sections of split cane were laid in a spiral pattern around the central pillar. Once lit, the length of the spiral equated with the anticipated duration of a meeting.

Bartram drew two sketches of Creek rotundas: one as a simple circle on "A Plan of the Muscogulge or Upper Creek Town" (see Figure 9.2), and another more elaborate outline in his "The Chunky Yard, Publick Square & Rotunda" (see Figure 9.7). This one showed two outer circles of posts, an inner circle of six to eight interior support posts, a central support post, a central spiral of cane fuel, and a door facing a corner of the nearby square ground.[29]

Bartram's circular rotunda was not the only form of winter council house among the Upper Creeks in the eighteenth century. Modern archaeological excavations have revealed that two types of rotundas were present. In addition to Bartram's circular form, other council houses had a squared floor plan, with an internal square of eight large support posts, and a square outer wall with broadly rounded corners. The squared rotunda style was the earlier form, with some dating from the seventeenth century. Both styles overlap in the second half of the eighteenth century, but why there are two forms and why Bartram describes only the circular type is unknown.[30]

Six squared rotunda council houses were found at the center of Fusihatchee. Presumably, only one of these was in use at any time. Averaging forty-five feet across, four of the rotundas overlapped in a ceremonial complex just north of the square ground. Each had a square floor plain with rounded corners, eight large pine (*Pinus palustris*) support posts, an outer wall of smaller posts covered with wattle and daub, sunken floor, and tunnel style entrances. Each of these structures was burned and replaced by another similar structure. These rotundas correspond closely with Taitt's 1772 description of the council house at the major town of Tuckabatchee, and with archaeological examples from the seventeenth-century occupation at the King site in west Georgia.[31]

In 1936, J. Y. Brame, an amateur archaeologist of the Alabama Anthropological Society, partially excavated a circular council house at the site of Otassee, possibly the same one described by Bartram. Uncovering a large area of discolored earth, Brame found large preserved pine posts arranged in an arc, which he projected would have a diameter of 94 feet. The number and positions visible in a contemporary photograph indicate a circular ring of support posts. Brame did not describe his discovery in any detail. There is no conclusive proof that this was the actual council house seen by Bartram; it may have predated or postdated 1775–1776.[32]

Forty feet to the west of the main rotunda complex at Fusihatchee was Structure 17, a very large circular building represented only by postholes. Agricultural plowing had destroyed the floor, hearth, and other architectural details. The outer wall was a 42-foot-diameter circle formed by small posts, 2.2 feet apart. Centered within this wall were eleven large support posts, averaging ten inches in diameter, arranged in a circle 28 feet in diameter. Two very similar circular council houses with internal rings of nine and ten large support posts were uncovered at the Hickory Ground site on the lower Coosa River in September 2004. These rotundas and Structure 17 at Fusihatchee appear to be smaller simplified versions of the circular Otassee council house described by Bartram. If Brame's reconstruction of the Otassee structure excavated in 1936 is correct, the Fusihatchee and Hickory Ground structures are half as large and have only one outer ring of posts, not the two mentioned by Bartram. They have nine to eleven support posts instead of six to eight posts, but do not have the single central support post described by Bartram. Some of the size differences probably result from the smaller populations of Fusihatchee and Hickory Ground.[33]

Chunky Yard

The third major component at the centers of Creek towns was the chunky yard. In his "Observations," Bartram wrote:

> The Chunky=Yard of the Cricks so called by the Traders is a cubiform Area generally in the center of the Town, because the Publick Square & Rotunda or Great Winter Council House, stands at two opposite corners of it. It is generally very extensive* especially in the large old Towns, is exactly level, and sunk, two,—sometimes, three, feet below the banks and terrace surrounding it, which are sometimes two—one above & behind the other, and is formed of the earth cast out of the area, at the time of its formation. These banks, or terraces serve the purpose of seats for the spectators—In the centre of the yard, there is a low, circular, mount, or eminence, in the center of which stands erect the Chunky Pole, which is a high obelisk, or four square pillar, declining upwards to an obtuse point . . . This is of wood—the heart or inward resinous part of a sound

pine tree—and is very durable—generally from thirty to forty feet in height . . . Near each corner of the lower, or farther end of the yard, stands erect a less pillar or pole, about twelve feet high—These are called <u>Slave Posts</u>, because to these are bound the captives condemned to be burnt.

[*The Chunkey=Yards are of different sizes, according to the Largeness & Fame of the Town they belong to.—Some are 200 or 300 yards in length & of porportionable width.][34]

At Otassee, he described another type of pole: "In the midst of a large oblong square adjoining this town is standing a high pillar, round like a pin or needle; it is about forty feet in height, and between two and three feet in diameter at the earth, gradually tapering upwards to a point; it is one piece of pine wood."[35]

At Fusihatchee, an area 49 by 160 feet extending west of the square ground and south from the rotundas was identified as the chunky yard. Agricultural plowing had destroyed all evidence of any bordering ridges or embankments. The small slave posts could not be identified. A very large posthole, three feet in diameter and four feet deep, located at the eastern end of the yard is probably one of Bartram's "Chunky Poles."[36] Bartram's use of the word "Chunky Pole" is problematic since the game does not require a pole. These poles likely served as goals for the single pole ball game.

According to Bartram, none of the local traders knew of the origin of the term "Chunky Yard." He was convinced that the yards were of "very ancient date" but maintained by frequent sweeping, a process which Vernon J. Knight claims produced the bordering low ridges or embankments. Bartram's ignorance that the yards were named after the game of Chunky played with a disk shaped stone and cane spears is surprising. Chunky stones have been recovered from late-eighteenth-century graves at Fusihatchee and other historic Creek sites. Perhaps Bartram did not witness chunky games because they were giving way in popularity to the stick ball game by the time of his visit. According to Bartram, "the [stick ball] game is exhibited in an extensively level plain, usually contiguous to the town." No clear evidence of a ball field is known from any of the historic Creek sites. Bartram does not say if the ball game was ever played on the Chunky Yard.[37]

Ponds

Man-made ponds were common in many towns. While Bartram was at Otassee, he reported the inhabitants were "fasting, taking medicine" in ritual fashion and he noted they ate only a "meagre gruel" and were "taking at the same time by way of medicine or physic, a strong decoction of the roots of the Iris versicolor. Bartram noted they held the root, a cathartic, in "high estimation, every town cultivates a small plantation of it, having a large artificial pond, just without the town, planted and almost overgrown with it, where they usually dig clay for pottery, and mortar and plaster for their buildings."[38]

Numerous irregular clay borrow pits, 6 to 10 feet across, are found at many historic Creek and other southeastern archaeological sites. Dug for red or yellow clay for daub and wall plaster, they are frequently located in close proximity to structures. Two of the largest daub pits at Fusihatchee were located immediately to the west of the trader's compound and the chunky yard. They supplied most of the clay plaster for the nearby public buildings and domestic houses. The sides and bottoms were irregular and pitted by many episodes of removing clay with digging sticks and iron trade hoes. Eventually measuring up to 95 by 141 feet across by 3.5 deep, the two pits soon filled with rain water, creating the type of ponds observed by Bartram. Subsequently, they served to water livestock, to support stands of the medicinal *Iris* plants, and ultimately for disposal of refuse.[39]

Ilex vomitoria Grove

The daily and ceremonial use of yaupon (*Ilex vomitoria*) or black drink as a caffeine stimulant and emetic by the Creeks is well known. Bartram stated that "the Ilex Casine is perhaps the most powerful & effiecacious vegetable Diuretick yet known." Used only by men, the beverage was drunk widely on a daily basis and in ceremonies in rotundas and square grounds. The natural distribution of *Ilex vomitoria* was confined to the coastal plain, but Benjamin Hawkins clearly stated that many Creek communities transplanted and cultivated groves of yaupon.[40]

A grove of yaupon or *Ilex Vomitoria*, over 72 by 85 feet in area, still stands on a slope between the southern edge of the chunky yard of Fusihatchee and a nearby backswamp. All of the individual plants are male, and may have originated vegetatively from one original transplanted specimen. Individual stems have bole diameters up to four and a half inches and heights of ten feet. First discovered by Peter Brannon in 1920, the grove has survived due to its unplowed marginal location and vegetative mode of reproduction in which new shoots grow from horizontal roots. Old stands of yaupon are extremely rare in the lower Tallapoosa River valley. The existing grove is almost certainly a surviving remnant of a transplanted grove established by the Fusihatchee community.[41]

European Trader's Compound

By the mid-eighteenth century most Upper Creek towns had resident European traders who were integral and often valued members of the community.

According to James Adair, traders in Indian communities had houses, corn-cribs, chicken houses, winter hothouses, and storehouses constructed in the Indian fashion.[42] At the town of Muccolossus on the north bank of the Tallapoosa River, Bartram wrote, "The trader's house and stores formed a compleat square, after the mode of the habitations of the Muscogulges, that is, four oblong buildings of equal dimensions, two opposite to each other, encompassing an area of about a quarter of an acre; on one side of this a fence enclosed a yard of near an acre of ground, and at one of the farther corners of which a booth or pavilion was formed of green boughs, having two laurel trees planted in front (Magnolia grandiflora)."[43]

At Fusihatchee, a probable European trader's compound was found 125 feet north of the rotundas and square ground (Figure 9.9). The first construction was a small rectangular structure or enclosure, 22.3 by 32.1 feet. It was constructed using a technique very similar to the French *poteaux en terre* method of erecting closely spaced small posts in narrow footing ditches. It could not be determined if this was a roofed structure or a small palisaded enclosure such as a corral. Following the destruction or abandonment of this structure, a very large rectangular enclosure, 88.6 by 121.4 feet, was erected using closely spaced small posts in narrow footing ditches. The posts averaged only two inches in diameter. The large enclosed area and the small size of the posts indicate that this was an enclosure and not a roofed structure. The entrance to the large enclosure was a 33.8-foot gap at the northwest corner. Posts in the center of the gap suggest that it was closed by a simple pole gate.[44]

The neatly arranged trader's complex of four dwelling houses described by Bartram was not found in or outside of the Fusihatchee enclosure, however a single large Creek-style rectangular house, 13.0 by 29.4 feet was located inside the compound, running parallel to the north wall. Within the house were beds at both ends, two storage pits and six graves. A short distance to the southeast, a scatter of postholes suggests the presence of a smaller rectangular structure, 15.3 by 22.1 feet. The patterns of posts suggests that this may have one of the elaborate "pavilions" with a raised floor, similar to that of the Boatswain on the Chattahoochee River. Further away, in the southeastern corner of the enclosure, there was a large arbor (13.6 by 16.1 feet) of the simpler bough-covered form. This may correspond to Bartram's "booth or pavilion" described for the trader's compound at Muccolossus.

Most resident European traders had Indian wives, which explains the combination of aboriginal and European structures and construction techniques at Fusihatchee.[45] Traditionally, domestic dwellings belonged to women and were constructed by their male relatives. Within the Fusihatchee trader's compound, the traditional house outline, bed posts, storage pits, and subfloor burials are indicative of the predominance of the Creek wife in the dwelling house. The nontraditional small building and large enclosure, perhaps, were constructed using an earthfast or *poteaux en terre* technique common on frontier colonial French sites such as Fort Toulouse at the junction of the Coosa and Tallapoosa rivers. The small structure may have served as a small storehouse or corral, while the later large enclosure was probably a corral for the trader's livestock or perhaps, a fence to control access to his trade goods. The proximity and large size of the elaborate compound to the ceremonial and social center of the community at the rotunda and square ground at Fusihatchee is indicative of the economic and social importance of the European traders.

Although 233 years and the humid southeastern climate have destroyed the indigenous architecture observed by William Bartram, recent archaeological investigations have found the subsurface remains or foundations of many of these buildings. Together, ethnohistory and archaeology have allowed unparalleled reconstructions of southeastern Indian architecture and buildings. They also enable us to evaluate the relative accuracy of Bartram as an observer of the southeastern scene. None of the archaeological information seriously conflicts with Bartram's descriptions. Bartram is most accurate when describing particular structures or features such as ponds. The greatest discrepancy comes with his most ambitious project—"A plan of the Muscogulge or Upper Creek Town" (Figure 9.2). Here, his bird's eye or schematic view unduly tidies up or regiments the arrangement of ordinary Creek houses, which archaeology has shown to be more irregular and scattered.

Compared to the writings of James Adair and Benjamin Hawkins, the other two major eighteenth-century observers of the Creek Indians, Bartram's descriptions hold their own. And no writer matches Bartram's ability to populate the houses and public buildings with people and activities. He tells of daily and ritual activities within the different structures, and where custom dictated how they and visitors should sit and act in the public spaces. With Bartram, the square ground comes alive: "One of these buildings is properly the council-house, where the mico, chiefs, and warriors, with the citizens who have business, or choose to repair thither, assemble every day in council, to hear, decide and rectify all grievances, complaints and contentions, arising betwixt the citizens; give audience to ambassadors, and strangers, hear news and talks from confederate towns, allies or distant nations; to consult about the particular affairs of the town, as erecting habitations for new citizens, or establishing young families, concerning agriculture &c."[46]

Acknowledgments

I want to thank John W. Cottier, Gregory A. Waselkov, and the many students, volunteers, and supporters who labored to collect and preserve the information gathered during eleven years of archaeological excavations at the

Fusihatchee site. Major funding for the excavations was provided by the National Science Foundation, the Alabama Historical Commission, and Auburn University. Special appreciation is extended to Gregory A. Waselkov and Sarah Mattics for providing digital illustrations of Bartram's drawings. I am very grateful to Kathryn H. Braund for her patience and careful editing.

Notes

1. Bartram's descriptions of historic Indian architecture are contained in two works: *Travels Through North and South Carolina, Georgia, East and West Florida* and "Observations on the Creek and Cherokee Indians, 1789." *Travels Through North and South Carolina, Georgia, East and West Florida: A Facsimile of the 1792 Edition*, edited and with introduction by Gordon DeWolf, was the primary edition used in this chapter. *Travels of William Bartram, Naturalist Edition*, edited by Francis Harper, contains corrected dates and other annotations. Bartram's second work, "Observations on the Creek and Cherokee Indians, 1789," was published and edited by E. G. Squier in *Transactions of the American Ethnological Society*, 1853. Earlier copies of Bartram's "Observations" manuscript are found in *William Bartram on the Southeastern Indians*, edited and annotated by Gregory A. Waselkov and Kathryn E. Holland Braund (Lincoln: University of Nebraska Press, 1995). I follow the recommendations by Waselkov and Braund that John Howard Payne's copy is more faithful to Bartram's text and that the copies by Edwin H. Davis of Bartram's drawings are more accurate. *William Bartram on the Southeastern Indians*, ed. Waselkov and Braund, 137.

Contemporary descriptions of eighteenth-century Creek architecture include those by James Adair, *The History of the American Indian Adair*, edited and with an Introduction by Kathryn E. Holland Braund (London: Charles and Edward Dilly, 1775; Tuscaloosa: The University of Alabama Press, 2005); David Taitt, "Journal of David Taitt's Travels to and through the Upper Creek Nation," in *Documents of the American Revolution, 1770–1783*, ed. K. G. Davies, volume 5, *Transcripts, 1772*, 251–272 (Dublin: Irish University Press, 1974); Caleb Swan, "Position and State of Manners and Arts in the Creek, or Muscogee Nation in 1791," in volume 5 of *Information Respecting the Condition and Prospects of the Indian Tribes of the United States*, ed. Henry Rowe Schoolcraft, 251–283 (Philadelphia: J. B. Lippincott, 1852–1857); Benjamin Hawkins, "A Sketch of the Creek Country in the Years 1798 and 1799," in *Collections of the Georgia Historical Society*, vol. 3, no. 1, Rpt. ed. (Americus: Americus Book Company, 1938); *The Collected Works of Benjamin Hawkins, 1796–1810*, ed. H. Thomas Foster II (Tuscaloosa: The University of Alabama Press, 2003); Sargent Wight, "Journal of the Passage of Serj't Wight to the Upper Creek Nation 1771," in *Colonial Captivities, Marches and Journeys*, ed. Isabel M. Calder (Port Washington, N.Y.: Kennikat Press, 1967), 236–243. John R. Swanton's "Social Organization and Social Usages of the Indians of the Creek Confederacy," in *Forty-second Annual Report of the Bureau of American Ethnology* (Washington, D.C.: Government Printing Office, 1928), 23–472, remains the best secondary treatment of historic Creek architecture.

2. For a similar treatment of Bartram's travels in the southern Appalachian Mountains, see Christopher N. Rodning, "William Bartram and the Archaeology of the Appalachian Summit," in *Between Contacts and Colonies,* ed. Cameron B. Wesson and Mark A. Rees, 67–89 (Tuscaloosa: The University of Alabama Press, 2002).

3. The most modern general treatment of Historic Creek archaeology is Gregory A. Waselkov and Marvin T. Smith, "Upper Creek Archaeology," in *Indians of the Greater Southeast, Historic Archaeology and Ethnohistory,* ed. Bonnie G. McEwan (Gainesville: University Press of Florida, 2000), 242–264. Other archaeology works relevant to historic Creek Indian architecture are Chad O. Bradley, "The Yuchi Town Site, 1RU63, A Summary of the 1958–1962 Excavations," Report to the National Park Service by Southeastern Archaeological Services, Athens, Georgia, 1994; Paul D. Jackson, ed., "Following in the footsteps of Gordon R. Willey, Excavations at the Town of Kasita (9CE1)," Report to the Headquarters United States Army Infantry Center by Panamerican Consultants, Inc. (Contract No. DABT10-01-D-0017), 2004; Vernon James Knight Jr., "Tukabatchee: Archaeological Investigations at an Historic Creek Town, Elmore County, Alabama, 1984," Report of Investigations 45, Office of Archaeological Research, Alabama Museum of Natural History, The University of Alabama, 1985; John W. Cottier, "The Display and Analysis of Spatial Data from Hoithlewaulee," in *Cultural Change on the Creek Indian Frontier,* ed. Gregory A. Waselkov, 34–55, Report to the National Science Foundation (Grant No. BSN-8305437), Auburn University, 1985; John Cottier, "Field Records, Hickory Ground (1EE89) Archaeological Investigations," Auburn University: Auburn University Archaeology Laboratory, 2006; Craig T. Sheldon Jr., "The Council Houses of Fusihatchee," in *Archaeological Excavations at the Early Historic Creek Town of Fusihatchee (Phase I, 1988–1989),* ed. G. A. Waselkov, J. W. Cottier, and C. T. Sheldon Jr., 45–76, Report to the National Science Foundation, 1990 (Grant no. BNS-8718934); Craig T. Sheldon Jr., "Public Architecture of the Historic Creeks," Paper presented at the 33rd meeting of the Southeastern Archaeological Conference, Mobile, Alabama, 1990; Craig T. Sheldon Jr., "Historic Creek 'Summer' Houses of the Historic Creek Indians," Paper presented at the 40th meeting of the Southeastern Archaeological Conference, Nashville, Tennessee, 1997; and Craig T. Sheldon Jr., "The Square Ground at Fusihatchee," Paper presented at the 45th meeting of the Southeastern Archaeological Conference, Biloxi, Mississippi, 2002; Gregory A. Waselkov, "Historic Creek Architectural Adaptations to the Deerskin Trade," in *Archaeological Excavations at the Early Historic Creek Town of Fusihatchee (Phase I, 1988–1989),* ed.

G. A. Waselkov, J. W. Cottier, and C. T. Sheldon Jr., 39–41. Report to the National Science Foundation, 1990 (Grant no. BNS-8718934); and Gregory A. Waselkov, "History of the Alabama Anthropological Society," *Archaeology* 13 (1994): 64–76.

4. See Sheldon, "Public Architecture," "Square Ground at Fusihatchee," and "Historic Creek 'Summer' Houses," 2; Waselkov, "Historic Creek Architectural Adaptations to the Deerskin Trade."

5. Archaeological sites in Alabama and Georgia are designated by unique site numbers indicating state, county, and order of discovery in that county. For Alabama, EE=Elmore County, MC=Macon County, MT=Montgomery County, and RU=Russell County.

6. Bartram, *Travels,* ed. DeWolf, 386–394 and 443–456.

7. See Adair, *History;* David Taitt, "Journal"; Swan, "Position and State"; Hawkins, *A Sketch of the Creek Country;* Hawkins, *Collected Works of Benjamin Hawkins,* ed. Foster; and Wight, "Journals."

8. Archaeological surveys and historic accounts indicate that each Upper and Lower Creek town controlled large valley-wide segments along major rivers. Surrounding each town's principal settlement or square ground were isolated households and hamlets, agricultural fields, forage areas for livestock, forests, and backswamps and bottomlands rich in natural resources. See Waselkov, "Lower Tallapoosa River Cultural Resources Survey, Phase I," and Sheldon, "Historic Creek 'Summer' Houses." After Bartram's visit, some Creek communities had begun to disperse as separate households and hamlets into the surrounding countryside and tributary stream valleys as adjustments to livestock raising. By the time of removal in the 1830s, many principal settlements had been reduced to only ceremonial square grounds and rotundas. Hawkins, *A Sketch of the Creek Country,* 26. Gregory A. Waselkov, "Changing Strategies of Indian Field Location in the Early Historic Southeast," in *People, Plants, and Landscapes, Studies in Paleobotany,* ed. Kristen J. Gremillion, 179–195 (Tuscaloosa: The University of Alabama Press, 1997).

9. Bartram, *Travels,* ed. DeWolf, 386. Archaeological investigations at the site of Yuchi in Russell County, Alabama, by Harold Huscher and David Chase in 1958–1963 uncovered scattered postholes, pits, and human burials reminiscent of the patterns found at Fusihatchee and Hickory Ground, but the excavation units were too small to reveal complete house outlines. Bradley, "The Yuchi Town Site."

10. Bartram, *Travels,* ed. DeWolf, 395.

11. See Wight, "Journals"; James Adair's *History,* 449–450; Swan, "Position and State."

12. Bartram, *Bartram on the Southeastern Indians,* ed. Waselkov and Braund, 180.

13. Ibid., 156.

14. Postholes are the most common archaeological features at historic Creek

sites, but only relatively large-scale excavations will reveal outlines of structures. See Bradley, "The Yuchi Town Site"; Jackson, ed., "Excavations at the Town of Kasita (9CE1)"; Knight, "Tukabatchee"; Cottier, "Hoithlewaulee" and "Field Notes, Hickory Ground Archaeological Investigations"; Sheldon, "Historic Creek 'Summer' Houses of Central Alabama," 12–16.

15. See Sheldon, "Historic Creek 'Summer' Houses"; Bartram, *Travels*, ed. DeWolf, 386 and 395; Wight, "Journals."

16. Sheldon, "Historic Creek 'Summer' Houses of Central Alabama," 12–16.

17. Bartram, *Travels*, ed. DeWolf, 513–514; Caleb Swan, "Position and State," 270.

18. John W. Cottier and Craig T. Sheldon Jr., "Field Records, Fusihatchee (1EE191) Archaeological Investigations" (Auburn and Montgomery: Auburn University Archaeological Laboratories, 1996); Bartram, *Bartram on the Southeastern Indians*, ed. Waselkov and Braund, 180.

19. Arbors have been identified at the sites of Hickory Ground, Hoithlewaule, Fusihatchee, and possibly, Kasita on the Chattahoochee River. Diane S. Muller, "Intrasite Settlement at the Historic Creek Town of Hickory Ground," *Journal of Alabama Archaeology* 41 (1995): 107–136; John W. Cottier and Rex Ogg, personal communication, September 2004; Cottier, "Hoithlewaulee"; Sheldon, "Historic Creek 'Summer' Houses," 11; and Thomas H. Foster II, "Structural Analysis at Cussetuh," in *Following in the Footsteps of Gordon Willey: Excavation at the Town of Kasita (9CE1)*, Draft Report Submitted to Fort Benning, Georgia, Panamerican Consultants, Inc. (Tuscaloosa, 2004), 465. Adjacent to many of the arbors were numerous small pits containing charred bark and corn cobs. Such features are very common on southeastern historic Indian archaeological sites and have been interpreted as pits for smoking deerskins.

20. The relationship between the large pre-European Mississippian mounds and the historic Creek square grounds is complex and not well understood. See John R. Swanton, "The Creek Indians as Mound Builders," *American Anthropologist*, 14:320–324; "The Interpretation of Aboriginal Mounds by Means of Creek Indian Customs," in *Forty-first Annual Report of the Bureau of American Ethnology*, 495–506 (Washington, D.C.: Government Printing Office, 1927); and Knight, "Symbolism of Mississippian Mounds," in *Powhatan's Mantle: Indians in the Colonial Southeast*, ed. P. H. Wood, G. A. Waselkov, and M. T. Hatley, 279–291 (Lincoln: University of Nebraska Press, 1989).

21. Bartram, *Bartram on the Southeastern Indians*, ed. Waselkov and Braund, 168.

22. John W. Cottier and Rex Ogg, personal communication, September 2004; J. Y. Brame to Peter A. Brannon, November 10, 1941, Brannon Manuscript Collection, Indians-Townsites, Autossee File, Alabama Department of Archives and History; Sheldon, "Public Architecture," 35–37, and "The Square Ground."

23. Bartram, *Travels*, ed. DeWolf, 452–454.

24. Bartram's drawing "Plan of the Publick Square" (Figure 9.8) was not gen-

erally available until it was published by Waselkov and Braund in 1995. Combined
elevation and plan views of historic southeastern Indian square ground structures
are rare. Only two other comparable illustrations of Creek square grounds are
known. The oblique view in the Bonar Map of 1757 actually shows Indians sitting
in the square ground structures. Louis De Vorsey, "Early Maps as a Source in the
Reconstruction of Southern Indian Landscapes," in *Red, White, and Black: Symposium on Indians in the Old South,* ed. Charles M. Hudson, 12–30, Southern Anthropological Society Proceedings, no. 5 (Athens: University of Georgia Press, 1971),
20. The earlier view of a single Alabama structure in a "Cabane du Conseil des
Alibamons" differs from Bartram in having four internal cabins or divisions, but
otherwise overlaps with his description. See "Extrait d'une letter de Diron, datée
du 28 Juin 1721," in Marc De Villiers, "Documents Concernant L'Histoire Des Indiens De La Région Orientale De La Louisiane," *Journal de la Société des Americanistes de Paris* n.s. 14 (1922): 127–140.

25. Sheldon, "Public Architecture," 35–37, and "The Square Ground."

26. The recently discovered square ground at the site of Hickory Ground dated
from the latter half of the eighteenth century and the early nineteenth century.
The rectangular structures and courtyard were similar in outline and arrangement
to those at Fusihatchee but were smaller and more clearly defined. The eastern-
most structure was probably the "principal council house" as described by Bartram.
Eight burials of unexplained origins were found under three of the structures. Perhaps they were of visitors to Hickory Ground who died without any local relatives
to bury them. John W. Cottier and Rex Ogg, personal communication, September
2004.

27. Bartram, *Travels,* ed. DeWolf, 448–449.

28. Ibid., 366–367. Bartram is wrong in stating that it was death for women to
enter the rotundas. At Cailedge Town on the Tallapoosa River, David Taitt saw
men and women dancing around the central fire in the "hot house." See Taitt,
"Journal," 261. According to Caleb Swan, "And poor old men and women, suffering from want of clothes, are entitled to sleep in the hot-houses of the town they
live in, if they please." See Swan, "Position and State," 265. Bartram's erroneous as-
sumption may have resulted from attending events in which women were not usually involved. Sheldon, "Public Architecture," 62–63.

29. Waselkov and Braund suggest that Bartram's unique description of a central
support pole in the Otassee council house may refer to an attempt to repair a sag-
ging roof. The proximity of a hearth to a highly resinous pine support post would
have been a major fire hazard. Bartram, *Travels,* ed. DeWolf, 175, 181, and 279.

30. For a contemporary description of a squared rotunda at Tuckabatchee, see
Taitt, "Journal," 254.

31. See Taitt, "Journal," 254; David Hally, "Archaeology and Settlement Pattern
of the King Site," in *The King Site: Continuity and Contacts in Sixteenth-Century*

Georgia, ed. Robert L. Blakely (Athens: University of Georgia Press, 1988), 15; David Hally, "As Caves Beneath the Earth: Making Sense of House Form in the Protohistoric and Historic Southeast," in *Between Contacts and Colonies,* ed. Cameron B. Wesson and Mark A. Rees (Tuscaloosa: The University of Alabama Press, 2002), 92–100; Charles H. Faulkner, "The Winter House: an Early Southeast Tradition," *Midcontinental Journal of Archaeology* 2 (1977): 41–59. One of the Fusihatchee council houses had a preserved flat-topped hearth of sand and clay measuring 4.7 by 6.4 feet by 7 inches high. On the floor of the same structure was a burned section of roof including pole rafters, overlain by woven cane and cypress bark. Coating the underside of the rafters was a two- to three-inch layer of clay plaster. See Sheldon, "Council Houses," and "Public Architecture," 37–52.

32. J. Y. Brame to Peter A. Brannon, November 10, 1941, Brannon Manuscript Collection, Indians-Townsites, Autossee File, Alabama Department of Archives and History. This feature is still visible in modern aerial photographs.

33. Sheldon, "The Council Houses," 37–50, and "Public Architecture." The Hickory Ground rotundas bear very close resemblance to Bartram's descriptions. Both had an inner circle of nine to ten large support posts, and a larger circle of smaller posts forming the outer wall. Plowing had destroyed the floor, hearth, and other features. John W. Cottier and Rex Ogg, personal communication, September 2004.

34. Bartram, *Bartram on the Southeastern Indians,* ed. Waselkov and Braund, 154. Bartram likely gave the pole this name because of its location in the "Chunky Yard." He apparently did not witness any games among the Indians but got information about them from deerskin traders. Several contemporary writers described the Chunky Yard but do not use the term "Chunky Pole."

35. Bartram, *Travels,* ed. DeWolf, 455. This may be another stick ball game goal or it could have served other purposes.

36. Sheldon, "Public Architecture," 1; John W. Cottier, personal communication, September 2004.

37. Bartram, *Bartram on the Southeastern Indians,* ed. Waselkov and Braund, 125, 154; Stewart Culin, "Games of the Southeastern Indians," in *Twenty-Fourth Annual Report of the Bureau of American Ethnology* (Washington, D.C.: Government Printing Office, 1907), 485–488; Swanton, "Social Organization and Usages of the Indians of the Creek Confederacy," 446. There is a possibility that Bartram's "Chunky Pole" was actually used in a single pole or men-against-women version of the stick ball game. The ball game was a southeastern forerunner of the game of lacrosse in which two teams, using racquets and a deerskin ball, attempted to score against an opponent's goal post. At the ceremonial grounds of Southeastern tribes in Oklahoma, single poles topped by cow or horse skulls or by an effigy fish are used in the men-against-women variation of the stick ball game. James H.

Howard, *The Southeastern Ceremonial Complex and Its Interpretation,* Memoir of the Missouri Archaeological Society, No. 6 (Columbus: Missouri Archaelogical Society, 1968), 62–63 and 142–148. An eighteenth-century example of a pole is illustrated on Bonar's 1757 map. DeVorsey, "Early Maps," 20. See Adair, *History,* 398–401.

38. Bartram, *Travels,* ed. DeWolf, 454 (quotation); Swan, "Position and State," 492.

39. Waselkov and Smith, "Upper Creek Archaeology," 253; Robert J. Scott, "Chapter 15, Characterizing Domestic Activities," in "Following in the Footsteps of Gordon R. Willey, Excavations at the Town of Kasita (9CE1)," 463–475, Report to the Headquarters United States Army Infantry Center by Panamerican Consultants, Inc. (Contract No. DABT10-01-D-0017), 2004, 465; Sheldon, "Historic Creek 'Summer' Houses," 7–8; Adair, *History,* 306. The large borrow pit ponds at Fusihatchee were eventually filled by silt and agricultural plowing. No remains of iris were identified in the archaeological excavations of the large borrow pits, but small stands of *Iris versicolor* were found in the freshwater swamp, 200 feet south of the square ground.

40. Bartram, *Bartram on the Southeastern Indians,* ed. Waselkov and Braund, 248 and 276 (quotation); Hawkins, *A Sketch of the Creek Country,* 29; Foster, *Collected Works of Benjamin Hawkins,* 32; Adair, *History,* 48–49, and Charles H. Fairbanks, "The Function of the Black Drink among the Creeks," in *Black Drink: A Native American Tea,* ed. Charles M. Hudson (Athens: University of Georgia Press, 1979), 127–129.

41. Peter A. Brannon, "Report on trip made to Foosihachi, Elmore County, May 1, 1920, Brannon Manuscript Collection, Report Files, Alabama Department of Archives and History; Sheldon, "Historic Creek 'Summer' Houses."

42. Kathryn Braund, *Deerskins and Duffels: Creek Indian Trade with Anglo-America, 1685–1815* (Lincoln: University of Nebraska Press, 1993), 83–86; Adair, *History,* 443. Benjamin Hawkins visited the trader at Fusihatchee in 1796: "I continued on to the Fusahatchees, and took up my residence with the trader Nicholas White, a native of Mersailles, but resident in this nation 30 years; he has an Indian woman, and 4 children, 2 of each sex, 3 of them married to Indians; he lives comfortable, has stables, and a kitchen, and his wife appears, tho' old, healthy, industrious and pretty cleanly," Hawkins, *Collected Works of Benjamin Hawkins,* 44.

43. Bartram, *Travels,* ed. DeWolf, 444.

44. Sheldon, "Historic Creek 'Summer' Houses," 8. The *poteaux en terre* technique of forming walls was very common at the nearby French post of Fort Toulouse (AD 1717–1763) and at the site of Old Mobile (AD 1702–1711). Craig T. Sheldon Jr., Ned J. Jenkins, and Gregory A. Waselkov, "French Habitations at the Alabama Post, Ca. 1720–1763," *Archéologiques, Collection Hors-Série* 2 (2008): 112–

127; Bonnie L. Gums, "Earthfast (Pieux en Terre) Structures at Old Mobile," in *French Colonial Archaeology at Old Mobile: Selected Studies, Historical Archaeology* 36, no. 1 (2002): 13–25, 15–17.

45. Braund, *Deerskins and Duffels,* 83–86.

46. Bartram, *Travels,* ed. DeWolf, 452.

10

E. G. Squier's Manuscript Copy of William Bartram's *Observations on the Creek and Cherokee Indians*

Mark Williams

Who doesn't love the work and legend of William Bartram? Even the sound of his name has come to imply adventure, beauty, and idyllic pride in the southeastern section of the United States. I first heard his wonderful prose about 1958 from my dad, who was reading sections from *Travels* to my brother and me while we were looking for the historic Cherokee town of Keowee in the Keowee Valley in upper South Carolina.[1] The sense of mystery and wonder I felt from Bartram's beautiful writing was and is almost palpable. As I grew up and became a professional archaeologist, I have obviously read and used Bartram's work many times over the years since that time. It was true joy when I discovered a document connected directly to the Bartram legacy—a previously unknown copy by Ephraim George Squier of the lost William Bartram original entitled *Observations on the Creek and Cherokee Indians*, the third such copy yet discovered.

This Bartram document was first published in 1853, some thirty years after his death. It has been reprinted in part or whole on a number of other occasions, most recently by Gregory A. Waselkov and Kathryn E. Holland Braund in their important 1995 compilation of Bartram's writings on the Southeastern Indians.[2] These authors expound upon the importance of this document to all later ethnographic study of these important Native American societies. Bartram had not actually written this for publication, but merely wrote it in response to a colleague's letter with questions about Bartram's personal recollections of Creek and Cherokee lifeways during his journeys in the South. Bartram's "Observations" has come to be and will continue to stand as one of our most important primary sources on Indian life in the American South. It is regularly used by anthropologists, archaeologists, and historians, and our collective knowledge of these Native Americans would be significantly poorer without its serendipitous existence.

I first saw the document discussed here in 1983 in what was then called the Rare Book Room of the University of Georgia Library, though in the years since, the name has become the Hargrett Rare Book and Manuscript Library. The document is part of the Charles C. Jones Jr. Collection. Jones was a Princeton-trained lawyer originally from Savannah and a colonel during the American Civil War. After the war he conducted business in New York for ten years before moving to Augusta, Georgia, where he spent the remainder of his life. He had been vitally interested in the archaeological remains of former Indian societies in Georgia for most of his life, and he published several books and papers on this topic.[3]

At the time, I was conducting archeological work on the Scull Shoals mound site (9Ge4) in Greene County, Georgia, and knew that Jones had briefly discussed the site in one of his published papers. Once I discovered the existence of the Jones papers in the University of Georgia Library, I wanted to see if additional unpublished information about his investigations at Scull Shoals was present. I did locate an important original hand-drawn map to the Scull Shoals site, and presented it in 1984.[4]

When I discovered this map, I noticed another object of interest in another folder. It was a bound hardback book with black leather and colored paper covers, 10 ½ by 8 ¼ inches in size, and just under 1 inch thick. The book's spine is labeled with both the title, *MSS American Antiquities,* and the author, *E. G. Squier,* in gold lettering. There are eight separate handwritten documents copied into what obviously was one of Squier's daybooks or commonplace books. The book also has a signature, E. Geo. Squier, in pen on the inside first page. Additionally it includes the phrase "Presented to Coln C. C. Jones Jr" in pencil well down the same page. I looked through the documents bound together in the volume, thought it was interesting, and did nothing more with it at that time. I am sure I saw the name Bartram, but was not very interested because I was reasonably sure even then that it was a copy, not an original. I also remember that I lacked the money to have much of it copied anyway.

I used the Jones papers again in 1986, when working on the well-known Shoulderbone site (9Hk1) in Hancock County, Georgia, and again found a previously unpublished hand-drawn map of that site.[5] I must have seen the Bartram document again at that time but have no clear recollection of that event. I did not think further about it until the republication in 1998 of Ephraim G. Squier's and Edwin H. Davis's 1848 book entitled *Ancient Monuments of the Mississippi Valley.* I purchased this volume, published on the 150th anniversary of its appearance as the first publication by the Smithsonian Institution's Classics in Smithsonian Anthropology series, and read the wonderful new introduction written by David Meltzer.[6] I took note of Squier's relation to the Bartram "Observations" document and vaguely associated it with the document in the Hargrett Library, but, again, lack of time prevented much additional investigation.

In the spring of 2002, I finally found time to investigate. It was at this time that I read the marvelous book by Waselkov and Braund entitled *William Bartram on the Southeastern Indians.* Although I remembered that my archaeological colleague Greg Waselkov had worked on Bartram's Indian material a few years before, I had not read their book. This reading provided me with the necessary background on the "Observations" document that I lacked, and I realized that what was in the Hargrett Library was likely Ephraim G. Squier's copy of the Bartram "Observations" document, apparently with editing comments in place on it.

It was not until February 2003 that I finally found the time to investigate the complex story of the document in detail and actually had it copied for the first time. Most of the story presented here is derived from either Waselkov and Braund or Meltzer, but some is from my own additional research. The story is a bit extended, quite curious, and still has a few loose ends, although the overall story is reasonably clear.

The story begins not with William Bartram himself, but with Benjamin Smith Barton (1766–1815). Barton was from Philadelphia. He began studies abroad in 1786 at the University of Edinburgh, where his emphases were on medicine and natural history. He first wrote Bartram from there on August 26, 1787, asking questions about Indian mounds. Receiving no answer, he rewrote him in February 1788 and soon received the brief Bartram manuscript now known as "Artificial Mounts and Eminences." Barton left Edinburgh probably by November 1788, apparently without a degree in hand. He wrote Bartram again on December 13, 1788, this time from Amsterdam. This letter apparently included the extended set of questions, the answers to which became the "Observations" manuscript. Bartram's work was hampered by poor eyesight, and his answers were not delivered to Barton until December 15, 1789, just over a year later. The manuscript also included five pencil sketches.[7]

Barton used some of the information in this manuscript in his 1797 publication, but not the majority of it.[8] He apparently did nothing further with the manuscript before his death from tuberculosis in 1815 at age forty-nine. Bartram died in 1823, eight years after Barton. We have no knowledge of what happened to the manuscript from the time of Barton's death until some time in the 1840s. It now seems reasonably certain that it was not found before 1847. We know from Squier himself that he did not see it until 1847.[9]

It is clear that the Bartram document was found by Dr. Josiah Nott (1804–1873), a doctor and ethnologist from Mobile, Alabama.[10] He reported in an 1854 letter to E. G. Squier that he found the manuscript as packing material in a box of books he had ordered from Philadelphia. Nott recognized the manuscript as potentially important, or at least a curiosity, and sent it back to his mentor and colleague, Dr. Samuel G. Morton in Philadelphia.[11] This event, I believe, took place most likely sometime in the spring of 1847. By that time the manuscript had been lost for some thirty-two years, perhaps more.

Samuel George Morton (1799–1851) was a famous Philadelphia doctor, who reputedly had the largest collection of human skulls in America. He was committed to discovering racial differences in humans based upon the measurements of their skulls. This now quaint and outdated practice was considered an important part of anthropology as an academic discipline even up to the middle of the twentieth century. Morton had published a book in 1839 on skulls of native peoples of North and South America, and maintained an interest in and communication with several antiquarians excavating mounds in the United States. He and Josiah Nott began communicating by letter about their common interest in racial matters by the fall of 1844, but probably not before. Their letters continued until Morton's death in 1851.[12]

In 1845, or before, Dr. Morton began communicating by letter with another medical doctor from Chillicothe, Ohio, Dr. Edwin H. Davis (1811–1888). Davis had been actively interested in conducting research on Indian mounds in Ohio since the early 1830s.[13] Morton was interested in obtaining skulls from Davis from mounds in Ohio to help with his racial theories of polygenesis.

Also in 1845, Ephraim G. Squier (1821–1888) moved to Chillicothe from New York as editor of the *Scioto Gazette,* the local newspaper. He and Edwin Davis soon became friends and began working on the antiquities and archaeological sites together. Squier was a quick writer and likely saw this field as one within which he could potentially make a name for himself. In the summer of 1846 he went east to attempt to raise money for a research project that he and Davis were planning.[14] He met Dr. Morton in either the spring or summer of 1846 on this trip east. He also met Benjamin Silliman (1779–1864) in Boston on this trip and began writing short articles for his journal, *The American Journal of Science and Arts.* One relevant article Squier published in this journal early in 1847, while he was still living in Chillicothe, makes no mention of Bartram's manuscript. Squier was unable to raise the funds they needed for more exploration, and he and Davis were encouraged to publish some of their existing data first.

In May 1847, Squier submitted the draft text for what became *Ancient Monuments of the Mississippi Valley* to Joseph Henry, secretary of the new Smithsonian Institution, for his consideration. One of the reviewers of the draft was their friend and colleague Samuel Morton. The book was accepted by the Smithsonian in June 1847, and the editing and printing processes were initiated. By September 1847, Squier and Davis were beginning what became a bitter falling out with each other over the relative importance of the contributions of each to the completed work. Their friendship and cooperation were at an end by later that fall.

The work of editing, plate preparation, and printing continued through the rest of 1847 and much of 1848.[15] Their landmark publication did not actually appear until September of that year. The Bartram manuscript is credited to Dr. Morton in Squier and Davis's preface, and portions of it are printed, along with three sketches, on pages 120–124 of the massive volume. Squier and Davis make it clear that the Bartram manuscript came into their hands after the bulk of their report had already been written and that the included information was added almost parenthetically.[16] One gets the sense that they felt it was just too good to omit, despite its late appearance.

Since Dr. Morton, as Squier and Davis state in their preface, had been working closely with them from 1845 on, it seems highly unlikely that he would wait until perhaps 1847 to spring this wonderful document on them when their book was almost completely finished, if he had had it in his possession all along.[17]

Following the September 1848 publication of *Ancient Monuments,* Squier decided that he needed to travel to Central America to find the ultimate origins of the Indian mounds. Unable to travel based upon his own resources, he applied for and received a U.S. Government post to Nicaragua in early May 1849, some eight months after *Ancient Monuments* had been published. With a quick change in presidential administrations, however, he was forced to return to the United States by mid-September 1850.

Waselkov and Braund located two manuscript copies of the Bartram document. The first of these, known as the "Davis copy" was given to the Smithsonian in 1898 by John Woodbridge Davis, the son of Edwin Davis. The elder Davis clearly obtained his copy through his direct connection with Morton as well as with Squier. The second copy, and the one more trusted and used by Waselkov and Braund, was a copy found in the possession of John Howard Payne after his death and called the "Payne copy."[18]

John Howard Payne (1791–1852) was an American actor, an author, an adventurer, and a United States government official during his rich life. He is best known as the author of the song "Home Sweet Home," prepared as part of an opera he wrote in 1822. Payne traveled through the Southeast in the 1830s and was deeply involved with the Cherokee people. He prepared a manuscript on them, and his writings include some of our most valuable ethnographic data on the Cherokee. Waselkov and Braund evidently assumed that Morton got the Bartram document from Josiah Nott before 1842. Although they don't explicitly state why, the implication is because they believed that Payne's copy of the document must have been obtained from Morton before Payne left in 1842 for Tunis as a U.S. Government consul.

Payne was indeed appointed to the consular position in Tunis on August 23, 1842, but did not actually leave for there from New York until February 11, 1843. He arrived in Tunis about April 1 of that same year. Payne lost this position in Tunis, however, after events following the presidential election of late 1844. He left Tunis in mid-October 1845. Payne toured Malta, Palermo, Rome, Naples, and Paris for twenty-one months and did not arrive back in New York until July 1847. He applied unsuccessfully for various jobs in New York and Washington until he was reappointed as consul to Tunis in late January 1851 as part of the Millard Fillmore administration. Fillmore had become president on July 9, 1850, through the untimely death of Zachary Taylor. A Jenny Lind concert in Washington on December 17, 1850, featuring his "Home Sweet Home" song, was apparently instrumental in him receiving the renewed appointment he dearly wanted. He left on May 9, 1851, arrived in Tunis on May 29, and was indeed there when he died on April 9 of the following year.[19]

The fact that Payne was in New York and Washington just when the Squier and Davis Smithsonian book was being produced provides strong circumstantial evidence of opportunity for Squier (or Davis) to have met with Payne during that period. There is more direct evidence, however. In two of Squier's early 1851 publications (*Monuments of New York* and *Serpent Symbol,* which was published in April 1851), Payne's Cherokee manuscript is mentioned and Squier even quotes from it.[20] Additionally, Squier quotes from the unpublished Payne manuscript in his notes at the end of his edited version of Bartram's document that was completed by July 1851. Payne's manuscript had not been published at that time and Squier likely could only have seen it in Payne's possession.[21] We know that Payne's Cherokee manuscript was ready for publication by July 1848, but that financial arrangements through a Cherokee named R. L. Delaware could not be satisfied.[22] As late as December 1899, the famous anthropologist James Mooney was writing Isaac Minis Hays, secretary at the American Philosophical Society, to see if he knew anything about the Payne manuscript mentioned in Squier's *Serpent Symbol* book.[23] Not finding the original, Mooney quoted extensively from Squier's *Serpent Symbol* extracts of the Payne manuscript in Mooney's *Myths of the Cherokee* published in 1900.

It seems highly likely, then, that Payne and Squier met and swapped access to the two manuscripts: Payne's unpublished Cherokee manuscript, and Bartram's "Observations" manuscript. My best guess for the date of the exchange is between July 1848 and March 1849, but it could also have been in the late fall of 1850 (see the appendix for a timeline). Payne probably saw the original Bartram manuscript owned by Morton, rather than Squier's copy. As Waselkov and Braund observe, "The Payne manuscript seems to preserve most fully the content of Bartram's original document. In spelling, grammar, punctuation, and style, the Payne manuscript resembles known Bartram documents much more closely than does the Davis copy. Furthermore, the Payne copy contains many words, phrases, and lines omitted from the Davis copy and the Squier editions."[24] In any event, Payne certainly took the manuscript that we know as the "Payne copy" with him when he left for what became his last trip to Tunis in May 1851.

After Squier arrived back in New York from Nicaragua in September of 1850, filled with new ideas, he immediately developed a project to publish the full Bartram manuscript.[25] He also was actively working on several other projects at the same time that fall that were published early in 1851. Several people began helping him raise money to publish the Bartram manuscript, still in the possession of the ailing Dr. Morton at that time. Indeed, Morton was supposed to write the preface to the publication, but he died on May 15, 1851, while the fund raising was still in progress.[26] Squier remained interested in this project, however, and finished the editing and preface by July of that same year. It was almost two more years, however, before the completed book could be published as *Transactions 3 of the American Ethnological Society*. Unfortunately, all but twenty-five of the printer's run were immediately destroyed by a fire.[27] Squier would have been the logical person to have acquired Bartram's original manuscript from Morton's estate, but nothing more is known of what happened to it.

There is little doubt that the manuscript in the Hargrett Library is the copy that Squier used to prepare at least part of the 1853 published account. There are pencil editing marks on it that perfectly match the wording in the 1853 published version. Further, there are some printer's marks. For example, the footnotes that Bartram added at the beginning of the document were specified to be set in 8 point Pica type. While the editing changes in the first part of the report seem minor, the published version of the Postscript[28] is massively different from that in the Hargrett manuscript. The location of Squier's original of the rewriting he did here is unknown. Also, there are some spelling differences between the Hargrett volume and the 1853 published one, so perhaps the Hargrett volume was merely a first edited draft. Also curious are a few numbered page breaks in the manuscript that match the same numbered page breaks in the actual 1853 publication. More detective work is certainly warranted here. In any event, it seems likely that Squier must have eventually recovered his edited manuscript from the printer after the book was published, but even this remains uncertain.

Squier's interest in the archaeology and ethnology of the eastern United States seems to have waned somewhat after 1853. Certainly the war eventually intervened, and by 1867 he began having family troubles. He was instrumental in killing the American Ethnological Society in the fall of 1869, yet he founded the short-lived Anthropological Society of New York the following spring.[29] This organization included his old friend Josiah Nott, who was appointed by Squier as vice president in the fall of 1872.[30] Squier and Nott had begun communicating with one another in the summer of 1848, and became friends for life after 1854. Dr. Nott had moved from Mobile to Baltimore after the war, and then to New York in May 1868, where he was a noted doctor and a good friend of Squier. Nott moved back to Mobile in early 1873 and died of tuberculosis soon afterward on March 31.[31]

That same year Squier went to Europe with his wife and the publisher Frank Leslie, for whom Squier was then working as a writer. Leslie and Squier's wife, Miriam, began an affair that culminated in her divorce from Squier in the summer of 1873.[32] He was distraught and examined by a neurological specialist who declared him to be a "lunatic." He was committed to an insane asylum by August 1874, and died on April 17, 1888, still a broken man. His wife, Miriam, who had also put her first husband in an insane asylum before marrying Squier, married Frank Leslie as soon as Squier was out of the picture, and then legally took her third husband's name after he died in 1880. As Frank Leslie she could continue to run his publishing empire until she died in 1914.[33]

The remaining question here is how did the Squier copy of Bartram's manuscript end up in the possession of Charles C. Jones Jr.? I have located two letters from Squier to Jones in the Hargrett library. The first is a polite note dated August 8, 1859, written to accompany the return to Jones of a loaned copy of an important address on antiquities Jones had given to the Georgia Historical Society earlier that year. The second is dated June 15. The year is unstated; it might be 1873, but this is not certain. It was bound by Jones into his own copy of his famous 1873 book, *Antiquities of the Southern Indians*, some time in early 1874. The letter itself is an abject apology from Squier to Jones for Squier having missed a diner engagement in New York. Internal evidence suggests that it may have been written as early as 1870, rather than 1873, but this is not completely clear. In his 1873 book Jones quotes from Squier's 1853 published and edited account of Bartram's *Observations*, but makes no mention of the Squier manuscript itself.[34] Perhaps Squier gave the Bartram volume to Jones to help atone for his social indiscretion or to congratulate him on his new publication, but it seems unlikely to me that Jones saw the manuscript before the summer of 1873. We know that Squier's books were sold by his brother after he was committed to a mental institution, presumably in the fall of 1874 at the earliest.[35]

The inside inscription of the Hargrett manuscript notes the volume was "presented" to Jones, but it is not completely clear by whom because there also is the name "Turner" listed on the inside cover page. There must remain some remote possibility that this "Turner" was an intermediate owner of the manuscript. Incidentally, the most likely candidate for the unknown "Turner" is the noted American Indian linguist William Wadden Turner (1810–1859). He was in the American Ethnological Society with Squier and is reported to have been in New York from 1842 to 1852.[36] We also know that Squier and Turner had an active correspondence between 1851 and 1857, with twenty-four letters now housed in the Library of Congress.[37] There is little chance that Charles C. Jones ever met William Wadden Turner, however, since he died before the war, or that he could have given the book to Jones. In the final analysis,

I believe it most likely that the volume was given directly to Jones by Squier in the summer of 1873.

The Squier volume presumably sat on Charles C. Jones's shelf in Augusta as a curio until he died on July 19, 1893. There is no indication that he ever referred to it or used any data from it in any of his own later writings. I do not yet know the history of the book from then until it was sold to the University of Georgia library in 1960 by the Waller family of Augusta. Presumably it was simply passed down as a family heirloom.

The job of comparing the newly discovered copy of Bartram's *Observations* with the Payne and Davis copies, as well as with the 1853 published version of Squier, is now underway. The manuscript consists of eighty-five pages, all told, and includes copies of all the drawings except for "*A Plan of the Muscogulge or Upper Creek Town.*"[38] While there are not apt to be any earthshaking new revelations in the text or the drawings here, the effort is certainly deemed worthwhile. Like Waselkov and Braund, I continue to hope that Bartram's original manuscript itself will eventually be discovered.[39] In the absence of that document, however, the newly discovered Squier copy is certainly a welcome addition to the growing collection of documents on the southeastern Indians by the famous William Bartram.

Appendix

Important dates establishing the Payne-Squier connection

ca. May 1847	Squier moves to New York
July 1847	Payne returns to New York from Europe
September 1847	Squier and Davis begin falling out over authorship of *Ancient Monuments*
July 11, 1848	Payne's Cherokee Manuscript is ready for publication
September 1848	*Ancient Monuments* is published
February 23, 1849	Date in Squier's Day Book title page
March 25, 1849	Payne moves to Washington, D.C.
May 1849	Squier moves to Nicaragua
September 15(?), 1850	Squier back in New York
Early January 1851	Payne back in New York
April 1851	Squier publishes *Serpent Symbol* with Payne quotes
May 9, 1851	Payne leaves for Tunis for the last time
May 15, 1851	Dr. Morton dies
July 1851	Squier completes editing of Bartram book with Payne quotes

Notes

1. William Bartram, *Travels of William Bartram,* ed. Mark Van Doren (New York: Macy-Masius, 1928; Rpt., New York: Dover, 1928), 269–271.

2. William Bartram, *William Bartram on the Southeastern Indians,* ed. Gregory A. Waselkov and Kathryn E. Holland Braund (Lincoln: University of Nebraska Press, 1995), 133–191.

3. For example, Charles C. Jones Jr., *Antiquities of the Southern Indians, Particularly of the Georgia Tribes* (New York: D. Appleton Company, 1873).

4. Mark Williams, *Archaelogical Excavations at Scull Shoals Mounds (9GE4), 1984 & 1985,* Lamar Institute Publication 1 (Watkinsville, Ga.: Lamar Institute, 1992). The map is on page 7.

5. Mark Williams, *Archaelogical Excavations at Shoulderbone Mounds and Village (9HK1),* Lamar Institute Publication 3 (Watkinsville, Ga.: Lamar Institute, 1990). The map is on page 15.

6. David J. Meltzer, "Ephraim Squier, Edwin Davis, and the Making of an American Archaeological Classic," in *Ancient Monuments of the Mississippi Valley,* ed. E. G. Squier and E. H. Davis (Washington, D.C.: Smithsonian Institution Press, 1998), 1–98.

7. Bartram, *Bartram on the Southeastern Indians,* ed. Waselkov and Braund, 134.

8. Benjamin Smith Barton, *New Views of the Origins of the Tribes and Nations of America* (Philadelphia: John Bioren, 1791).

9. Waselkov and Braund speculated that it came into Nott's possession prior to 1842. Bartram, *Bartram on the Southeastern Indians,* ed. Waselkov and Braund, 135; William Bartram, "Observations on the Creek and Cherokee Indians, 1789," with Prefatory and Supplementary Notes by E. G. Squier, *Transactions of the American Ethnological Society,* vol. 3, pt. 1, 3.

10. For Nott's biography, see Reginald Horsman, *Josiah Nott of Mobile: Southerner, Physician, and Racial Theorist* (Baton Rouge: Louisiana State University Press, 1987).

11. Bartram, *Bartram on the Southeastern Indians,* ed. Waselkov and Braund, 135.

12. Morton's book, *Crania Americana* was published in Philadelphia by Dobson in 1839. Horsman, *Josiah Nott,* 85–94.

13. Meltzer, "Ephraim Squier," 7.

14. Ibid., 6–9.

15. Ibid., 23–33.

16. Squier, *Ancient Monuments,* 120.

17. Ibid., xxxvi.

18. Bartram, *Bartram on the Southeastern Indians,* ed. Waselkov and Braund, 136–137.

19. Grace Overmyer, *America's First Hamlet* (New York: New York University Press, 1957), 335–337, 360–362, 365–370.

20. Squier 1851b:239–240 and Squire 1851c:191.

21. Bartram 1853:74–77.

22. Overmyer, *America's First Hamlet,* 356.

23. James Mooney to Isaac Minis Hays, December 16, 1899, American Indian Manuscript 4167, American Philosophical Society, Philadelphia. Available on-line at http://www.amphilsoc.org/library/guides/indians/info/cha.htm.

24. Bartram, *Bartram on the Southeastern Indians,* ed. Waselkov and Braund, 137.

25. Bartram, "Observations," ed. Squier, 4; Bartram, *Bartram on the Southeastern Indians,* ed. Waselkov and Braund, 135.

26. Bartram, *Bartram on the Southeastern Indians,* ed. Waselkov and Braund, 136.

27. Ibid.

28. Bartram, "Observations," ed. Squier, 51–58.

29. Meltzer, "Ephraim Squier," 676.

30. Horsman, *Josiah Nott,* 334.

31. Ibid., 108, 203, 319–335.

32. Meltzer, "Ephraim Squier," 66–67.

33. Ibid., 50.

34. Charles C. Jones Jr., *Antiquities of the Southern Indians, Particularly of the Georgia Tribes* (New York: D. Appleton Company, 1873), 178–181.

35. Meltzer, "Ephraim Squier," 67.

36. James Grant Wilson and John Fiske, eds., *Appleton's Cyclopedia of American Biography,* 6 volumes (New York: D. Appleton and Company, 1887). Available on-line at http://www.famousamericans.net/ (accessed February 1, 2003).

37. Martin J. Manning, "William Wadden Turner," American National Biography Online. http://www.anb.org/articles/20/20-01644-article.html (accessed February 5, 2003). As of 2008, I have not had the opportunity to examine these letters.

38. For the drawings, see Bartram, *Bartram on the Southeastern Indians,* ed. Waselkov and Braund, 181–183.

39. Ibid.

IV
Botanical Discoveries

11

William Bartram's *Oenothera grandiflora*

"The Most Pompous and Brilliant Herbaceous Plant yet Known to Exist"

Joel T. Fry

William Bartram observed an astonishing array of new plants in his travels through the largely unexplored floral paradise of the Carolinas, Georgia, and East and West Florida from 1773 to 1776. His exploration introduced a number of new plants to science and horticulture, and many of his discoveries are popular garden shrubs today, including oakleaf hydrangea, flame azalea, bottlebrush buckeye, Fothergilla, and of course Franklinia. Of all his discoveries, Bartram singled out the largeflower evening primrose, *Oenothera grandiflora*, as "the most pompous and brilliant herbaceous plant yet known to exist." This is a glowing description even for Bartram, who of course is known for his florid prose. He repeated praise for his golden evening primrose on more than one occasion, and lamented when it failed in cultivation in the family garden sometime before 1788.

For a flower that might well have a claim to be William Bartram's favorite among many favorites, it is surprising how little attention has been paid to *Oenothera grandiflora* by the world of horticulture. It is not readily available commercially as seed or plant in North America or perhaps anywhere in the world. This might be attributable to the easy growth of the largeflower evening primrose and its large sprawling habit, or to its too close family resemblance to a ubiquitous weed, the common evening primrose, *Oenothera biennis*. In North America, Bartram's *Oenothera grandiflora* has a much more limited range, and never seems to have become a problem weed; perhaps it is muscled out by its smaller relative, the common evening primrose. As if to signify the failure of the plant in gardens, it does not have a simple or catchy common name. Even William Bartram tried out different names for his favorite plant from *"Oenothera speciosum"* to *"Oenothera speciosa"* to *"Oenothera grandiflora,"* and "Great Tree Primrose from Florida," and "Golden Oenothera." The modern common name, "largeflower evening primrose," is not particularly engaging, and in truth is only a verbatim translation of the Latin scientific name.

In the rather humble position as an inhabitant of old fields and disturbed land, *Oenothera grandiflora* remains in the vicinity of Stockton, in Baldwin County, Alabama, where William Bartram first found it in the summer of 1775. For over two centuries this area along the east bank of the Tensaw River above Mobile Bay has proved a reliable place to find the large-flowered plant whenever curious botanists or gardeners have gone to look for it. And in what is a surprising twist in the story of this Bartram discovery, in the early twentieth century *Oenothera grandiflora* came to play a supporting role in the development of modern genetics—including the rediscovery of Mendelian inheritance, the theory of mutation, and a proposed mechanism for Darwinian evolution. The influential Dutch botanist Hugo de Vries (1848–1935) spent several decades beginning in the 1890s in large-scale experiments with evening primrose plants, including William Bartram's *Oenothera grandiflora* and hybrids developed from it.

Discovery of *Oenothera grandiflora*

William Bartram approached the British colonial settlement of Mobile, in West Florida in late July 1775, from the east through the Creek country. Sometime in the last week of the month he "arrived at Taensa, a pretty high bluff, on the Eastern channel of the great Mobile river, about thirty miles above fort Conde, or city of Mobile, at the head of the bay."[1] "Taensa" or Tensaw Bluff, also known as Farm Hall, was the plantation of Major Robert Farmar, the retired military commander of Mobile. Farmar was living near the northern frontier of British West Florida on lands that had once been occupied by French planters and before that by Native Americans. Bartram spent only the evening at Tensaw Bluff at this time, then continued on to the town of Mobile with the goal of reaching the Mississippi.

"Not having an immediate opportunity from hence to Manchac" on the Mississippi, Bartram took the intervening month for explorations around Mobile Bay, largely on the east side in what is now Baldwin County, using Major Farmar's plantation as his base. On August 5 he "set off from Mobile up the river in a trading boat, and was landed at Taensa bluff . . . to make good my engagements, in consequence of an invitation from that worthy gentleman, to spend some days in his family."[2] Farmar provided Bartram with a light canoe to further explore the Tensaw River, upriver from Farm Hall. During one of these frequent explorations William Bartram observed the new evening primrose. He wrote in *Travels:*

11.1. *Oenothera grandiflora,* William Bartram's largeflower evening primrose in late season flower along the road from Stockton to Rice Creek Landing on the Bartram Canoe Trail, Baldwin County, Alabama, October 28, 2007 (Photo courtesy of Joel T. Fry).

Early one morning, passing along by some old uncultivated fields, a few miles above Taensa, I was struck with surprise at the appearance of a blooming plant, gilded with the richest golden yellow, stepping on shore, I discovered it to be a new species of the Oenothera . . . perhaps the most pompous and brilliant herbaceous plant yet known to exist. It is an annual or biennial, rising erect seven or eight feet, branching on all sides from near the earth upwards, the lower branches extensive, and the succeeding gradually shorter to the top of the plant, forming a pyramid in figure; the leaves are of a broad lanceolate shape, dentated or deeply serrated, terminating with a slender point, and of a deep full green colour; the large expanded flowers, that so ornament this plant, are of a splendid perfect yellow colour; but when they contract again, before they drop off, the underside of the petals next the calyx becomes of a reddish flesh colour, inclining to vermilion, the flowers begin to open in the evening, are fully expanded during the night, and are in their beauty next morning, but close and wither before noon. There is a daily profuse succession for many weeks, and one single plant at the same instant presents to view many hundred flowers. I have measured these flowers above five inches in diameter, they have an agreeable scent.[3]

Leaving the "splendid fields of the golden Oenothera" Bartram passed abandoned plantations for over ten miles and noted peach and fig trees among the "ruins of ancient habitations." According to the account in *Travels* this particular canoe exploration of the Tensaw delta extended for about a week up and back. On the day following his return to Farmar's plantation, Bartram noted he "felt symptoms of a fever, which in a few days laid me up and became dangerous."[4]

Bartram recovered enough to continue his explorations but does not seem to have been well for months to come. He had recurring crises with this or a similar fever, possibly scarlet fever, although a precise diagnosis has never been put forth. Bartram returned to Mobile by the beginning of September "very ill," and after a brief sailing trip to Pensacola, left Mobile for Manchac and the Mississippi River at the end of the first week of September. Bartram's health continued to decline and his eyesight was particularly affected. Close to death, he was forced to rest for over a month at the plantation of James Rumsey on Pearl Island.[5] Fortunately for posterity Bartram was eventually able to continue to the Mississippi, traveling as far north as Pointe Coupee in modern-day Louisiana.

The history of the largeflower evening primrose, *Oenothera grandiflora*, picks up on William Bartram's return from the west to Mobile in mid-November 1775. Bartram spent a little short of two weeks in Mobile preparing for his return east, and "having made up my collections of growing roots, seeds and curious specimens, left them to the care of Messrs. Swanson and M'Gillavry, to be forwarded to Dr. Fothergill of London."[6] It is impossible to say for certain when William Bartram collected seed of his new *Oenothera*. In early August 1775 when he first saw the flower, the fields of evening primrose had only recently begun to bloom and likely had not developed ripe seed. Before the end of August, when Bartram returned from Tensaw to Mobile, he may have been able to find seed. If not, he also could have arranged for someone from the Farm Hall plantation to gather seed for him.

It is certain Bartram did collect seed and at least one specimen of the new flower in bloom for his patron Dr. John Fothergill in London. These must have been included in the collections left in the care of Swanson and M'Gillavry to be forwarded to Fothergill. No acknowledgment survives from Fothergill that he received these collections from Mobile, but a dried specimen of *Oenothera grandiflora* survives in a bound book of West Florida specimens now at the Natural History Museum in London (see Fig. 11.2).[7] And as will be seen Dr. John Fothergill is credited with introducing the "great-flower'd Oenothera" into cultivation in England in 1778.

William Bartram set off from Mobile for his return east on November 28, 1775, and arrived at Tensaw Bluff the same day. The next day he took leave of Major Farmar and joined a company of traders and pack horses traveling east to Augusta, Georgia. He probably carried seed of the new *Oenothera,* and he may have had time to collect more en route. Bartram likely carried the precious seed of his new plant with him for the rest of his time in the South. He certainly brought seed of the "pompous and brilliant" plant back to his father's house on the banks of the Schuylkill in Philadelphia, when he returned in January 1777.

Cultivating the New Evening Primrose

William Bartram without doubt planted seed of the new largeflower *Oenothera* in the spring of 1777 at Bartram's Garden. The year 1777 was eventful in many ways, and William's arrival, probably unannounced and unexpected, was a singular happy event for the year. William's father, John, had retired in the spring of 1771 and turned the garden business over to his son John Jr. Two generations—John and his wife, Ann, and John Jr. and wife, Elizah, and young daughter Mary—shared the large stone house. William would have met his niece Mary for the first time, and would learn of another niece, Ann, who had died the year before. Another niece Elizabeth would be born in August 1777, and die in the fall (more children followed in the future).[8]

With luck, William Bartram and his father might have seen the brilliant new evening primrose in flower toward the end of the summer in 1777. *Oenothera* species are generally biennial, producing a large low rosette of leaves the first year with a deep storage root, followed by a great burst of height and flowers the second year, but under ideal conditions, they can grow large enough to flower in one year. William was also busy propagating the many valuable seeds he brought back from the South, including *Franklinia alatamaha, Fothergilla gardenii, Cyrilla racemiflora, Cliftonia monophylla, Litsea aestivalis, Kalmia hirsuta, Lyonia lucida, Nyssa ogeche, Osmanthus americanus, Oxydendrum arboretum, Philadelphus inodorus, Prunus angustifolia, Robinia viscosa, Vaccinium arboreum, Aesculus sylvatica, Styrax grandifolius, Sideroxylon lycioides,* and many more. This may seem a long list, but is really only a partial selection of the significant shrubs Bartram brought back as seed from his travels.[9] From long experience the Bartram family knew the prime value of these new plants. These

11.2. Dried specimen of largeflower evening primrose, *Oenothera grandiflora,* collected by William Bartram in August 1775 and sent to Fothergill from Mobile in late November. The *Oenothera* was on page 10 of a book of West Florida specimens. There is no surviving annotation by Bartram for these specimens. The handwritten identification from 1914 is by the Canadian biologist R. R. Gates (Courtesy the Natural History Museum, London).

were important new capital for the family plant business, and in the midst of war William and his brother planted and cultivated their garden looking forward to future peace.

The year 1777 came to a sad conclusion. The American army under Washington failed to stop a British advance from the south at the Battle of Brandywine on September 11. In two weeks the city of Philadelphia would be occupied by the British under Lord Howe. On September 22 John Bartram died, and family tradition records he feared British retribution would destroy his garden. Instead, British officers may have been assigned to protect the garden, although the events of the war remain poorly documented at Bartram's Garden. October and the first half of November saw daily fighting and a month-long siege of Mud Island or Fort Mifflin on the Delaware River, south of the garden at the mouth of the Schuylkill. The Darby Road, which formed the west boundary of the Bartram farm, served as a no-mans-land between the two armies, with frequent guerrilla raids and sniping. The Bartrams were hunkered down in the midst of an international war. In spite of this a British Captain of Guards, E. S. Fraser, wrote the Bartrams in mid-December requesting information on a list of more than two hundred species of North American plants he wanted to acquire for his property in England.[10]

At the same time, seeds and plants William Bartram sent to Dr. John Fothergill were growing in Fothergill's garden at Upton in Essex, perhaps the premier plant collection of the day in London. The fate of Bartram's plants in Fothergill's garden is also not well researched, but it is clear the British gardeners had success with the new evening primrose, probably from seed. In 1778, *Oenothera grandiflora* flowered for Fothergill, presumably at Upton. A dried specimen of *Oenothera grandiflora* in the Banks Herbarium at the Natural History Museum in London has the year "1778" and "Oenothera grandiflora MSS" noted on the rear in the botanist Daniel Solander's hand. Fothergill's introduction in 1778 is also credited in *Hortus Kewensis,* the first catalogue of the Royal Botanic Gardens at Kew issued in 1789.[11]

An unsolved puzzle remains—who coined the name "*Oenothera grandiflora?*" The note in Solander's hand on the 1778 specimen seems to be the earliest known use of the name, but it refers to another manuscript. The question remains, was this a Solander manuscript or a lost William Bartram manuscript naming or describing the plant in the wild? Solander, or later European botanists, are credited as the source of the botanic name, but it is possible William Bartram suggested the name in correspondence with Fothergill. Over the next few years Bartram was inconsistent in the Latin names he used for the new plant, but he did eventually print an engraving in Philadelphia around 1786 illustrating the new plant under the name *Oenothera grandiflora,* prior to any European publication.

The American Revolution cut off trade with the Bartrams' major customers in Europe for a considerable time, for at least eight years, and possibly for as much as a decade. Shipping from Philadelphia declined in the early 1770s as non-importation agreements were enforced, and all trade stopped in 1775. Still in the midst of war, the Bartram brothers had an opportunity to send new plants to France in 1779. The first French ambassador, Joseph Matthias Gérard de Rayneval, or Sieur Gérard, prepared to return to Paris in the fall of 1779. Draft catalogue lists for four shipments from the Bartrams for Sieur Gérard survive in William Bartram's handwriting on the backs of some of his father's letters.[12] A July 1779 "List of Seeds" for Gérard included "Oenothera speciosum" as well as "Mimosa Mississipi."[13] "Speciosum" means beautiful in Latin, and here certainly refers to what will later be officially named *Oenothera grandiflora*. The Mississippi Mimosa is now called prairie mimosa, *Desmanthus illinoensis*. William Bartram had encountered this plant while recuperating on Pearl Island, near the Rigolets. An herbaceous perennial, Bartram was also particularly taken with the new mimosa, "in respect of the elegancy of its pinnated leaves, cannot be exceeded by any of that celebrated family."[14]

A month later in August 1779, "Oenothera speciosa, Great Tree Primrose from Florida," appears in a list of "growing roots" prepared for Gérard by Bartram.[15] All told, six boxes of plants and seeds were packed by the Bartram brothers for Sieur Gérard in 1779. Some may have been shipped earlier in the spring, but most probably accompanied Gérard on his return to Paris in the fall of 1779, protected by convoys of the French fleet. A number of William Bartram's new discoveries from his travels in the South made it to Paris with surprising speed. Franklinia and the largeflower evening primrose probably survived the trip and are later reported growing at the Trianon Garden at Versailles and other French royal gardens. Documentation connecting these plants with William Bartram and his explorations seems to have been lost, however. Later French accounts are often unclear where the plants came from, even what continent.[16]

Efforts to publicize William Bartram's botanic discoveries including *Oenothera grandiflora* next surface in Philadelphia, circa 1786. Bartram had prepared a draft manuscript for his travels by as early as 1783. Johann David Schöpf, a surgeon with Ansbach troops serving with the British army, visited Bartram's Garden at the close of hostilities in summer 1783 and mentioned an "unprinted manuscript on the nations and products" of Florida by William.[17] By 1786 the Philadelphia printer Enoch Story Jr. was mounting a subscription effort to publish the work, perhaps with support from Benjamin Franklin, who had returned from France in 1785.[18] Story wrote Franklin at some point in 1786, announcing progress in his planned subscription and the letter indicates William Bartram had already prepared a printed illustration of the

Franklinia—intended for the volume of travels: "I am about publishing the Travels of Mr. Bartram Bottanist—I have inclosed proposals for the same and hope it will meet with your approbation . . . —I have some of the cuts viz. The Indian Warrior, the Paroquet of Carolina & the Franklinia which are done by Mr. Bartram in etching for the Vol. If you choose can let you see them."[19]

A set of eight engravings based on William Bartram drawings survives in the Barton Delafield Collection at the American Philosophical Society, with most labeled "Bart. Journ." and signed "W. Bartram Delin. Trenchard Sculp." James Trenchard (b. 1746) was a well-known Philadelphia engraver, active from 1777 onward. These engravings are captioned "Franklinia alatamaha," "Æsculus polygamia," "Aonymos & Kalmea celiata," "Bignonia bracteata," "Magnolia awriculata," and "Œnothera grandiflora." Two additional engravings in the same format of the Gopher Turtle, *Gopherus polyphemus,* are likely part of this set, but are not marked "Bart. Journ." Although not certain, it seems reasonable to assume these engravings are related to the "cuts" Story mentioned to Franklin in 1786. The Indian Warrior was probably reused as the frontispiece for the 1791 edition of *Travels,* and the Carolina paroquet seems lost, but the Franklinia is represented in this collection at the American Philosophical Society.

There is no other known engraving (or "etching" as Story described it) of Franklinia by William Bartram. Engravings were expensive to produce and the prints valuable. In at least two cases sets of these additional prints were included in bound copies of the 1791 edition of *Travels.*[20] These engravings are larger than the octavo size of the 1791 edition and when bound in the volume were folded in thirds. It remains a mystery why so few copies of these fine engravings are preserved. They are valuable additions to the illustrations in Bartram's book and would have supported his botanic descriptions and naming for several new species. Franklin tree, bottlebrush buckeye, coco plum, wicky, fevertree, mountain magnolia, and the largeflower evening primrose were included along with views of the upper and lower shell of the gopher tortoise. The image of *Oenothera grandiflora* is a particularly stylish drawing of the plant in bloom. If these drawings had been included in the general run of the first edition of *Travels* they would almost certainly have been copied in the European reprint editions that followed, and they would have enhanced Bartram's reputation as an American artist. As it stands, a few copies of *Travels* are illustrated with hand-colored engravings, including at least two with Bartram's primrose (see Fig. 11.3).

The initial subscription to publish William Bartram's manuscript with Enoch Story failed for unknown reasons. There may have been financial difficulties, and young Benjamin Smith Barton was also criticized for interfering with the publication. In the fall of 1786 William Bartram's problems were com-

11.3. Engraved image of *Oenothera grandiflora* produced in
Philadelphia. Drawing by William Bartram, engraved by
James Trenchard, ca. 1786, and probably intended for inclusion
in *Travels*. This rare image was included in a few copies of
the book, which served as presentation copies from the author
(Courtesy of the American Philosophical Society).

pounded with a life-threatening fall. He wrote later, describing the accident: "I
broke my Leg & was near loosing my life in consequence of it I fell near 20 feet
from a Cypress Tree in the garden where I was gathering seeds. I am recovered so as to be able to walk about pretty well tho it being a compound fracture
& as near as possible to the Ankle joint which is Yet stiff & troublesome after
much walking."[21]

    In another letter written almost a decade later to Lachlan McIntosh, William
again recalled the fall, "a violent fracture of my Right Leg by a fall from a tree
where I was collecting seeds, which laid me up for near 12 months."[22]

In 1788, with no clear prospects for publishing his research, William Bartram packed most of his remaining duplicate plant specimens from the South, together with colored illustrations and detailed descriptions of four of his most significant discoveries, and sent them to Robert Barclay in London. Barclay, from a prominent London Quaker family, had actually been raised in Philadelphia, and he may have had some acquaintance with the Bartrams. Barclay was an amateur botanist and friend of Sir Joseph Banks and a supporter of William Curtis in his new serial, *The Botanical Magazine*.[23]

Bartram remarked that letters from Fothergill and Solander had reported most of his plants were new genera or new species.[24] And in November 1788, over a decade after his return, still few of his plants had been published in Europe. He sent his duplicates "cheerfully," "for the inspection & amusement of the curious, expecting or desiring no other gratuity than the bare mention of my being the discoverer, a reward due for traveling several thousand miles mostly amongst Indian Nations which is not only difficult but Dangerous, besides suffering sickness cold & hunger. But with a perfect Sence of gratitude I with pleasure acknowledge that the Noble Fothergill liberally supported me whilst in his employ with ample pecuniary assistance."[25]

Bartram's four drawings for Barclay included *Franklinia alatamaha*, *Pinckneya bracteata*, *Hydrangea quercifolia*, and *Oenothera grandiflora* and are among his most finished works. The Franklinia drawing was rediscovered early in the twentieth century and has been widely reproduced as one of Bartram's masterpieces. The other three drawings for Barclay were missing for some time and have only recently surfaced in the Natural History Museum in London.[26] The largeflower evening primrose is "Tab IV" of this set.

Bartram's descriptions are in Latin and English, and he may have hoped they would be published in Curtis's *Botanical Magazine*. The English notes on *Oenothera grandiflora* actually precede the description in *Travels* by a few years, but strike the same tone, "a Plant which perhaps exhibits the most brilliant shew of any yet known to exist." Bartram explained to Barclay: "I found it growing in the old fields, of the Rich low lands on the Mobile River W.t. Florida. I never saw it but at one plantation where the old fields of many acres in extent appear'd exceedingly splendid, decorated with them."[27]

William Bartram's notes for Robert Barclay also document that his new evening primrose had grown happily for a while in Philadelphia at Bartram's Garden. He reported: "I bro't the Ripe seeds to Pensylvania where they grew in equal perfection in the open garden, sowing themselves as an indiginous Plant; but through inattention we have lost it."[28]

It may have been a while before *Oenothera grandiflora* returned to Bartram's Garden, but it was back in the catalogue of the garden in 1807.[29]

William Bartram did not get much of a response from the drawings and specimens he sent to Barclay. Bartram's documentation for the new genus

"Franklinia" was ignored, largely at the insistence of Joseph Banks. None of his descriptions or drawings were published, and they seem to have had little or no impact on the botanic community in Britain. The next year, 1789, *Oenothera grandiflora* was published for the first time in William Aiton's, *Hortus Kewensis*. The "Great-flower'd Œnothera," a greenhouse biennial, was described as a native of North America, and introduced to England in 1778, by John Fothergill, M.D. There was no mention of William Bartram, or use of his data on the discovery and growth of the plant.[30] Bartram did get at least one thing in return from his correspondence with Robert Barclay, a copy of the three-volume *Hortus Kewensis* in 1790.[31]

As authority for naming the new species, *Oenothera grandiflora*, Aiton referenced L'Héritier's *Stirpes Novae*, vol. 2, tab. 4. Charles Louis L'Héritier de Brutelle (1746–1800) was a French aristocrat and amateur botanist living in Paris. He began a project publishing folios of plates illustrating and describing rare and interesting new plants in 1783. Six sets or fascicles of these plates forming one volume were issued between 1785 and 1791. The second volume never appeared, although some plates were prepared and printed and distributed after L'Héritier's death. There never was a second volume of *Stirpes Novae*, so the author of the Kew catalogue referenced a nonexistent book, apparently confident it would appear in the future. L'Héritier had traveled to England in 1786–1787 with the young artist Pierre-Joseph Redouté, who was preparing illustrations for the publication, *Stirpes Novae*. The pair spent a great deal of time at Kew, and could have seen *Oenothera grandiflora* there. And both L'Héritier and Redouté had likely seen plants of the new largeflower evening primrose in Paris as well.[32]

William Bartram's *Travels* was finally published in Philadelphia in 1791 after a second subscription effort was organized by the publishers James & Johnson. The account of his arrival at "Taensa" and the description of his exploration of the delta and discovery of *Oenothera grandiflora* were located between pages 403 and 407. Bartram used the name *Oenothera grandiflora* for his new evening primrose and repeated the same Latin description of the characters of the plant he had sent to Robert Barclay in November 1788.

In recent biography William Bartram has been portrayed as slow to publish, and not assertive about his priority, and perhaps not serious enough about his science. A careful analysis of his efforts with *Oenothera grandiflora* (and this is just one of his new plants) disproves this thesis. Bartram sent specimens and seeds and probably a description of the new evening primrose to Fothergill and Solander in England in 1775. He sent seeds and plants to French botanists via the ambassador Sieur Gérard in 1779. He had a drawing of the plant engraved in Philadelphia circa 1786. He sent a colored drawing of the plant and a detailed botanical description to Robert Barclay in 1788. And Bartram published his own account of the plant in *Travels* in 1791. This summarizes his efforts that are currently documented. There may well have been further attempts to communicate his discoveries that have not survived.

It seems more likely that William Bartram's failure to be heard was a result of changing relationships between European and North American science and scientists in the last quarter of the eighteenth century. William Bartram was never able to establish a cooperative trans-Atlantic correspondence like his father had with Peter Collinson. There is plenty of evidence William Bartram attempted to make connections abroad, but wars and revolutions interrupted the flow of letters. European science was growing professionalized in large capital cities and universities and showed little cooperation if not outright condescension toward provincials. From 1787 onward, Bartram's most successful correspondence was with a local Philadelphian, Benjamin Smith Barton. In Europe, William Bartram's book drew a large literary audience, but less regard from natural scientists.

Following the publication of *Travels* in 1791 there is little evidence for the history of the largeflower evening primrose, *Oenothera grandiflora*, at Bartram's Garden. At some point toward the end of the century the plant was reintroduced to the Bartram collection, perhaps by a Philadelphia area collector who traveled through its natural range. *Oenothera grandiflora* is listed in catalogues from Bartram's Garden through the close of business at the garden in the 1840s.

Occasional notice of Bartram's "pompous" plant appeared in later generations of North American botanic writing. Frederick Pursh notably credited Bartram with the plant, in his *Flora Americae Septentrionalis* in 1814, but located the plant "in the woods and fields of Carolina."[33] William Paul Crillon Barton, a nephew of B. S. Barton, published a figure and description of *Oenothera grandiflora* in his *Flora of North America* in 1821, but did not seem to know the connection with William Bartram. Barton was only familiar with the species as a cultivated plant. He took his habitat information "the vicinity of habitations in South Carolina and Georgia" from Stephen Elliott's *A Sketch of the Botany of South-Carolina and Georgia* of 1821 but included a note from Elliott "certainly not indigenous in the low country."[34] This sort of confusion about the origins of *Oenothera grandiflora* continues for many years, perhaps due to its limited natural distribution.

Science and the Largeflower Evening Primrose

The largeflower evening primrose remained a rather obscure plant through much of the nineteenth century. It was occasionally grown as a garden plant; it occasionally escaped and naturalized for a time around the world; but it was certainly not a focus of scientific research. All that changed in the last decade of the century. A young Dutch botanist, Hugo De Vries began growing and crossing multiple generations of largeflower evening primroses, with a passion. De Vries's Ph.D. dissertation of 1889 was entitled *Intracellular Pangenesis* and was an attempt to define the ultimate units of heredity. Charles Darwin had proposed a provisional mechanism for inheritance entitled "pangenesis" in 1868.[35] This was a clumsy, extracellular hypothesis that allowed for the accumulation of "gemmules" that were transported around the body. De Vries placed his units of heredity, "pangenes" paired within the cell, and usually in the cell nucleus, cleaving during cell division. De Vries's book was a powerful springboard for experimental work in heredity and evolution, and in time his "pangenes" were simplified into the modern gene concept. De Vries was also one of three researchers who stumbled onto the same laws of inheritance Gregor Mendel had published in obscurity in the 1860s. De Vries, Carl Correns, and Eric von Tschermak all published plant research in 1900 that confirmed and revived Mendel's earlier laws.

Hugo De Vries worked with many plants as part of his own research, but became fascinated with a weedy population of evening primroses he observed in vacant lots in Amsterdam that he identified as "*Oenothera lamarckiana.*" He collected seed and began growing *Oenothera* over several decades. Generations of these evening primroses varied so greatly that De Vries became convinced he was seeing the creation of new species. He developed a theory of mutations as the major mechanism of evolution and his results were published in German in 2 volumes, 1901–1903 as *Die Mutationstheorie* or "Mutation Theory: Research and Observations on the Origin of Species in the Plant Kingdom."[36]

Mutation theory was a scientific phenomenon of its own and widely read around the world. De Vries's major examples of mutation were taken from experiments with the largeflower evening primrose he called *Oenothera lamarckiana.* His publication in 1901 set off a furor to test and repeat his experiments, and largeflower evening primroses were soon in experimental plots around the world. Extensive research was carried out at the New York Botanical Garden, the Station for Experimental Evolution at Cold Spring Harbor, Long Island, and other research laboratories of the Carnegie Institution of Washington.[37]

De Vries initially thought *Oenothera lamarckiana* was a synonym for *Oenothera grandiflora* and that he was dealing with a native North American plant, naturalized in northern Europe. North American botanists disagreed and could find no American plant that corresponded with De Vries's mutating *Oenothera.* But at the same time it turned out no one in North America was familiar with William Bartram's largeflower evening primrose, *Oenothera gran-*

diflora. The botanist Samuel Mills Tracy, living near Biloxi, was dispatched to identify and collect samples, and on August 16, 1904, he "re-discovered the locality" of Bartram's "most pompous and brilliant herbaceous plant yet known to exist" in Alabama. Or at least he thought he had. "Abundant material was sent to the New York Botanical Garden" and plots of *Oenothera grandiflora* were begun.[38] With specimens from Alabama in hand, it was clear Bartram's *Oenothera grandiflora* was not the same as De Vries's experimental plant. Even De Vries "unhesitatingly" agreed they were not like his *Oenothera lamarckiana* when he saw Alabama specimens in the fall of 1904 in New York.

Hugo De Vries and plant researchers in the United States and elsewhere continued to experiment and grow *Oenothera* species on a large scale for the next two decades. Seed of Alabama-collected *Oenothera grandiflora* was added to the mix and the Bartram species appears often in plant experiments after 1904. In 1918 Hugo De Vries published an article particularly on mutations observed in *Oenothera grandiflora*, after visiting a wild population of the plant in the vicinity of Castleberry, Alabama, and collecting seed in September 1912.[39]

Much like Mendel's peas and later fruit fly experiments, *Oenothera* plants became a stock reference for genetic research, and intensive research on *Oenothera* species continues to the present. Hugo De Vries's "mutations" are now thought to be the result of a hybrid origin for the European plants he observed, and the peculiar genetic nature of *Oenothera* species. Some of the fourteen chromosomes of *Oenothera* do not always pair during meiosis, but form a closed circle that shares genetic data in odd unexpected ways. This coupled with additional genetic material in cell organelles or plastids—the chloroplasts and mitochondria produced the "mutations" that De Vries and others carefully and accurately described.[40]

De Vries's favorite test subject, *Oenothera lamarckiana*, now renamed as *Oenothera glazioviana*, is thought to be a hybrid, perhaps a complex hybrid including some of William Bartram's *Oenothera grandiflora* as a parent stock. It remains something of a mystery where and when it developed. Carl Linnaeus and Philip Miller described a largeflower evening primrose wild on wastelands in the Netherlands in the 1730s. By 1800 a similar plant was growing wild on dunes near Liverpool. Lamarck's name was associated with these European weeds in the early nineteenth century after a description in his *Encyclopédie Méthodique: Botanique*, which incorrectly used the name "Oenothera grandiflora" to describe the species.[41] Today *Oenothera glazioviana* is common across northern Europe, particularly on coastal dunes and sandy wastelands. It is also now found in the United States. This hybrid may have developed more than once, in light of the apparent early populations in the 1730s, but it may also owe something to a fashion for William Bartram's "pompous and brilliant herbaceous plant" in London and Paris gardens in the later eighteenth century.

There still remains a bit more to the story of Bartram's plant. By 1960 *Oenothera grandiflora* had again largely fallen out of cultivation. A young biology graduate student, Paul Biebel, who was teaching at Spring Hill College in Mobile, Alabama, was dispatched to find and collect seed and specimens from Bartram's original location in the summer of 1962. Seeds were requested by Ralph E. Cleland of Indiana University, and for his colleagues Wilfried Stubbe at the University of Düsseldorf, Eric Steiner at the University of Michigan, and others. Biebel seems to be the first to accurately read the text of William Bartram's *Travels* to help locate the 1775 discovery of *Oenothera grandiflora*. Biebel realized that all the earlier twentieth-century searches for the largeflower evening primrose had started from the modern town of Tensaw near the site of Fort Mims on the Alabama River, a considerable distance upstream from the actual location of Major Farmar's Tensaw Bluff. S. M. Tracey had gathered specimens and seed twenty-five miles above Fort Mims at Dixie Landing, on the Alabama River. Biebel also consulted local historians about the location of Major Farmar's plantation and made contact with two sisters, Bernice McMillan and Mrs. Pierce Holmes, who ran the Stockton, Alabama, store.[42] An overgrown field behind the Stockton Store proved to provide the best source of seed. Beibel collected *Oenothera grandiflora* specimens and seed from the rear of the Stockton Store, from Seabury Creek, and from Martin's Branch in Baldwin County, Alabama, in fall 1962. Plant lines from these seeds have remained in cultivation since and continue to be used in a wide variety of botanic and genetic research.[43] Bernice McMillan also recorded her memories of visits from Paul Biebel and his search for Bartram's *Oenothera grandiflora* in a short article "The Evening Primrose" that appeared in *Fort Mims and the Tensaw Settlement* in 1988.[44]

Old fields and overgrown land around Stockton, Alabama, continue to be a reservoir of William Bartram's largeflower evening primrose. In late October 2007, a few plants were found in bloom en route to a day of canoeing on the Bartram Canoe Trail on the road from Stockton to Rice Creek Landing as part of the biennial Bartram Trail Conference. A healthy rosette was collected and returned to Philadelphia and bedded down for the winter in the garden in front of the Bartram House. For the first time in over 150 years *Oenothera grandiflora* returned to Bartram's Garden. It bloomed in 2008 and we will make every effort not to lose it through "inattention."

Notes

1. William Bartram, *Travels Through North & South Carolina, Georgia, East & West Florida, the Cherokee Country, the Extensive Territories of the Muscogulges, or Creek Confederacy, and the Country of the Chactaws; Containing An Account of the Soil*

and Natural Productions of Those Regions, Together with Observations on the Manners of the Indians. Embellished with Copper-Plates (Philadelphia: James & Johnson, 1791), 403.

2. Bartram, *Travels,* 405. The location of Tensaw Bluff and Robert Farmar's plantation has been well documented in recent years. Edward J. Cashin, *William Bartram and the American Revolution on the Southern Frontier* (Columbia: University of South Carolina Press, 2000), 176, credits Baldwin County historian Davida Hastie with locating the plantation at Lower Bryant Landing. This location was also determined by the botanist Paul Biebel in the summer of 1962 when he was tasked with recollecting William Bartram's evening primrose. Biebel to Dr. Ralph E. Cleland, Dept. of Botany, Indiana University, December 27, 1962, John Bartram Association Collections. See also the Bartram Trail Conference's *Bartram Heritage: A Study of the Life of William Bartram* (Montgomery: Bartram Trail Conference, 1979), 127–128. The location of the plantation is shown on two maps of the period: a British survey of the Mobile River Delta by Elias Durnford, engineer: "Field Survey of the River Mobile and Part of the Rivers Alabama And Tensa with the Different Settlements and Lands marked thereon," 1770 (British National Archives, Colonial Office 700, Florida 40) as well as "A Plan of Part of the Rivers Tombicbe, Alabama, Tensa, Perdito & Scambia in the Province of West Florida," by David Taitt, 1771 (British National Archives, MPG 6). Both are discussed in Gregory A. Waselkov and Bonnie L. Gums, *Plantation Archaeology at Rivère aux Chiens, ca. 1725–1848* (Mobile: University of South Alabama Center for Archaeological Studies, 2000), chap. 3. (Thanks to Kathryn Braund for providing map references.) The Durnford map reproduced in Archer Butler Hulbert, *The Crown Collection of Photographs of American Maps: A Collection of Original Photographs, Carefully Mounted, of maps important historically yet hitherto unpublished, contained in the British Museum and other foreign Archives especially chosen and prepared to illustrate the early history of America* (Cleveland: Arthur H. Clark Co., 1909), plate #93, catalogue #40. (Thanks to John A. Jackson of the Baldwin County Department of Archives and History for providing the Hulbert reference.) Francis Harper seems to have misread this map and placed Tensaw Bluff further north at the mouth of Hall Creek, today's Upper Bryant Landing, four miles north of Stockton. William Bartram, *The Travels of William Bartram,* Naturalists's Edition, ed. Francis Harper (New Haven, Conn.: Yale University Press, 1958), 640. For Farmar, see Robert R. Rea, *Major Robert Farmar of Mobile* (Tuscaloosa: The University of Alabama Press, 1990).

3. Bartram, *Travels,* 406–407.

4. Ibid., 411.

5. Cashin, *William Bartram,* 191; Harper places this plantation on modern Prevost Island, Bartram, *Travels,* ed. Harper, 407–408.

6. Bartram, *Travels,* 438.

7. Joseph Ewan, ed., *William Bartram Botanical and Zoological Drawings, 1756–1788* (Philadelphia: American Philosophical Society, 1968), 163. *Oenothera grandiflora* appears on folio 10 of this book of specimens, labeled "Book [D]" for Fothergill. Unlike the five other books of specimens Bartram prepared for Fothergill, there is no annotation on any of these West Florida plants. This suggests William Bartram was in a hurry in packing materials for shipment to Fothergill in late November 1775. The evening primrose is accompanied by specimens of many of Bartram's important discoveries: oakleaf hydrangea, *Hydrangea quercifolia;* bottlebrush buckeye, *Aesculus parviflora;* flameflower, *Macranthera flammea;* scarlet calamint, *Clinopodium coccineum;* and crimson pitcherplant *Sarracenia leucophylla,* among others. If William Bartram were considered the valid author of the name *Oenothera grandiflora,* this specimen would be considered the type specimen. In any case the specimen is an important document of the wild population Bartram first sampled and described.

8. For information on Bartram family history, see Joel T. Fry, "Historic American Landscapes Survey, John Bartram House and Garden (Bartram's Garden), HALS No. PA-1, History Report," MS report, U.S. Department of the Interior, National Park Service, HABS/HAER/HALS/CRGIS Division, Washington, D.C., 2004.

9. Most of these shrubs and trees appear in a broadside *Catalogue* issued by the Bartram brothers in 1783; others are found on shipping lists and catalogues of sales. Joel T. Fry, "An International Catalogue of North American Trees and Shrubs: The Bartram Broadside, 1783," *Journal of Garden History* 16, 1 (January–March 1996): 3–66.

10. E. S. Fraser to William or John Bartram Jr., Bartram Papers, Historical Society of Pennsylvania (HSP), 4:1; William Darlington, *Memorials of John Bartram and Humphry Marshall: With Notices of Their Botanical Contemporaries* (Philadelphia: Lindsay & Blakiston, 1849), 465–466.

11. Ewan, ed., *William Bartram Botanical and Zoological Drawings,* 163. William Aiton, *Hortus Kewensis, or a Catalogue of the Plants Cultivated in the Royal Botanic Garden at Kew,* 3 vols. (London: Printed for George Nicol, 1789), 2:2.

12. March 3, 1779, Bartram Papers, HSP, 4:106; July 1779, Bartram Papers 1:75; August 20, 1779, Bartram Papers, HSP, 4:82; October 16, 1779, Bartram Papers, HSP, 4:75.

13. William Bartram, "List of Seeds collected for the Minister of France, July Ano. 1779," Bartram Papers, Historical Society of Pennsylvania, 1:75. A numbered list of eleven species and varieties of seeds.

14. Bartram, *Travels,* 421–422. William Bartram would later call the new mimosa "Mimosa virgata" a valid Linnaean name for a related Asian species. *Desmanthus illinoensis* remained in cultivation for many years at Bartram's Garden, and it was likely a favorite plant. It was a frequent part of plant shipments from

the garden, including a collection sent to Mount Vernon for George Washington in March 1792.

15. William Bartram, "List of growing Roots of Trees Shrubs & Plants, for his Excelly Gerard Minister of France, August 20, 1779," Bartram Papers, HSP, 4:82. A numbered list of forty-one species and varieties of live plants in two boxes.

16. The 1788 description of Franklinia, as *Gordonia pubescens*, in the *Encyclopédie Méthodique: Botanique*, suggested rather reservedly that the plant "is believed in all likelihood to come from America." Jean Baptiste Pierre Antoine de Monet de Lamarck, *Encyclopédie Méthodique: Botanique*, vol. 2 (Paris: Panckoucke, 1788), 770.

17. Johann David Schöpf, *Travels in the Confederation, 1783–1784*, trans. and ed. Alfred J. Morrison (Philadelphia: William J. Campbell, 1911), 1:91.

18. Francis Harper, "Proposals for Publishing Bartram's Travels," *American Philosophical Society Library Bulletin 1943–1945*, 27–28.

19. Enoch Story to Benjamin Franklin, ca. 1786. Benjamin Franklin correspondence, American Philosophical Society.

20. Both copies of the 1791 edition of *Travels* that contain these extra engravings are known to be presentation copies, given directly by the author. One was presented to the Darby Library Company and a letter from the trustees of the library to William Bartram records receipt of the gift, March 14, 1793. (This copy is now housed at the Library Company of Philadelphia.) A copy of *Travels* with fine colored versions of the extra plates was given to William Hamilton of The Woodlands. (This copy is now owned by the Sterling Morton Library, Morton Arboretum, Lisle, Illinois.) A colored, unbound set of the engravings was once owned by Benjamin Smith Barton and is now part of the Barton-Delafield Collection at the American Philosophical Society. A fourth set of the engravings, probably once owned by the Bartram family, was apparently presented to the Historical Society of Pennsylvania in 1896 and is now missing. There may be other undiscovered sets.

21. William Bartram to Benjamin Smith Barton, undated draft, probably a response to a letter of August 26, 1787. Item 104A, Jane Gray Autograph Collection, Archives, Gray Herbarium, Harvard University.

22. William Bartram to Lachlan McIntosh, May 31, 1796, Misc. Mss. Bartram, The New-York Historical Society.

23. Ewan, ed., *William Bartram Botanical and Zoological Drawings*, 154, notes Barclay's connections. Ewan seems to have made an error in using 1786. The letter that accompanied the drawings and specimens is clearly dated 1788 and he quotes it. There are also other William Bartram letters around the time that confirm the 1788 date.

24. This correspondence from Fothergill and Solander is now lost. Some of Solander's notes remain in the Natural History Museum in London.

25. William Bartram to Robert Barclay, November 1788, Natural History

Museum, London. Ewan, ed., *William Bartram Botanical and Zoological Drawings,* 164.

26. Judith Magee, *The Art and Science of William Bartram* (University Park: The Pennsylvania State University Press in association with the Natural History Museum, London, 2007), 69, 117, 143, 144.

27. William Bartram to Robert Barclay, November 1788. Natural History Museum, London.

28. William Bartram to Robert Barclay, November 1788. Natural History Museum, London. The complete text of this letter is included in Ewan, ed., *William Bartram Botanical and Zoological Drawings,* Appendix A, 151–153.

29. [William Bartram], *A Catalogue of Trees, Shrubs, and Herbaceous Plants, Indigenous to the United States of America; Cultivated and Disposed of By John Bartram & Son, At their Botanical Garden, Kingsess, near Philadelphia: To Which is Added A Catalogue of Foreign Plants, Collected From Various Parts of the Globe* (Philadelphia: Bartram and Reynolds, 1807).

30. By the second edition of *Hortus Kewensis* in 1811 it was clear *Oenothera grandiflora* was a hardy biennial in London.

31. The copy, inscribed "For Wᵐ· Bartram from Robᵗ· Barclay 1790" is in the McLean Library of the Pennsylvania Horticultural Society. Bartram passed the book on to Colonel Robert Carr in 1819.

32. A manuscript description for *Oenothera grandiflora* by L'Héritier does survive, and possibly one or more copies of the engraved illustration intended for the second volume. R. R. Gates, "Early Historico-Botanical Records of the Oenotheras," *Proceedings of the Iowa Academy of Science for 1910* 17:105, and plate V reproduces L'Héritier's manuscript description of *Oenothera grandiflora* from the DeCandolle library.

33. Frederick Pursh, *Flora Americae Septentrionalis* (London: White, Cochrane, and Co., 1814), 1:261.

34. William P. C. Barton, *A Flora of North America* (Philadelphia: M. Carey & Sons, 1821), 1:21–24, tab. 6; Stephen Elliott, *A Sketch of the Botany of South-Carolina and Georgia,* 2 vols. (Charleston: J. R. Schenk, 1821), 1:442. Elliott's habitat information reads: "Grows in gardens around buildings. Certainly not indigenous in our low country."

35. Charles Darwin, *The Variation of Animals and Plants under Domestication,* 2 vols. (London: J. Murray, 1868). See "Provisional Hypothesis of Pangenesis," vol. 2, chapter 27.

36. Hugo De Vries, *Die Mutationstheorie: Versuche und Beobachtungen über die Enstehung von Arten im Pflanzenreich,* 2 vols. (Leipzig: Veit & Co, 1901–1903). (English edition 1909–1910.)

37. D. T. MacDougal, A. M. Vail, G. H. Shull, and J. K. Small, *Mutants and Hybrids of the Oenotheras,* Publication No. 24 (Washington, D.C.: Carnegie Insti-

tution of Washington, 1905); D. T. MacDougal, A. M. Vail, and G. H. Shull, *Mutations, Variations, and Relationships of the Oenotheras,* Publication No. 81 (Washington, D.C.: Carnegie Institution of Washington, 1907).

38. Anna Murray Vail, "*Onagra grandiflora* (Ait.): A Species to be Included in the North American Flora," *Torreya,* vol. 5 (1905), 9–10. [Onagra is a synonym for Oenothera.] MacDougal, assisted by Cail, Shull, Small, *Mutants and Hybrids,* 1905, p. 8, prints Tracey's report on locating *Oenothera grandiflora.*

39. Hugo De Vries, "Mass mutations and twin hybrids of *Oenothera grandiflora* Ait.," *Botanical Gazette* 65 (May 1918): 377–422.

40. Jaroslav Mráček, "Investigation of interspecific genome-plastome incompatibility in Oenothera and Passiflora" (Ph.D. dissertation, Biology Faculty, Ludwig-Maximilians University, Munich, 2005).

41. Lamarck, *Encyclopédie Méthodique: Botanique,* 554. (The description is thought to be by Poiret, not Lamarck.) R. R. Gates, "Early Historico-Botanical Records of the *Oenotheras,*" *Proceedings of the Iowa Academy of Science for 1910,* vol. 17, 85–124, covers much of the early history of *Oenothera* species in Europe, but is not entirely accurate. It oddly argues that *Oenothera lamarckiana* was once native to Virginia, but has been exterminated.

42. Paul Biebel to Ralph E. Cleland, Dept. of Botany, Indiana University, December 27, 1962; Bernice McMillan and Mrs. Pierce Holmes to Paul Biebel, August 13, 1962; and Ralph E. Cleland to Paul Biebel, January 3, 1963. Copies of Biebel's correspondence and 35 mm color slides relating to collecting *Oenothera grandiflora* are on deposit at Bartram's Garden. Biebel went on to a career as professor of biology at Dickinson College, Carlisle, Pennsylvania, and lectured on Bartram's *Oenothera grandiflora.*

43. W. Stubbe and E. Steiner, "Inactivation of Pollen and other effects of genome-plastome incompatibility in Oenothera," *Plant Systematics and Evolution,* vol. 217 (1999), 259–277, lists a large number of strains of *Oenothera grandiflora* on 261, used in investigations with Paul Biebel's October 1962 collections from Stockton and Seabury Creek as the oldest in cultivation after a 1944 Tuscaloosa collection. Stubbe and Steiner published extensively on *Oenothera.*

44. Dess L. Sangster and Tom Sangster, compilers, *Fort Mims and the Tensaw Settlement* (Bay Minette, Ala.: Lavender Publishing, 1998), 3rd printing, second revision, 23–25.

12

The Mystery of the Okeechobee Gourd

Marc C. Minno and Maria Minno

The River

The St. Johns River is the longest river in Florida. It begins in the marshes surrounding Blue Cypress Lake in Indian River County and flows northward through a series of lakes. Along the way, springs and creeks, some fresh, some salty, join the river's flow to the sea. The river water is generally black and tea-like and enriched with dissolved minerals.[1]

The last lake through which the river flows is Lake George, the second largest lake in Florida. From Jacksonville the river turns eastward and forms an expansive estuary that empties into the Atlantic Ocean. In 1765–1766, John Bartram and his son William traveled into Florida and up the St. Johns River. Later, in 1774, William followed his father's footsteps and canoed up the St. Johns River to explore and collect plants. In *Travels,* William Bartram wrote: "It is very pleasing to observe the banks of the river, ornamented with hanging garlands, composed of varieties of climbing vegetables, both shrubs and plants, forming perpendicular green walls, with projecting jambs, pilasters, and deep apartments, twenty or thirty feet high, and completely covered with Glycine frutescens, Glyc. apios, Vitis labrusca, Vitis vulpina, Rajana, Hedera quinquifolia, Hedera arborea, Eupatorium scandens, Bignonia crucigera, and various species of Convolvulus, particularly an amazing tall climber of this genus, or perhaps an Ipomoea."[2]

Today, in spite of power boats, jet ski riders, and barges, Bartram's descriptions of the river can still be recognized in many places. Near Hontoon Island both John and William noticed evidence that native Florida Indians had once lived there.[3] Also of interest was a "Wild Squash" growing along the riverbanks. In *Travels,* William Bartram recorded that it was "exceedingly curious to behold the Wild Squash* climbing over the lofty limbs of the trees; its yellow fruit, somewhat of the size and figure of a large orange, pendant from the extremities of the limbs over the water." In a footnote (that he noted with an asterisk), Bartram identified the "wild squash" as "Cucurbita peregrina."[4]

For a long time, no one knew which plant William Bartram was talking about, since there was no specimen to study and botanists had not found a species that matched his brief description. Indeed, over a century passed until John Kunkel Small found a gourd that matched the description, but the location was in southern Florida. He discovered the gourds between 1913 and 1917 during expeditions to Lake Okeechobee. He found a gourd climbing into pond apple trees (*Annona glabra* L.) in dense hammocks along the southern shore of Lake Okeechobee. Small called this plant the Okeechobee gourd (*Pepo okeechobeensis*).[5]

The botanist L. H. Bailey, working in the next decade, changed the plant's name and moved the Okeechobee gourd into the genus *Cucurbita*. As had been the case for both Bartram and Small, Bailey found that learning about this rare gourd required an adventuresome spirit. In 1943 he published an account of his experience in the wild Florida swamps where the gourd had been found. Bailey was trying to collect a female flower from the plant, since none was yet known to science. He wrote:

> In October 1929 I was accompanied by E. G. Hume, son of Dean H. H. Hume of the University of Florida. Diligent search had failed to discover a pistillate flower. Finally we saw one about ready to expand, swinging on the limb of a dead tree about 30 feet or more above the ground, and hanging over the water. We could find nothing long enough to reach it. The vine would not rip loose. The tree was covered with poison ivy. The day was dark and the tail end of a hurricane was blowing itself out. Hume had a 22 Colt automatic pistol, woodsman model. He climbed the tree a short distance to get above the brush and gripped himself tight. Then he fired away. A bullet cut the stem cleanly and the flower floated to my feet in perfect condition. . . . It is the only pistillate flower of *Cucurbita okeechobeensis* I have ever seen in the wild.[6]

It took people who worked both in botany and history to link the find to William Bartram. In an article entitled "In Defense of the Validity of William Bartram's Binomials," published in 1944, E. D. Merrill postulated that Bartram's wild squash from the St. Johns River was probably *Pepo okeechobeensis* Small or *Cucurbita okeechobeensis*.[7] In 1958, Bartram scholar Francis Harper found a note on the squash in a letter from William Bartram to Henry Muhlenberg (a well-known eighteenth-century botanist) dated September 6, 1810. In the letter, Bartram remarked upon the "*Cucurbita peregrina*, a new species un-

12.1. Habitat of the gourd at Lake Okeechobee (Photo courtesy Marc C. Minno).

doubtedly. The hunters call it the Wild squash." Based on notes, letters, and other writings, Harper determined that Bartram had seen the wild squash a few miles south of Lake Dexter.[8]

Because the Okeechobee gourd was so rare, D. B. Ward included it in his 1979 book on the rare plants of Florida. He thought the gourd may have disappeared from where the Bartrams had found it along the St. Johns River because it had been killed off by freezing weather.[9]

Recent studies of *C. okeechobeensis* have indicated it is closely related to *C. martinezii* from Mexico and *Cucurbita lundelliana* from Central America.[10] In fact, in a study where gourd seeds from Hontoon Island were examined closely, seeds resembling those of the Okeechobee gourd were found at archaeological sites estimated to have been occupied from 500 BC to AD 1750. These were not the seeds of *Cucurbita pepo*, the Seminole pumpkin cultivated by the Indians.[11]

On July 12, 1993, the U.S. Fish and Wildlife Service put *Cucurbita okeechobeensis* on the Endangered Species list, because it is so rare and its habitat around Lake Okeechobee has been so extensively destroyed. It is also on Florida's Endangered Species list.[12]

Who would have thought the rare and endangered Okeechobee gourd could have gone unnoticed, living along the banks of the St. Johns River, for two hundred years since Bartram first described it? And yet it is still there. On September 28, 1993, Marc C. Minno, Palmer Kinser, and Gregory Dambek rediscovered the Okeechobee Gourd along the St. Johns River near Lake Beresford.[13] This seems to be approximately ten to fifteen miles south of where William Bartram had observed a wild squash in 1774. Daniel B. Ward, at the time a botany professor with the University of Florida, examined specimens collected by Minno, Kinser, and Dambek, and confirmed that they were indeed the Okeechobee gourd.

The Okeechobee Gourd: Distribution and Habitat

Since the 1990s, the authors have sighted the Okeechobee gourd, *Cucurbita okeechobeensis,* at about a dozen sites, mostly marshy islands, in Lake Okeechobee. The Okeechobee gourd has also been found at 14 sites along the St. Johns River from Lake Beresford to Lake Monroe in Lake, Volusia, and Seminole counties. For the most part, the habitat bordering the St. Johns River and its tributaries and lakes is bottomland swamp. Ash (*Fraxinus caroliniana* and *Fraxinus profunda*), red maple (*Acer rubrum*), water hickory (*Carya aquatica*), elm (*Ulmus americana*), and bald cypress (*Taxodium distichum*), are the most important trees in this community. The most abundant shrubs are Carolina aster (*Symphyotrichum carolinianum*), saltbush (*Baccharis halimifolia*), buttonbush (*Cephalanthus occidentalis*), swamp dogwood (*Cornus foemina*), *Itea virginica,* wax myrtle (*Myrica cerifera*), Carolina willow (*Salix caroliniana*), and elderberry (*Sambucus canadensis*). Vines such as moon flower (*Ipomoea alba*), hempvine (*Mikania scandens*), and cowpea (*Vigna luteola*) are abundant.[14]

Along the St. Johns River, the Okeechobee gourd grows in openings in the swamp forest that are dominated by elderberry, or along the habitat edges between the swamp and marsh communities. The Okeechobee gourd is not usually found at the river's edge. Rather, most are found ten to thirty feet from the river.

The gourd may have been overlooked for two hundred years because it blends in so well with other vegetation. Its leaves look like those of the ubiquitous moon flower.

The Okeechobee Gourd: Results of Observations

Stems of Okeechobee gourd trail along the ground and climb into shrubs, holding themselves aloft with tendrils. The gourds sometimes grow in thick sheets, densely covering the woody plants they use for support. Their favored supports were elderberry, ash, and red maple.

Roots grew from the nodes of trailing stems. When the stems were im-

12.2. Okeechobee gourd with closed flower (Photo courtesy of Marc C Minno).

mersed in water or touching moist soil, severed stems quickly produced new roots and continued to grow.

Unlike most other wild gourds, the flowers are creamy in color. During the day the flowers are usually partially or completely closed. It may be that the insects that visit the flowers come at night or early in the mornings and evenings.

Numerous fruits were produced, as many as 191 from a single gourd patch. Okeechobee gourds are the size of oranges, dark green with pale stripes at first, but aging to a grayish color.

The vines are attacked by few herbivores and disease. The fruit, stems, and leaves are extremely bitter tasting. The larvae of the melonworm, *Diaphania hyalinata* (L.), and a close relative, *Diaphania indica* (Saunders), sometimes eat the young leaves or bore into the tips of shoots or developing fruit. The leaves are also a host for powdery mildew fungus, especially on mature plants.

Our studies show that the colonies along the St. Johns River are slowly disappearing. Of the fourteen sites found since 1994, we only found the gourd at two locations in 2005. We hypothesize that Okeechobee Gourd plants tend to disappear during wet times, but survive in the soil as seeds that later sprout, flower, and fruit during periods of drought.

The Mystery

Many questions remain surrounding the distribution and biology of the Okeechobee gourd. Why is this vigorous vine so rare? It produces many fruits. Could it be that it has a difficult time finding a suitable spot for seed germination?

Do mature plants survive the winters and floods and droughts, or are plants killed back such that they have to grow again from seed?

Was the gourd used by the Florida Indians? If so, was it used as floats for their fishing nets or perhaps other purposes? Did people originally carry it all the way from Mexico?

Could the Okeechobee gourd be used for plant breeding? Could the species we eat be made more resistant to pests and diseases by crossing with the Okeechobee gourd, which already seems to be resistant?

Could this endangered plant be cultivated? Could its range be increased by bringing seeds or cuttings to suitable spots?

We are still pondering Bartram's discovery, and much about the Okeechobee Gourd remains a mystery.

Notes

1. Ronald L. Myers and John J. Ewel, eds., *Ecosystems of Florida* (Orlando: University of Central Florida Press, 1991), 397–403.

2. William Bartram, *Travels,* ed. Mark Van Doren (New York: Macy-Masius, 1928; Rpt., New York: Dover, 1928), 128.

3. Bartram, *Travels,* ed. Van Doren, 130; Edmund Berkeley and Dorothy Smith Berkeley, *The Life and Travels of John Bartram: From Lake Ontario to the River St. John* (Tallahassee: University Presses of Florida, 1982), 258–260.

4. Bartram, *Travels,* ed. Van Doren, 129.

5. J. K. Small, "The Okeechobee Gourd," *Journal of the New York Botanical Garden* 31 (1930): 10–14. See also J. K. Small, "Exploration in the Everglades and on the Florida Keys," *Journal of the New York Botanical Garden* 15 (1914): 63–79, as well as his "Narrative of a Cruise to Lake Okeechobee," *American Museum Journal*

18 (1918): 685–700, and "Wild Pumpkins," *Journal of the New York Botanical Garden* 23 (1922): 19–23.

6. L. H. Bailey, "Species of *Cucurbita*," *Gentes Herbarium* 6 (1943): 266–322.

7. E. D. Merrill, "In Defense of the Validity of William Bartram's Binomials," *Bartonia* 23 (1944): 25.

8. William Bartram, *The Travels of William Bartram*, Naturalists's Edition, ed. Francis Harper (New Haven, Conn.: Yale University Press, 1958), 633.

9. D. B. Ward, "Okeechobee Gourd," in *Rare and Endangered Biota of Florida*, ed. Peter C. H. Pritchard, 6 vols. (Gainesville: University Presses of Florida, 1979), 5:81–83.

10. T. W. Walters and D. S. Decker-Walters, "Systematics of the Endangered Okeechobee Gourd (*Cucurbita okeechobeensis: Cucurbitaceae*)," *Systematic Botany* 18 (1993): 175–187. Walters, Decker-Walters, and Katz, "Seeking the Elusive Okeechobee Gourd," *Fairchild Tropical Garden Bulletin*, January 1992, 22–30.

11. D. S. Decker and L. A. Newsom, "Numerical Analysis of Archaeological *Cucurbita pepo* seeds from Hontoon Island, Florida," *Journal of Ethnobiology* 8 (1988): 35–44. For more information, see T. C. Andres and G. P. Nabhan, "Taxonomic Rank and Rarity of *Cucurbita okeechobeensis*," FAO/IBPGR Plant Genetic Resources Newsletter, vol. 75/76 (1988): 21–22, and T. W. Walters and D. S. Decker-Walters, "Systematics of the Endangered Okeechobee Gourd (Cucurbita okeechobeensis: Cucurbitaceae)," 175–187. See also Gary Paul Nahbah's chapter, "Lost Gourds and Spent Soils on the Shores of Okeechobee," in *Enduring Seeds: Native American Agriculture and Wild Plant Conservation* (San Francisco: North Point Press, 1989).

12. N. C. Coile, *Florida's Endangered and Threatened Plants*, Florida Department of Agriculture and Consumer Services, Division of Plant Industry, Bureau of Entomology, Nematology, and Plant Pathology, Botany Section Contribution No. 29 (Gainesville, Fla., 1993).

13. J. Klinkenberg, "Seeds of Doubt," *St. Petersburg Times*, November 28, 1993, Section F, 1 & 6; D. B. Ward and M. C. Minno, "Rediscovery of the Endangered Okeechobee Gourd (*Cucurbita okeechobeensis*) along the St. Johns River, Florida, where last reported by William Bartram in 1774," *Castanea* 67 (2002): 201–206. See also T. Walters, D. Decker-Walters, and S. Katz, "Seeking the Elusive Okeechobee Gourd," *Fairchild Tropical Garden Bulletin*, January 1992, 22–30.

14. Ibid.

V

Natural History Writing in the Twenty-first Century

13
The Role of Digital Specimen Images in Historical Research

Stephanie C. Haas, Kent D. Perkins, and Michael Bond

In 1999, an article by Vincent Kiernan in the *Chronicle of Higher Education* addressed the value of the "International Plant Names Index," a joint Web database project of Harvard University Herbaria; the Royal Botanic Gardens, Kew, England; and the Australian National Botanic Gardens in Canberra. In that article, Kiernan touched on the possibility that the database's function of providing an authoritative record on the names of every flowering plant on earth could be expanded to include digital photographs of each plant. Kiernan pointed out that "a researcher who wants to determine if a plant specimen belongs to a known species faces a big task in resolving the issue. The researcher must compare the newly found plant with a 'type specimen,' a preserved sample of the older plant, collected by its discoverer. But that sample could be in a herbarium halfway across the globe. The researcher either has to travel to the herbarium or persuade officials there to send a sample by mail."[1] Dr. David Boufford of the Harvard University Herbaria expressed support for digitizing specimens: "Having the images could save a lot of time and effort . . . [and make for] less wear and tear on the specimens."[2] A decade later, botanic gardens and herbaria across the globe are digitally capturing their specimens and making them available over the Internet.

Field photographs and line drawings of plants are excellent resources for study, but specimen images offer a number of advantages:

- The specimens these images are based on are permanently preserved in museums and may include details on plant form, locality, habitat, flowering and fruiting period, frequency, and distribution. The individual specimens may be part of a set of specimens with added historical context.
- The images of voucher specimens offer particular potential in resolving taxonomic discrepancies and can be used as a stable reference for ongoing scientific discussions.

- Specimen images generally depict diagnostic characteristics better than photographs. Typically, the specimens are pressed with attention to appropriate features. Images reveal aspects of the plant not discernable in drawings; textures, for example.
- Digitized images provide researchers the opportunity to study specimens from multiple collections.
- Costs associated with taxonomic projects may be significantly reduced because initial screening of plants can be done on-line.
- Multiple researchers can discuss taxonomic issues related to a specific displayed specimen.

In addition to the advantages for current botanical research, the use of digital images offers substantial assistance to historical research.

In 2000, the University of Florida Digital Library Center developed a pilot digital project entitled *The Bartrams' Florida* (http://www.uflib.ufl.edu/digital/collections/bartram/Default.htm). The purpose was to create an integrated digital portal to the Bartrams' travels in Florida by digitizing and linking text, maps, aerial photography, specimen images including botanical specimens, and manuscript transcriptions. John Bartram's travel in 1765–1766 established an East Florida route later traversed by the most notable European and American naturalists in the eighteenth and nineteenth centuries including his son William. Digital representation of John's travels provided the content focus for the pilot project. According to Francis Harper, John Bartram "was probably the first botanist to examine and report on the flora of Florida and the greater part of Georgia. In South Carolina he had apparently been preceded only by Mark Catesby and Dr. Alexander Garden."[3]

To digitally enrich John's travels, textual references were linked to specimen images and other digital objects. The passage below, including Harper's extensive annotations, is taken from John Bartram's *Diary of a Journal through the Carolinas, Georgia, and Florida, from July 1, 1765 to April 1766.* It records the botanical sightings made on a trip from St. Augustine to Fort Picolata on November 15, 1765:

[November 15[.] A lovely cool day[.] wind N. West[.] never was A finer day to travail[.] fine clear morning[.] therm[.] 65[.] set out for picolata[,] sun one hour high[.] rode over much poor ground[.] about one half way crossed severall narrow bay swamps mixed with some small Cypresses[,] ye higher ground being generally white sand[.] many shrubs of evergreen oaks[,] *vacciniums*[,] andromedas of several kinds[,] chinquapins[,] small stragling pines[,] & some oakes very scrubby[,] of ye black Jack kinds[,] & A few scrubby white oaks[;] but ye country generaly open[,] so as to se[e] round for several miles[,] & very little grass but plenty of y^e *dwarf palmeto*[,] & few savanahs[.] y^e, swamps contains[,] in ye higher part[,] *live oaks prety large*[;] ye inner parts[,] small lobloly bay [,]sweet bay[,] *our red maple*[,] common crategus[,] *dahoon holly[,]* nissa[,] *sweet gum*[,] andromedas[.] I saw one viburnum or arrowwood & severall of our screw orchis & *pontedera*[,] all small[,] but toward St Johns ye soil[,] alltho to all appearance seems very sandy[,] yet ye pines is much larger & grows thicker & ye grass is much better[,] covering ye ground midle leg deep or more[,] & ye swamps broader & richer[,] & ye timber larger[,] & ye creeks better or larger[,] & thair current deeper[.]^4

The italicized plant names are linked to representative specimen sheets in the University of Florida Herbarium located in the Florida Museum of Natural History. Much of the initial determination of species fell to Michael Bond, the primary botanist associated with the project. Kent Perkins, the manager of the University of Florida's Herbarium, provided the specimens to be digitized. A preliminary matrix of botanical species information can be viewed at http://www.uflib.ufl.edu/digital/collections/bartram/botany.htm.

Interpreting the botany of Bartram's travels offers untold opportunities for historical researchers, ecologists, and botanists. Bartram knew and corresponded with most of the leading botanists both in the colonies and abroad. He was a true naturalist describing soils and environs he encountered, as well as the plants. By studying environmental clues and plant common names, we get a fairly good picture of the ecology possibly witnessed in 1765.

The first and most obvious clues lie in the plant names assigned by John Bartram. Once spelling inconsistencies are accounted for, such as "oakes" to "oaks" and accepting that "nissa" is probably "nyssa," the task became more challenging. With nearly thirty species of oaks and three nyssa in Florida, the specific ones encountered are a matter of conjecture.

We do know that John Bartram and Carl Linnaeus were correspondents; therefore, Bartram may have been naming plants based on Linnaeus's binomial system. If that is the case, only specimens named by Linneaus prior to 1765 would have been recorded by John Bartram. While taxonomists have reevaluated many of Linneaus's species, it is probable that we can, for the most part, accept Bartram's names at the generic level.

Further refinement of species identification resulted after consulting the first edition of Richard P. Wunderlin's *Guide to the Vascular Plants of Florida*^{5} and his online *Atlas of Florida Vascular Plants* (http://www.plantatlas.usf.edu/).^{6} The species distribution maps in the *Atlas* give some indication where species occurred historically. However, since these distributions are based on voucher specimens, the absence of location does not mean that the species doesn't or couldn't grow there, it just hasn't been recorded as being there.

Additional references consulted to help decipher and corroborate names used include Robert K. Godfrey's *Trees, Shrubs, and Woody Vines of Northern Florida and Adjacent Georgia and Alabama,* the monocot and dicot volumes of his *Aquatic and Wetland Plants of Southeastern United States,* and Ronald L. Myers's and John J. Ewel's *Ecosystems of Florida.* A final check was done in John T. Kartesz' *A Synonymized Checklist of the Vascular Flora of the United States, Canada, and Greenland* to confirm synonym and nomenclature changes. (See the bibliography.)

Many of the plants mentioned in the diary are consistent with our current nomenclature. As an example, John Bartram mentions "our red maple," which is the vernacular name commonly used for the species, *Acer rubrum.* Figure 13.1 is a specimen sheet of *Acer rubrum* found at http://www.uflib.ufl.edu/ufdc/?b=UF00084109. This image is served as a JPG2000 format, which allows specimen images captured at 140 MB to be compressed to 63.6 KB and served over the Internet. By clicking on the image, viewers can enlarge it to the original size, or 1:1 capture, and finer details become evident. For research purposes, images must be captured at a sufficiently high resolution (at least 400 dpi) to permit online study of details.

Some common names offer serious challenges to researchers. Bartram's reference to "our screw orchis" uncovered no leads in the literature. John Bartram was from Pennsylvania and perhaps "our" refers to a common species in the northeastern United States. Upon further scrutiny "orchis" is found to have been used by Linnaeus in naming orchids from several genera. A search of the Linnaean Plant Name Typification Project database (http://www.nhm.ac.uk/research-curation/projects/linnaean-typification/) indicates thirty-eight species that were included in the genus *Orchis.* Based on their current scientific name, three of these species occur in Florida: *Platanthera ciliaris, Platanthera flava,* and *Zeuxine strateumatica.*[7] *Zeuxine strateumatica,* an introduced species native to Asia, does not occur in Pennsylvania and was not likely to be present in Florida in 1765, so it can be excluded. Both species of *Platanthera* occur in Pennsylvania, but according to Wunderlin's online atlas only *Platanthera ciliaris* was recorded in St. Johns County, Florida. Members of the genus *Platanthera* are also commonly called bog orchids or fringed orchids. It appears from the Bartram excerpt above that the "screw orchis" was encountered in the inner part of a swampy area so bog may be an appropriate adjective.

Ideally, to settle the issue we would access digital images of *Platanthera ciliaris* collected in Pennsylvania, Florida, and the Bartram images at the Natural History Museum, London, for comparison. Unfortunately, at the time of the pilot project specimen images were not widely available. However, the Natural History Museum had digitized specimen sheets of John Clayton, a Virginia contemporary and friend of John Bartram. These are available online for scholarly study (http://www.nhm.ac.uk/research-curation/projects/

Herbarium of the University of Florida
Gainesville, Florida, U.S.A.

PLANTS OF: FLORIDA   COUNTY: ALACHUA
FLORA OF PAYNES PRAIRIE STATE PRESERVE

Acer rubrum L.

S. of Gainesville.T10S, R2OE, sec 25, NW ¼.
N.E. of Bison Pen, N.E.of road, near
inlet.
Scattered trees to 7 m tall. Bark
gray, smooth.

7 Feb 1982

coll. Janet C. Easterday # 795

13.1. Specimen sheet of *Acer specimen* (Red Maple), University of Florida Herbarium digital image (Image courtesy of the University of Florida Herbarium, Florida Museum of Natural History).

clayton-herbarium/). Clayton collected two specimens of *Orchis ciliaris,* now treated as *Platanthera ciliaris,* in 1753. He sent many of his specimens to Johann Frederick Gronovius, who in turn shared them with Linnaeus.[8] These "were among the earliest North American specimens that he had seen . . . Consequently, many of Clayton's specimens are types of Linnaean names."[9]

The on-line Biodiversity Heritage Library (http://www.biodiversitylibrary. org/About.aspx) includes searchable full text of historic taxonomic literature. This resource is of particular assistance in tracing early nomenclature variations in plant names. A search of *Orchis ciliaris* enabled us to identify and retrieve Linnaeus's 1753 entry from his *Species Plantarum,* volume 2, page 939. In Linnaeus's work, the habitat referenced is "Virginia, Canada."[10]

While the solution to this puzzle rests in finding a specimen collected by John Bartram, the distribution, habitat, and knowledge of this species by leading botanists and Linnaeus certainly seems to indicate that John Bartram's "screw orchis" is *Platanthera ciliaris.*

Other descriptions present similar puzzles. In his November 21, 1765, diary entry, Bartram refers to the "water dragon" plant he encountered in the "very rich low swamp" bordering the St. Johns River near Picolata. Harper notes in his annotations that Major John Eatton Le Conte suggested this was *Arum virginicum,* currently known as *Peltandra virginica,* or green arrow arum.[11] Another intriguing possibility is *Saururus cernuus,* a species that is vernacularly known as water dragon, or lizard's tail. Both species were collected by Clayton, described by Linnaeus, and both have been recorded in St. Johns County, Florida. The Clayton plant specimen for *Saururus cernuus* is not available. The University of Florida Herbarium has preserved type specimens and perhaps, in the future, as more digital images and descriptions become available, botanists and historians will arrive at consensus on the identity of this and other plants. (The specimen is available for viewing on-line at the University of Florida Herbarium Web site.)

Ultimately, many of the species identification questions can only be answered by reviewing the botanical specimens that John Bartram collected in 1742–1743 and those that were collected by William Bartram on subsequent trips to East and West Florida, South Carolina, and Georgia.

Considerable time has elapsed since the original drafting of this manuscript. The work for this pilot project reinforced the need for accessible, digitized images of specimens to clarify historic natural history documents. As a result, the University of Florida libraries have been able to negotiate the digitization of the Bartram herbarium specimens at the Natural History Museum, London. The specimen images have been received and initial re-determinations have been made. Metadata creation and mounting of the individual images is cur-

13.2. Flower head from Clayton's *Platanthera ciliaris* specimen collected in 1753 (Courtesy the Natural History Museum, London).

rently underway. As completed, images may be viewed as part of *The Roving Naturalists* Web site (http://www.uflib.ufl.edu/UFDC/?s=bart).

As historic botanical collections are digitized and made available on-line, the sightings by the early naturalists will lead to taxonomic revisions or revalidations, enrich our understanding of plant distribution, and suggest cases of species extirpation. These collections are the true "baseline" studies for floristic inventories. As such, their research value will never be equaled.

Notes

1. Vincent Kiernan, "An Encyclopedic Database about Plants Will Soon Flower on the Internet," *Chronicle of Higher Education* 46, 6 (1999): A33.

2. Ibid.

3. Francis Harper, "Other Early Investigations by Naturalists on Bartram's Route of 1765–66," in Introduction to John Bartram, "Diary of a Journey Through the Carolinas, Georgia, and Florida, from July 1, 1765, to April 10, 1766," edited and annotated by Francis Harper, *Transactions of the American Philosophical Society,* new series, vol. 33, part 1 (Philadelphia: American Philosophical Society, 1942): 5–8.

4. John Bartram, "Diary," 35.

5. Richard P. Wunderlin, *Guide to the Vascular Plants of Florida* (Gainesville: University of Florida Press, 1998).

6. Atlas of Florida Vascular Plants http://www.plantatlas.usf.edu/ (accessed 2005).

7. A full-color image of the specimen is available on-line at http://www.flmnh.ufl.edu/herbarium/cat/imageserver.asp?image=11768a1 (accessed October 25, 2005).

8. A full-color image of the specimen is available on-line at http://www.nhm.ac.uk/resources/research-curation/projects/clayton-herbarium/lgimages/BM000051650.JPG (accessed October 22, 2005).

9. *The John Clayton Herbarium,* http://www.nhm.ac.uk/research-curation/projects/clayton-herbarium/ (accessed October 22, 2005).

10. Carl von Linné, *Species plantarum* (Holmiae: Impensis Laurentii Salvii, 1753), 2:939. Accessed via Biodiversity Heritage Library (http://www.biodiversitylibrary.org/) in 2008.

11. John Bartram, *"Diary,"* 106.

14
Bartram's Legacy

Nature Advocacy

Charlotte M. Porter

A Long Book

In 1791, Bartram's book of *Travels,* a volume of some four hundred pages, was the largest work of natural history published in the United States. The author recorded over six hundred species of plants, birds, amphibians, and reptiles, as well as many geological features.[1] Famous passages described north-central Florida, in Bartram's day, home to Creeks and allied Seminoles, groups Bartram referred to as "Lower Creeks, or Siminoles," and associated Yamassees.[2] Their mico, or chief, Ahaye, whom the British called Cowkeeper, Bartram described as a statesman, "a tall, well made man, very affable and cheerful, about sixty years of age, his eyes lively and full of fire, his countenance manly and placid."[3]

Readers of the *Travels* still find much interesting information. Alas, reading the book from cover to cover is not an easy task. Trail enthusiasts expecting a precise itinerary are disappointed by the flowery style, and social historians puzzle over Bartram's verbose and herbose narrative. Many biologists find the scientific descriptions too poetic to pass current muster, and poets groan under Greek and Latin cognates, fond baggage of Bartram's education at the Philadelphia Academy, a school founded by Benjamin Franklin.[4] Readers seeking a love interest will have to settle with Bartram's love of nature or rent the movie *Cold Mountain,* adapted from Charles Frazier's recent novel of the same title.[5]

In a work of four distinct parts, Bartram fused compelling landscape descriptions, engaging ethnography, and poetic vision with a value system recognized today as environmental. Family connections included some of the nation's Founding Fathers, Benjamin Franklin, Thomas Jefferson, and Charles Thomson, but William's idiom differed from their rhetoric of nature. Unlike

"Poor Richard," or Franklin, his father's longtime friend, Bartram was neither humorist nor homilist in print.[6] Unlike Jefferson, a sometime neighbor on the Schuylkill River, he did not redeploy language of Newtonian physics.[7] Unlike his schoolteacher Thomson, the nation's leading classicist and second signer of the Declaration of Independence, William was neither purist nor grammarian.[8] To the contrary, Bartram fearlessly mixed metaphors with obscure vocabulary, biological nomenclature, vibrant adjectives, and romantic aesthetics.[9]

Bartram did not attempt succinct definition of nature, natural, or natural history. As an author, he was a demonstration artist: his book is a presentation of American nature, beautiful, complex, and untidy. Mindful of Bartram's mature views on human rights, this essay will address his contributions to nature advocacy in Florida. In the *Travels*, the naturalist confessed, "within the circle of my acquaintance, I am known to be an advocate or vindicator of the benevolent and peaceable dispositions of animal creation."[10] With language scientific, classical, poetic, and private, even politically incorrect, Bartram described changes that white settlement and nationhood portended for sentient biological communities and the peoples dependent upon them.

In 1791, publication of Bartram's *Travels* culminated more than a century of Quaker observation in the North American Southeast. An older generation might have referred to transformation of field notes into a book-length narrative as the effects of Inward Light, God's Light Within.[11] George Fox, founder of the Religious Society of Friends, ventured as far south as North Carolina between 1671 and 1673. Quakers Thomas Chalkely, Thomas Story, John Farmer, Samuel Bownas, John Griffith, Benjamin Holmer, and William Edmundson followed.[12] Published accounts of their journeys, for the most part presented in terms of their ministries, interested British officials because of their attention to the Creeks and Cherokee.

Bartram's book delivered the promise of a long title, discussions of Southeastern Indian peoples, but departed from the missionary bent of predecessors. Cherokees and Creeks Bartram found to be "frank, cheerful, and humane" and "tenacious" of "liberties." In 1791, his addition of "natural rights" to "liberties" were concerned words of warning as well as respect.[13]

Fictive Kinship

In the spring of 1774, Bartram arrived with deerskin traders in the Great Alachua Savanna in present-day Alachua County, Florida.[14] At the Creek town of Cuscowilla, Cowkeeper greeted the party and gave Bartram a guest name, transliterated as Puc Puggy and translated as the Flower Hunter in the *Travels*.[15] This name, a visa, permitted Bartram to collect flowers and medicinal plants in safety and distinguished the designated flower hunter from the rough crowd with whom he traveled. A form of fictive kinship, the name related Bartram to other human groups in Cowkeeper's community and established his credentials among Creek commercial deer hunters. Coincidentally, Bartram received his gift name in April about the date of his birthday. Unlike the traders, Bartram posed no real threat to the lifestyle of Cowkeeper's people or to the mico's authority, but if circumstances warranted, he was a convenient hostage. As long as the traders kept their agreements with the Creek elders, the guest name granted privilege and safe passage.

Cowkeeper was a crafty veteran of British diplomacy and Spanish relations, and Creeks routinely honored visiting dignitaries with honorific titles. Bartram's Creek title was "Puc Puggy," which he translated as "flower hunter." But perhaps there could be another side to Bartram's title. Possibly, Cowkeeper found Bartram's scientific rhetoric amusing. Related to modern Creek words for white, seedy, and puffy, the name Puc Puggy may have been a pun, a good-natured tag for Fluffy Head, Seedy, or Whitey (white being a Creek peace color).[16] Even passing familiarity with the English language allowed enjoyment of the homonymic relationship of the nouns Flower Hunter and Florida.[17] Furthermore, the name might also have referred to flour, a white, seed-based, powdery Pennsylvania commodity, because of recent hurricanes, then in short supply in Spanish Cuba.[18] Whatever Cowkeeper's frame of reference, the term flower hunter carried additional English meanings as botanist, florist, plant merchant, and herbalist. Bartram was both naturalist and nurseryman, but not a medical practitioner like many other eighteenth-century botanists.[19] In this regard, Cowkeeper may have expected or felt entitled to *gratis* medical advice, but there is no evidence that Bartram reciprocated Creek courtesies with data or drawings.

Pack animals transported Bartram's natural history collections and trade goods, and this association of science and commerce reinforced commercialization of North American species in Creek lands. The brisk traffic in partially cured deerskins enabled Bartram's scientific travels and specimen procurement. As a naturalist working without shelter from bad weather, Bartram drew plants, parsed flower parts, counted stamens and pistils, and sewed pressed specimens in linen herbarium books.[20] Cloths and kettles, valued by Creeks, held no excitement for him, and objects of natural history, exciting to Bartram, held no novelty for Creeks and Seminoles familiar with local plants and animals. For hired factors, fearful of ambush and indifferent to species designations, scientific objects were more cumber to haul.[21]

During the summer of 1774, commercial flower hunting and commercial deer hunting, science and the deerskin trade, went hand in hand in a hot humid climate. Bartram left behind specimens, especially animals, which he could not preserve. Commercial Creek hunters, pressured to harvest more deerskins to assuage ever-mounting community debts at trade stores, had to kill and skin as many animals as possible in a yearlong hunt.[22] No longer only hunting seasonally in traditional family groups for subsistence, they left behind the meat, horns, bones, and sinew which they could not transport or preserve.[23] Vultures, Bartram mused, were their constant companions, their "shade."[24] His description and fine drawing of the black vulture (*Coragyps atratus*) introduced the scavenger to science, *sui generis,* with at least three different English names: carrion crow, vulture atratus, and black buzzard.[25]

In recorded Creek Trickster tales, Buzzard was a sham doctor who got a bad taste of his own medicine.[26] Crossing and re-crossing geographical, cultural, ethnic, and political borders, Bartram, an unlikely candidate for Trickster, also had to reconfigure his credentials. In 1765, he and his father, John Bartram, traveled a small section of the English province of East Florida to promote plantation prospects along the St. Johns River.[27] By 1766, physical ailments curtailed John's fieldwork.[28] William, captivated by the region, stayed on, and with slaves reluctantly purchased by his father, attempted to start up a plantation on the St. Johns.[29] William abandoned the ill-suited venture. To the distress of father and friends, the fiasco cost him his birthright and self-esteem, and his name disappears from his father's scientific correspondence.[30] William's work ethic seemed less reliable than his spelling, but, in 1772, a London physician, Dr. John Fothergill, took a chance and sponsored thirty-something William to collect plants, species suitable for horticulture, in the Georgia colony.[31] After one year's work, an independent Bartram disregarded Fothergill's instructions and returned to East Florida, like a culprit to the scene of a crime.[32]

Three years of travels in East Florida, Alabama lands, and West Florida changed the late bloomer, exercised his powers of observation, enlarged his focus and, by 1791, his language skills.[33] Summoning delight and humility, he frequently invoked readers in the present tense to "behold" reverie-like phenomena which he knows "to be matter of real fact."[34] Because readers lacked access to the same data and experiences, Bartram had to establish himself as a trustworthy witness in landscapes of shifting human populations. Dangerous confrontations with rattlesnakes, alligators, and renegades were truth-tests, as were grand-scale confrontations with ancient Mississippian culture earthwork, mounds.[35] He knew that he was seeing "pensile banks" and "grassy verges" at just the verge of their permanent settlement by men and women of European origin.[36]

Nature's indicators, shifting biological populations, also intrigued Bartram. As he crossed southern latitudes, he described the approach of springtime in the Northeast as quickening of landscape by birds arriving from Florida flyways. "The greatest variety and abundance of these winged emigrants," he wrote, "choose to celebrate their nuptials" in East Florida.[37] Bartram and his contemporaries did not understand avian migrations, but Bartram recognized their guest status, happier than his own.

Willing to merge science and sentiment, Bartram described his summer months in the Alachua Savanna as an Arcadian experience, the magical literary invention of Elizabethan poet Philip Sidney.[38] Arcadia was an imaginary landscape of renewal and redemption, in which heroes underwent disguise, name change, potion, and often amorous entanglement. Bartram changed his plain Quaker dress to don the attire of traders; he gained a new name, Puc Puggy; and he drank the "thin drink" of hospitality with Creek elders.[39] In 1775, he would imbibe the more powerful "white drink," a vomitive called "black drink" by Europeans.[40]

Arcadia became Arden, a mirror of society, in William Shakespeare's *As You Like It,* and like love-struck Orlando of that play, Bartram, fond of lists, discovered books in trees and loves in species. Word stacks, such as "Live Oak, Mulberry, Magnolia, Palm, Zanthoxylon," were his way of describing the composition of forests and other habitats.[41] Word stacks helped him record natural history at a time when many intellectuals regarded the trained human memory as sufficient to the task of species identification and inventory. Associations were key.

Names

Natural history nomenclature reflected the debt of eighteenth-century arts and letters to classical literature. In the middle years of the century, the Swiss scientist Carl Linnaeus successfully proposed standard binomials, two-part Greek and Latin names for genera and species.[42] For example, for the two-part scientific name, *Zanthoxylon clava-herculis,* Linnaeus derived the genus name from Greek words meaning yellow wood.[43] The species descriptor for this shrubby Florida tree with knobs and dreadful thorns takes its meaning from the club of Hercules, the laboring hero of Greek mythology. A common name for a second Florida species, *Z. americanum,* is toothache tree, the twigs of which persons of African descent have chewed to treat toothaches. Puc Puggy, too, was a binomial and perhaps a gentle rebuke. Greek and Latin descriptors chosen by a distant scientific elite too often ignored the names, traditions, and classifications used by Creeks and other Amerindian peoples. Viewed through lenses of dead languages, they were names without local context.

For Bartram, scientific nomenclature, the tool of biological classification, was a bonanza, an opportunity to generate a large body of vocabulary and neologisms. Many of the plants and animals that Bartram observed in East Florida had no English names. His nomenclature qualified them for entry into the imperial fold, the British natural history press, which, following Mark Catesby's magnificently illustrated volumes, was centered in London.[44]

The material bases for species designations, type specimens, were critical objects that Bartram forwarded to his patron, Fothergill. Acquired in the early 1780s for the British Museum at Montagu House, already an overcrowded facility, they were accessible for study in London, but unpublished, they remained outside science.[45] Bartram lost control of these specimens. Publication of the *Travels* restored Bartram's scientific authority, but separated from his original specimens, his ornate descriptive language created confusion among late-nineteenth-century revisionists.[46]

After the treaty ending the War of Independence, Bartram also lost control of his intellectual property, drawings and notes, housed in the United States. Engaged in the life of the new republic, he was no recluse. At the family garden, he entertained many visitors, including members of the Constitutional Convention in 1787, traveling scientists, and more than three decades of medical students on field trips.[47] Shared conversations, notes, drawings, and plant displays kept Bartram in the loop and enabled the publications of others, notably, Humphrey Marshall, Bartram's second cousin; Dr. Benjamin Smith Barton, professor of natural history at the University of Pennsylvania; C. S. Rafinesque, a zealous polymath; as well as the French father and son, André and Francois André Michaux.[48] Alexander Wilson, a well-known poet, turned ornithologist after drawing lessons with Bartram and his niece at Kingsessing, repeatedly expressed his debt in letters, popular magazine poems, and his groundbreaking elegant multivolume *American Ornithology.*[49] The English traveler and frequent guest, Thomas Nuttall, retraced parts of Bartram's southeastern route in the autumn of 1815 and republished passages from the *Travels* in his popular bird manual.[50] The naturalist Titian Ramsay Peale, familiar from youth with Bartram, the garden, and the *Travels,* traveled to Florida with a group of naturalists from the Philadelphia Academy of Natural Sciences and later published George Ord's biography of Bartram in an illustrated periodical which he coedited in 1831–1832.[51] Indeed, ambitious John James Audubon arrived in Florida in 1831 to outdo Bartram's bird records for his own great book then in progress.[52]

In addition to observation of individual species, admiration of nature as assemblage was basic to Bartram's mode of expression. All living things, large and small, possessed "importance," manifested in the integrity of "inimitable workmanship," his phrase for intelligent design.[53] This workmanship was the plentitude of Creation, the fullness of nature that Bartram imitated and reflected in his writings and drawings. To his thinking, life seeped into all natural spaces like a fluid or subtle ether, imbuing organisms with their distinctive worth and bounteousness. Biodiversity, wealth of life was "happy," "virtuous," and "beautiful," adjectives found frequently throughout the *Travels,* and this "superabundance" encouraged human contentment.[54] As a result, parsimony, the working principle of modern-day biological cladists, was not a necessary discipline for Bartram. To the contrary, the language of his book intentionally mirrored bounteousness in an idiosyncratic form of prayer.[55]

Placing the American frontier within the bounds of science, literature, and religion, Bartram's words were instruments of English culture as powerful as the broad axe and froe. On opposing shores of the St. Johns River, Bartram observed British officials and horse thieves, plantation owners and their agents, deerskin traders and Creek hunters, and free men and slaves (both Negro and Indian). He collected, recorded, and drew nature seemingly oblivious to political turmoil and dangers about him. Scientific language proffered essential, if singular, elements of ongoing negotiation and Creek relocation. Linnaean binomials sanctioned species status as a form of novelty and provided two-worded contracts for English recognition and appropriation of living things in lands controlled by Creeks. In East Florida, in 1774, they did not yet preempt the Middle World of Creek cosmos, the human interface with fire above and water below.[56] Some of Bartram's manuscripts and drawing captions recorded Creek animal names, but with the exceptions of "Ephouskyca" (hokoseyc, cry baby) for "the crying bird" (the limpkin) and "echo" (eco) for the deer, these words did not surface in the *Travels.*[57] In their stead, species descriptions offered fictive kinship, scientific impunity, to readers, by 1791, citizens of the United States.

In the *Travels,* Bartram ended his introduction with a plea to the federal government to send envoys to Indian peoples to learn their languages and life ways, but, as Congress debated the war powers of the president, he was proposing too little too late.[58] The national responsibility of orderly settlement and treaty involved jurisprudence. Witness to routine destruction of snakes, bears, and wolves and commercial decimation of deer, he feared overkill which he bravely termed "criminal."[59] Abetted by British interests in East Florida, Creeks of his observations were waging "war" on wildlife, strong words from a pacificist.[60] Furthermore, species destruction involved two paired dangers: (1) hubris (despoiling of divine workmanship) and self-destruction (decimation of peoples dependent upon targeted species) and (2) ignorance (distain for species-based science) and cruelty (nullification of humane qualities, including the animal instincts). Because he considered plant sensitivity the basis for animal sensibility and animal behavior the basis for human morality, Bartram believed that legal framework had to recognize species status. Even at their best, science and Creek alliances were inadequate barriers. The logical conclusion was grim: depletion of biological reservoirs.

Comparisons

Creek hunting territories, land swaps for debt, and white settlement were current spatial crises that also jeopardized temporal continuum of the "divine . . . workmanship."[61] News of "Big Bones," fossilized remains of giant mammals, posed profound questions about the past.[62] Bartram made miscellaneous mention of fossils when he discussed soil types and he took time to observe Big Shells, giant fossil oysters in strata at Silver Bluff in South Carolina.[63] Pondering both ends of the continuum of divine workmanship, land mammals and marine bivalves, Bartram, unlike his father, declined to speculate in print.[64] Other thinkers less modestly seized on parallels to an antique past irrelevant to the American experience. Before the leading British scientific organization, the Royal Society of London, Sir Hans Sloane, for example, could explain Big Bones in Europe as remains of elephants in the entourage of Alexander the Great in part because of archaeological finds of Roman coins in Yorkshire.

Lofty connections to an idealized past resonated with fashionable taste for neoclassical design, a revival of antiquarianism receiving grand expression in expensive English homes and formal gardens.[65] Incorporating exotic species as well as sculptural and architectural elements from colonized landscapes around the world, estate designers lifted the physical arrangements from celebrated canvasses of the French artist Claude Lorraine and developed an aesthetic called the picturesque.[66] Full effects required serial imitation in a form of admiration and competition: designers recreated vistas that Lorraine recreated from the Latin authors Virgil and Ovid.[67] They built faux temples and other edifying ruins leading to the garden's end marked by a hut and hired hermit, whose situation visitors could envy or despise.

In Kingsessing, John Bartram's garden, a nursery business, was a direct beneficiary. Fashion, desire to revamp garden real estate, not abstract science motivated Fothergill's initial patronage of William in Georgia, and after Jefferson toured English estates in 1786, he, too, designed fake temples for his garden planned at Monticello, Virginia.[68] William could not feign ignorance of English garden trends. He repeatedly used the word picturesque to describe landscapes of his travels, uncovered imagined "porticos" among the vines, recycled Roman place names, and his wonderful description of the snakebird, or anhinga (*Anhinga anhinga*), eluded to Ovid.[69]

Pseudo Greco-Roman landscapes required pseudo Greco-Romans as well as species designated with Greek and Latin nomenclature. Long before

Horatio Greenough unveiled his monumental sculpture of a bare-chested George Washington in a Roman toga, artists painted the figures of more ordinary mortals from plaster casts of antique statues.[70] Neither William nor his father traveled the Grand Tour in Europe, but Bartram described Indian men as statues embodying classical virtues ensconced in southern American landscapes. These word pictures borrowed vocabulary and vanities in vogue.[71] For example, museum founder Charles Willson Peale, painter of the famous fluffy haired portrait of William Bartram, portrayed himself in his eighties, standing beside Big Bones like a Caesar with the muscular legs of a gladiator.[72]

Plain Truths

True to his Quaker background, Bartram also offered antidotes to fanciness and affected tastes, and, for present readers, many of the finest passages in the *Travels* celebrate transparency. In north-central Florida, the medium, the beautiful spring runs, matched the message in a way consistent with the Inward Light. Following one of his few biblical references, Bartram wrote of a "paradise of fish" observed in a spring, "here the water or element in which they live and move, is so perfectly clear and transparent, it places them all on an equality."[73] Besides his aesthetic appreciation of freshwater spaces, Bartram's use of the word "nursery" to describe wetlands, marshes, and swamps was ahead of its time.[74] While his countrymen drained bogs, he valued these landscape features as productive habitats.

A striking passage in the *Travels* described a wetland bird that Bartram called the wood ibis.[75] Nuttall published this description almost verbatim in 1834: "Here, alone the feathered hermit stands listless, on the topmost limb of some tall and decayed cypress, with his neck drawn in upon his shoulders, and his enormous bill resting like a scythe upon his breast."[76] Slogging about salt marshes near St. Augustine, Audubon, tired of eating "Poor Jobs" [herons] and wearing wet socks, assured his wife, Lucy Bakewell Audubon, that his reports would "be far, very far from" Bartram's "*flowery sayings.*"[77] Bartram's wood ibis, he decided, was actually a brown pelican (*Pelicanus occidentalis*), which he drew as a solitary bird perched with its neck drawn in and its enormous (but pouched) beak resting "like a scythe" upon its breast. The "feathered hermit" in decayed abode hearkened English garden theory, and Audubon benefited by association. Volume three of *Birds of America* paid mixed tribute with a handsome plate of "Bartram's sandpiper," *Totanus Bartramius* (now the upland sandpiper, *Bartramia longicauda*), and remarked about gastric risks of dining on the bird's flesh.[78]

Bartram's emphasis on freshwater habitats found more welcome accommodation in the landscape paintings of Martin Johnson Heade. Heade studied frontier expansion from the vantage of extensive travels in North and South America, including proposed sites for the Panama Canal. Intrigued by the biological diversity of the neotropics, he produced many pictures of Central and South American subjects. Moving to St. Augustine in the 1880s, Heade found acceptable resolution of art, nature, and personal contentment and enjoyed the benefits of railroad magnate Henry Flagler. In popular flower paintings, Heade celebrated the beauty of the "glorious" *Magnolia grandiflora,* one of Bartram's favorite species in East Florida.[79] An amateur ornithologist and collector, Heade was a skilled illustrator of hummingbirds, aware of competition in the international scientific press.[80]

Similarities between Heade's studies of hummingbirds and flowers and Bartram's work are not fortuitous. Traveling at least twice to London on the business of art and natural history, Heade may have sought out Bartram's drawings at the British Museum. Early oil paintings included hunting themes, but his signature wetland panoramas, the largest, 52 x 96 inches, presented luminescent vistas worthy of Bartram's descriptions. Hazy green and pink wet meadows, not beaches, beckon with radiant fullness.

As a youth in Pennsylvania, Heade had painted with Thomas Hicks, nephew of Edward Hicks, a Quaker artist. In 1826, Edward Hicks's famous painting of Niagara Falls commemorated the much-publicized travels and poetry of Alexander Wilson, Bartram's student.[81] A series of paintings illustrating the Peaceable Kingdom described by the Old Testament prophet Isaiah established his reputation. Hicks was not only addressing the past. To the lion and the lamb and other peace-making animal pairs mentioned in the biblical prophecy, Hicks added historic Quaker and Indian treaty groups, mounted animals from Peale's Philadelphia Museum, and atlas images of recognizable landscape features.[82] The fact that his sources were not obscure was key to his success.

Had Hicks also read Bartram's ideas in the *Travels,* in Wilson's other poems, or in passages excerpted in magazines and other books by naturalists associated with Peale's museum? Bartram, too, had tried to reconcile current frontier issues with peaceable traditions of his Quaker background. He recognized that treaty, or social contract, was necessary to uphold nature as repository for the best human values. Bartram wanted a peace treaty between species and human beings, and, like Hicks, he desired, indeed, demanded a meaningful environmental context.

Stewardship

In 1791, Bartram's *Travels* was a large book with many audiences. For land speculators, the account offered a meandering armchair tour of the Southeast. For patriots, the work explored a wealth of American possibilities. For female readers, the book was literary surrogate for the circuit walk, an expository narrative in fashionable terms of the picturesque. For nurserymen, descriptions of nature's beauties promoted plants with commercial potential. For politicians, the *Travels* advocated rights of Indian "nations" and cautioned against annexation of their lands.[83] For romantics, the *Travels* anticipated new aesthetics. Sightseeing in the United States at the time of the book's publication, the French author René de Chateaubriand immersed his didactic novella *Atala* (1801) in the Alachua Savanna, in his thesis, a theme park of good and evil, tradition and transgression. Indeed, *The Burial of Atala* (1813), a grand tableau painted by the French master Anne-Louis Girodet-Trioson, exaggerates the relief of the limestone typography with correct botanical detail, species known in France, thanks to the Michauxes and Bartram's Kingsessing garden.[84]

After the Civil War, travel to Bartram's literary garden, Florida, became part of a national healing process, and artists, writers, and photographers led the way. Like Heade, they promoted railroad and steamboat tourism along the St. Johns River.[85] The poet and composer Sidney Lanier prepared a guide to Florida, which included the great sinkhole at the northern end of the Alachua Savanna, an imperative stop for photographers.[86] After the novelist and spiritualist Harriet Beecher Stowe moved to a cottage on the banks of the St. Johns River, she published a volume of chatty letters to women friends. When Mrs. Stowe described fishing picnics along the river slews, she enjoyed an old food chain described in Bartram's *Travels*.[87] At Magnolia Springs, the grand hotel boasted a state-of-the-art photographic dark room as well as tennis courts.[88] In St. Augustine, Heade and a staff of studio artists offered art lessons and afternoon entertainments at the Ponce de Leon Hotel, only a short walk from the house where Bartram gagged on a dinner of rattlesnake with the English governor.[89] At Silver Springs, the great photographer of the western surveys, William Henry Jackson, was on hand to take stunning black-and-white photographs.[90] Colored in Detroit, Michigan, as early penny postcards, Jackson's views popularized the Florida tourist trail.

The message was "Wish you were here," but chatty notes, art lessons, and scenic views of springs and Spanish moss were not the real tourist draws. They were compensations for the women left at hotels after their men departed on hunting and fishing excursions. The sporting habits that provided Heade with his sinecure at the Ponce de Leon studios also came under fire in acerbic letters penned for *Forest and Stream*. Writing under the *nom de plume* Didymus, Heade advocated bag limits, management of game and nongame species, and an end to commercial wildlife exploitation, especially plume hunting. Attacking the nineteenth-century legacy of the eighteenth-century British deerskin trade, Heade exhorted other sportswriters to expose "game butchers."[91]

Heade, a sportsman himself, warned that hotel-sponsored competitions for gargantuan trophy catches, five hundred redfish per day per person, were both bad business and bad nature policy. Making extinction a political issue, he roasted entrenched attitudes and demanded legal solutions, "sensible game laws and their strict enforcement."[92] With sad conviction, he wrote that sea turtles "like their friends, the manatee, seem to have a limited future."[93] In October 1898, he condemned Florida as "a State in the Union where everything in the shape of a bird and beast is being so rapidly exterminated, regardless of common sense or common interests."[94] Like Bartram he observed that native peoples "know that [hunting], one of their sources of income is being destroyed, but what can they do to prevent it?"[95]

Writing from wetlands along the St. Johns River, Heade voiced frustrations and fears that Bartram had expressed a century earlier. The Creeks of Bartram's observations depended upon high-volume commercial hunting, because like white settlers living on their lands, they needed European goods. Heade's readers, tourists, had no hardship excuse, and a northern public began to boycott plume hunting for the fashion industry. Stowe chided a young woman too loaded down with wildlife products—palmetto hats, "orange wood cane tipped with an alligator's tooth," and assortment of plumes—to notice Florida's wildflowers.[96] "All women who have souls worth saving," Heade goaded the all-male hunt clubs, "have joined the Audubon Society."[97] One type of club activity had hatched another. "Criminal excess," Bartram's concern and Heade's mantra, had not been Audubon's worry, but seeking a charismatic icon, educated women of Massachusetts chose the wrong man's name for their organization.

The new ethic was conservation, and Florida was the focus. During the twentieth century, the mission of the Audubon Society widened. Other outspoken citizen groups joined ranks to organize stewardship of the environment, and thanks to their commitment, wildlife and natural areas have gained legal status, scientific management, and a future. Today, if William Bartram returned to north-central Florida, he would not encounter Creek communities in the Alachua Savanna, but he would recognize the prairie basin and surrounding mesic hammock, now managed as Paynes Prairie Preserve on the basis of descriptions in the *Travels*.

All natural history is to some degree nostalgic, and Bartram's book is a souvenir in the best sense of the word. Among the Bartram Family Papers, undated advice to a nephew interested in natural history addressed the character of his own pursuits: "Be moderate in all thy aims, & acquisition, with respect to reputation, riches or gratification of the passions." In fact, Bartram gained "security and confidence," as well as acquisitions, from his work, and the *Travels* stand as a cornerstone of American nature writing.[98] The aim of his book was not moderate. The author approached his subject with indulgence, rich with passion for living things and gratifying in kindly intelligence.

Notes

1. Over the years, students and I have made recounts. The exact number of Bartram's technical contributions will remain, indeed, should remain in friendly dispute.

2. William Bartram, *The Travels of William Bartram*, Naturalists's Edition, ed. Francis Harper (New Haven, Conn.: Yale University Press, 1958), 134. William Bartram, *William Bartram on the Southeastern Indians*, ed. Gregory A. Waselkov and Kathryn E. Holland Braund (Lincoln: University of Nebraska Press, 1995), 47–72; Charlotte M. Porter, "William Bartram's Travels in the Indian Nations," *Florida Historical Quarterly* 70, 4 (April 1992): 436–440.

3. Bartram, *Travels*, ed. Harper, 118.

4. Thomas P. Slaughter, *The Natures of John and William Bartram* (New York: Vintage Books, 1996), 117–118.

5. Ada and Inman are the sweethearts in Charles Frazier, *Cold Mountain: A Novel* (New York: Atlantic Monthly Press, 1997).

6. See David E. Shi, *The Simple Life: Plain Living and High Thinking in American Culture* (New York: Oxford University Press, 1985), 71.

7. Charles A. Miller, *Jefferson and Nature: An Interpretation* (Baltimore: Johns Hopkins University Press, 1988), 11, 78, 80, 91, 113–115, 256, 273.

8. Ernest Earnest, *John and William Bartram, Botanists and Explorers* (Philadelphia: University of Pennsylvania Press, 1940), 89–90, and J. Edwin Hendrick, *Charles Thomson and the Making of a New Nation* (Canbury, N.J.: Associated University Presses, 1979), 7–8, 136–137. Thomson devised the motto for the Great Seal.

9. Christoph Irmscher, *The Poetics of Natural History from John Bartram to William James* (New Brunswick, N.J.: Rutgers University Press, 1999), 39–41. See also L. Hugh Moore, "The Aesthetic Theory of William Bartram," *Essays in Arts & Sciences* 12 (March 1983): 19.

10. Bartram, *Travels*, ed. Harper, 135.

11. Arthur J. Worral, *Quakers in the Colonial Northeast* (Hanover: University Press of New England, 1980), 5.

12. J. Ralph Randolph, *British Travelers among the Southern Indians, 1660–1763* (Norman: University of Oklahoma Press, 1973), 49–51.

13. Bartram, *Travels*, ed. Harper, 307.

14. Ibid., 117.

15. Ibid., 118.

16. See Charlotte M. Porter, "An Eighteenth-Century Flower Child: William Bartram," in Jack E. Davis and Raymond Arsenault, eds., *Paradise Lost? The Environmental History of Florida* (Gainesville: University Presses of Florida, 2005), 52, an interpretation based upon Jack B. Martin and Margaret McKane Maud-

lin, *A Dictionary of Creek/Muskogee* (Lincoln: University of Nebraska Press, 2000), 97, 239, and requiring more input from native Creek speakers. For kinship terms, see Charles Hudson, *The Southeastern Indians* (Knoxville: University of Tennessee Press, 1976), 189.

17. For the naming of Florida, see Michael Gannon, "First European Contacts," in *The New History of Florida,* ed. Michael Gannon (Gainesville: University Press of Florida, 1996), 19, 21–23.

18. Sherry Johnson discussed the flour crisis of the 1770s, "Hurricanes in Cuba," George E. Pozzetta Lecture, December 1, 2006, History Department, University of Florida, Gainesville.

19. For the organizing role of individuals with medical training in colonial scientific communities, see Raymond Phineas Stearns, *Science in the British Colonies of America* (Urbana: University of Illinois Press, 1970), 671–672.

20. Bartram, *Travels,* ed. Harper, 91.

21. Kathryn E. Holland Braund, *Deerskins and Duffels: Creek Indian Trade with Anglo America* (Lincoln: University of Nebraska Press, 1993), 82, 95–96, 103.

22. Braund, *Deerskins,* 97–102; Steven C. Hahn, *The Invention of the Creek Nation, 1670–1763* (Lincoln: University of Nebraska Press, 2004), 76–80.

23. J. Leitch Wright Jr., *Creeks and Seminoles: Destruction and Regeneration of the Muscogulge People* (Lincoln: University of Nebraska Press, 1986), 41–71.

24. Bartram, *Travels,* ed. Harper, 128.

25. Reproduced as plate 56 in Joseph Ewan, ed., *William Bartram: Botanical and Zoological Drawings, 1756–1788* (Philadelphia: American Philosophical Society, 1968); see 82 for annotation.

26. Earnest George, *Totkv Moevse/New Fire: Creek Folktales,* ed. Jack B. Martin, Margaret McKane Maudlin, and Juanita McGirt (Norman: University of Oklahoma Press, 2004), 89.

27. Edmond Berkeley and Dorothy Smith Berkeley, *The Life and Travels of John Bartram: From Lake Ontario to the River St. John* (Tallahassee: University Presses of Florida, 1982), 236–254.

28. Berkeley and Berkeley, *John Bartram,* 265.

29. Ibid., 262–267; Slaughter, *The Natures,* 155–165. The site under management is Six-mile Creek near present-day Doctors Bridge, Jacksonville, Florida.

30. John Bartram to William Bartram, April 5, 1766, The Bartram Family Papers, Historical Society of Pennsylvania, Philadelphia.

31. See letters of October 22, 1772, and n.d. 1775, in Betsy C. Corner and Christopher C. Booth, eds., *Chain of Friendship: John Fothergill of London, 1735–1780* (Cambridge, Mass.: Harvard University Press, 1971), 391, 464.

32. Charlotte M. Porter, "Philadelphia Story: Florida Gives William Bartram a Second Chance," *Florida Historical Quarterly* 71, 3 (January 1993): 319.

33. Porter, "Philadelphia Story," 321–323.

34. Bartram, *Travels*, ed. Harper, 105.

35. Robin F. A. Fabel, "British Rule in the Floridas," in Gannon, ed., *New History*, 134–135.

36. Bartram, *Travels*, ed. Harper, 32, 174.

37. Ibid., 179.

38. T. W. Craik, ed., *Sir Philip Sidney: Selections from Arcadia and Other Poetry and Prose* (New York: Capricorn Books, 1965), 1–6.

39. Bartram, *Travels*, ed. Harper, 118.

40. Hudson, *Southeastern Indians*, 226.

41. Bartram, *Travels*, ed. Harper, 141.

42. Gunnar Ericksson, "Linnaeus the Botanist," in Tore Frangsmyr, ed., *Linnaeus: The Man and His Work* (Berkeley and Los Angeles: University of California Press, 1983), 77–85.

43. Andre F. Clewell, *Guide to the Vascular Plants of the Florida Panhandle* (Tallahassee: Florida State University Press, 1985), 476.

44. Joseph Kastner, *A Species of Eternity* (New York: Alfred A. Knopf, 1977), 16–18.

45. Marjorie Cayhill, *The Story of the British Museum* (London: British Museum Publications Ltd., 1981), 13.

46. Elliot Coues, "Fasti ornitholgiae redivivi. No. 1 Bartram's 'Travels,'" *Proceedings of the Academy of Natural Sciences* 27 (1875): 338–358, and "The Finishing Stroke to Bartram," *Auk* 16 (1899): 83–84.

47. Porter, "Philadelphia Story," 321; Kastner, *Eternity*, 112.

48. Henry Savage Jr. and Elizabeth J. Savage, *André and Francois André Michaux* (Charlottesville: University Press of Virginia, 1986), 104.

49. For Bartram's influence, see Clark Hunter, *The Life and Letters of Alexander Wilson* (Philadelphia: American Philosophical Society, 1983), 71–72, 85, 105, 202, 283, and William B. O. Peabody, "Life of Alexander Wilson," in Jared Sparks, ed., *The Library of American Biography* (Boston: Hillard Gray & Co.; London: Richard James Kennett, 1834), 2: 61–62. Wilson studied drawing with Bartram and "Miss Nancy" (Ann Bartram) to combat in his own word, "depression," an ailment also of Bartram, discussed by Slaughter, *Two Natures*, 242–243. See also numerous references to Bartram throughout Alexander Wilson's 9-volume *American Ornithology* (Philadelphia: Bradsford and Inskeep, 1808–1814), especially vols. 1, 2, and 5.

50. Jeannette E. Graustein, *Thomas Nuttall, Naturalist: Explorations in America* (Cambridge, Mass.: Harvard University Press, 1967), 19–20, 194.

51. George Ord, "Biographical Sketch of William Bartram," *Cabinet of Natural History and Rural American Sport* 2 (1832): i–vii, a rare work.

52. As confided to Lucy in letters excerpted by Kathryn Hall Proby, *Audubon in Florida with Selections from the Writings of John James Audubon* (Coral Gables: University of Miami Press, 1974), 13, 31.

53. Bartram, *Travels,* ed. Harper, lii.

54. Ibid., xiv, 7, 134, 168.

55. Ibid., li.

56. Term used by George E. Lanford, ed., *Native American Legends: Southeastern Legends: Tales from the Natchez, Caddo, Biloxi, Chickasaw and Other Nations* (Little Rock, Ark.: August House, 1987), 106.

57. Bartram, *Travels,* ed. Harper, 93, 136.

58. Abraham D. Sofaer, *War, Foreign Affairs and Constitutional Power* (Cambridge: Ballinger Pub. Co., 1976), 94–101, 117–118, 327, 341.

59. Bartram, *Travels,* ed. Harper, 135.

60. Ibid., 135.

61. Ibid., lii.

62. John C. Greene, *American Science in the Age of Jefferson* (1984; Claremont, Calif.: Regina Books, 2004), 32, 34, 289, 318.

63. Bartram, *Travels,* ed. Harper, 199.

64. Ibid., 201.

65. Francis Haskell and Nicholas Perry, *Taste and the Antique: The Lure of Classical Sculpture, 1500–1900* (New Haven, Conn.: Yale University Press, 1981), 87–88, 94–98.

66. James D. Kornwolf, "The Picturesque in the American Garden and Landscape before 1800," in Robert P. Maccubbin and Peter Martin, eds., *British and American Gardens in the Eighteenth Century: Eighteen Illustrated Essays on Garden History* (Williamsburg: Colonial Williamsburg Foundation, 1984), 93–95.

67. For "Ovid in the Garden," see John Dixon Hunt, *Garden and Grove: The Italian Renaissance Garden in the English Imagination: 1600–1750* (Princeton, N.J.: Princeton University Press, 1986), 42–43, 93, and Mavis Batey, "The High Phase of English Landscape Gardening," in Maccubbin and Martin, eds., *British and American Gardens,* 44–45.

68. William L. Beiswanger, "The Temple in the Garden: Thomas Jefferson's Vision of the Monticello Landscape," in Maccubbin and Martin, eds., *British and American Gardens,* 180.

69. Bartram, *Travels,* ed. Harper, 85.

70. Russell Lynes, *The Art-Makers: An Informal History of Painting, Sculpture, and Architecture in Nineteenth-Century America* (New York: Dover Publications, 1970), 120–121.

71. Bartram, *Travels,* ed. Harper, 306.

72. Charles Willson Peale, *The Artist in His Museum,* oil, Philadelphia Academy of Fine Arts.

73. Bartram, *Travels,* ed. Harper, 106.

74. Ibid., 145.

75. Ibid., 94–95.

76. Thomas Nuttall, *A Popular Handbook of the Ornithology of Eastern North America,* ed. Montague Chamberlain, 2d rev. ed. (Boston: Little, Brown, 1896), I: xxxvi–vli.

77. Quoted in Proby, *Audubon in Florida,* 31.

78. Plate 160; see useful discussion in Roger Tory Peterson and Virginia Marie Peterson, *Audubon's Birds of America: The Audubon Society Baby Elephant Folio* (New York: Cross River Press / Abbeville Press, 1981), Section V, unpaginated.

79. Didymus [Martin Johnson Heade], "On the Chagres River," *Forest and Stream,* September 23, 1899, 244.

80. Katharine Emma Mathorne, *Tropical Renaissance: North American Artists Exploring Latin America, 1839–1879* (Washington, D.C.: Smithsonian Institution Press, 1989), 42–49, and Barbara Novak and Timothy A. Eaton, *Martin Johnson Heade: A Survey: 1840–1900* (West Palm Beach: Eaton Fine Art, n.d.), 13, 22–25, 26–29, 64–69.

81. Charlotte M. Porter, *The Eagle's Nest: Natural History and American Ideas, 1812–1842* (University: University of Alabama Press, 1986), 164.

82. Porter, *Eagle's Nest,* 169–174.

83. Bartram, *Travels,* ed. Harper, 307–308.

84. An exhibition that opened May 24, 2007, at the Metropolitan Museum of Art, New York, N.Y., featured works by Girodet (1767–1824) from Museé Girodet, Montargis, France.

85. Charlotte M. Porter, "Martin Johnson Heade, An Early Voice for Florida Conservation," *Proceedings of the 90th Meeting of the Florida Historical Society,* St. Augustine, May 1992, 186–187.

86. Sidney Lanier, *Florida: Its Scenery, Climate and History,* 1875 facsimile ed. (Gainesville: University of Florida Press, 1973), 140–147.

87. Harriet Beecher Stowe, *Palmetto-Leaves,* 1873 facsimile ed. (Gainesville: University of Florida Press, 1968), 69–86.

88. Floyd and Marion Rinhart, *Victorian Florida: America's Last Frontier* (Atlanta, Ga.: Peachtree Publishers, 1986), 57.

89. Porter, "Heade," 187; Bartram, *Travels,* ed. Harper, 170.

90. Floyd and Marion Rinhart, *Victorian Florida,* 11, 70–71.

91. Didymus, "Concerning Big Bags of Ducks," *Forest and Stream,* December 2, 1899, 449.

92. Didymus, "Walloping the Citizens," *Forest and Stream,* May 12, 1900, 336.

93. Didymus, "The Florida Manatee," *Forest and Stream,* August 15, 1896, 125.

94. Didymus, "Florida Turtle Eggs," *Forest and Stream,* October 22, 1898, 325.

95. Didymus, "Florida Plume Birds," *Forest and Stream,* April 17, 1898, 90.

96. Stowe, *Palmetto-Leaves,* 98.

97. Didymus, "Birds and Bonnets," cited in Porter, "Heade," 188.

98. William Bartram to Moses Bartram Jr., Bartram Papers (Historical Society of Pennsylvania); Bruce Silver, "William Bartram's and Other Eighteenth-Century Accounts of Nature," *Journal of the History of Ideas* 39, 4 (1978): 597–614; Michael P. Branch, ed., *Reading the Roots: American Nature Writing before Walden* (Athens: University of Georgia Press, 2004), 184; Pamela Regis, *Describing Early America: Bartram, Jefferson, Crevecoeur, and the Influence of Natural History* (Philadelphia: University of Pennsylvania Press, 1992), 40–78.

Bibliography

Primary Sources

Alabama Department of Archives and History, Montgomery.
    Brannon Manuscript Collection, Indians—Townsites, Autossee File.
American Philosophical Society, Philadelphia.
    Barton-Delafield Collection.
    Benjamin Franklin Correspondence.
Bartram's Garden, Philadelphia.
    John Bartram Association Collection.
British National Archives (Public Record Office).
    Kew Colonial Office, 5/76, 5/556.
William L. Clements Library, Ann Arbor, Michigan.
    Gage Papers.
Georgia Archives, Morrow, Georgia.
    Colonial Plat Book C (1748–1771).
Gray Herbarium, Archives, Harvard University, Cambridge, Massachusetts.
    Jane Gray Autograph Collection.
Hargrett Rare Book and Manuscript Library, University of Georgia, Athens, Georgia.
    Charles C. Jones Jr. Collection.
Hege Library, Guilford College, Greensboro, N.C.
    Friends Historical Collection, Minutes of the Cane Creek Monthly Meeting (1760–1900).
Historical Society of Pennsylvania, Philadelphia.
    Bartram Papers.
Library of Congress, Washington, D.C.
    Benjamin Wailes, *Extracts from the Letter Book of William Dunbar of the Forest*

from 18 June 1775 to 20 March 1802. Together with a Biographical Sketch, com-
piled by B. L. C. Wailes [uncertain]. William Dunbar, MMC-alpha. MSS
92–498.
Natural History Museum, London.
Barclay Materials.
National Anthropological Archives, Smithsonian Institution, Washington, D.C.
J. Woodbridge Davis Papers.
New-York Historical Society, New York City.
Bartram Papers.
Henry Knox Papers of the Gilder-Lehrman Collection, on deposit at the
New-York Historical Society.
South Caroliniana Library, Columbia, S.C.
Miscellaneous Collections.
University Libraries, Cambridge, England.
Arthur Dobbs, "A Scheme to Increase the Colonies and Commerce of
Britain," *Cholmondeley Houghton* 84, pp. 18–19, Ms. No. 68.

Newspapers

Augusta (Georgia) Chronicle and Gazette of the State of Georgia, 1796.
Georgia Gazette, February 2, 1774.
South Carolina and American General Gazette (Charleston), 1780.

Published Primary Sources

Adair, James. *The History of the American Indian Adair,* ed. and with an Introduc-
tion by Kathryn E. Holland Braund. London: Charles and Edward Dilly, 1775;
Tuscaloosa: The University of Alabama Press, 2005.
Aiton, William. *Hortus Kewensis, or a Catalogue of the Plants Cultivated in the
Royal Botanic Garden at Kew.* 3 vols. London: Printed for George Nicol, 1789.
Anderson, William L. "Cherokee Clay from Duché to Wedgwood: The Jour-
nal of Thomas Griffiths, 1767–1768." *North Carolina Historical Review* 63
(1986): 501.
Barton, Benjamin Smith. *New Views of the Origins of the Tribes and Nations of
America.* Philadelphia: John Bioren, 1797.
Barton, William P. C. *A Flora of North America,* vol. 1. Philadelphia: M. Carey &
Sons, 1821.
Bartram, John. *A Journal kept by John Bartram of Philadelphia, Botanist to His
Majesty for the Floridas; upon a Journey from St. Augustine up the River St. John's.*
In William Stork, *An Account of East-Florida.* London: W. Nicoll, 1766.
———. "Diary of a Journey Through the Carolinas, Georgia, and Florida, from

July 1, 1765, to April 10, 1766." Edited and annotated by Francis Harper. *Trans-actions of the American Philosophical Society,* new series, vol. 33, pt. 1. Philadel-phia: APS, 1942.

———. *Observations on the Inhabitants, Climate, Soil, Rivers, Productions, Animals, and Other Matters Worthy of Notice Made by Mr. John Bartram in His Trav-els from Pensilvania to Onondago, Oswego and the Lake Ontario in Canada, To which is annex'd, a curious Account of the Cataracts at Niagara by Mr. Peter Kalm, a Swedish Gentleman who travelled there.* London: Printed for J. Whiston and B. White, in Fleet-Street, 1751. Reprinted with the addition of one map and one plate, Geneva, N.Y.: George Perkins Humphrey, 1895, and in Whitfield J. Bell Jr., *A journey from Pennsylvania to Onondaga in 1743, by John Bartram, Lewis Evans [and] Conrad Weiser.* Barre, Mass.: Imprint Society, 1973.

———. *The Correspondence of John Bartram, 1734–1777,* ed. Edmund Berkeley and Dorothy Smith Berkeley. Gainesville: University of Florida Press, 1992.

[Bartram, William]. *A Catalogue of Trees, Shrubs, and Herbaceous Plants, Indige-nous to the United States of America; Cultivated and Disposed of By John Bartram & Son, At their Botanical Garden, Kingsess, near Philadelphia: To Which is Added A Catalogue of Foreign Plants, Collected From Various Parts of the Globe* (Phila-delphia: Bartram and Reynolds, 1807).

Bartram, William. "Observations on the Creek and Cherokee Indians, 1789 with Prefatory and Supplementary Notes by E. G. Squier." *Transactions of the American Ethnological Society,* vol. 3, pt. 1, 1–81. New York, AES: 1853.

———. "Travels in Georgia and Florida, 1773–74: A Report to Dr. John Fother-gill." Edited and annotated by Francis Harper. *Transactions of the American Philosophical Society,* new series, vol. 33, pt. 2. Philadelphia: APS, 1942.

———. *Travels Through North & South Carolina, Georgia, East & West Florida, the Cherokee Country, the Extensive Territories of the Muscogulges, or Creek Confed-eracy, and the Country of the Chactaws; Containing An Account of the Soil and Natural Productions of Those Regions, Together with Observations on the Man-ners of the Indians. Embellished with Copper-Plates.* Philadelphia: James & Johnson, 1791.

———. *The Travels of William Bartram,* Naturalists's Edition, ed. Francis Harper. New Haven, Conn.: Yale University Press, 1958.

———. *Travels and Other Writings,* ed. Thomas P. Slaughter. New York: Library of America, 1996.

———. *Travels of William Bartram,* ed. Mark Van Doren. New York: Macy-Masius, 1928; Rpt., New York: Dover, 1955.

———. *Travels Through North and South Carolina, Georgia, East and West Florida: A Facsimile of the 1792 Edition.* Introduction by Gordon DeWolf. Savannah: Beehive Press, 1973.

———. *William Bartram The Search for Nature's Design: Selected Art, Letters, &*

Unpublished Writings, ed. Thomas Hallock and Nancy E. Hoffmann. Athens: University of Georgia Press, 2010.

———. *William Bartram on the Southeastern Indians,* ed. Gregory A. Waselkov and Kathryn E. Holland Braund. Lincoln: University of Nebraska Press, 1995.

Candler, Allen D., et al., eds. *The Colonial Records of the State of Georgia.* 30 vols. Atlanta: various printers, 1904–1916, 1979–1982.

Candler, Allen D., comp. *The Revolutionary Records of the State of Georgia.* 3 vols. Atlanta: Franklin, 1908.

Catesby, Mark. *The Natural History of Carolina, Florida and the Bahama Islands.* 2 vols. London: Printed for the author, 1731–1743 [1729–1747].

Coldham, Peter W., comp. *American Loyalist Claims.* Washington, D.C.: National Genealogical Society, 1980.

———. *American Migrations.* Baltimore: Genealogical Publishing Company, 2000.

Collections. 20 vols. Savannah: Georgia Historical Society, 1840–1980.

Corner, Betsy C., and Christopher C. Booth, eds. *Chain of Friendship: Selected Letters of Dr. John Fothergill of London, 1735–1780.* Cambridge, Mass.: Harvard University Press, 1971.

Dalrymple, Fisher, ed. *The Merchant of Manchac: The Letterbooks of John Fitzpatrick, 1768–1790.* Baton Rouge: Louisiana State University Press, 1978.

Darlington, William. *Memorials of John Bartram and Humphry Marshall: With Notices of Their Botanical Contemporaries.* Philadelphia: Lindsay & Blakiston, 1849.

Darwin, Charles. *The Variation of Animals and Plants under Domestication,* 2 vols. London: J. Murray, 1868.

Davidson, Grace G., comp. *Early Records of Georgia: Wilkes County.* 2 vols. Macon: Burke, 1933.

Davies, K. C., ed. *Documents of the American Revolution 1770–1783.* 21 vols. Shannon: Irish University Press, 1972–1981.

Davis, Robert S., ed. "A Georgia Loyalist's Perspective on the American Revolution: The Letters of Thomas Taylor." *Georgia Historical Quarterly* 81 (1997): 118–138.

———. "Letters from St. Paul Parish." *Richmond County History* 10 (Summer 1978): 19–35.

———. *The Wilkes County Papers, 1773–1833.* Easley, S.C.: Southern Historical Press, 1979.

———, comp. *Quaker Records in Georgia.* Augusta: Augusta Genealogical Society, 1986.

De Villiers, Le Baron Marc. "Extrait d'une letter de Diron, datée de Juin, 1721." In "Documents Concernant L'Histoire Des Indiens De La Région Orientale De La Louisiane." *Journal de la Société des Americanistes de Paris* (1922): n.s., vol. 14: 127–140.

De Vries, Hugo. *Die Mutationstheorie: Versuche und Beobachtungen über die En-stehung von Arten im Pflanzenreich.* 2 vols. Leipzig: Veit & Co, 1901–1903.

Drayton, John. *Memoirs of the American Revolution.* 2 vols. 1821; reprint, New York: New York Times and Arno Press, 1969.

Dunbar, William. *Life, Letters, and Papers of Willigam Dunbar of Elgin, Moray-shire, Scotland, and Natchez, Mississippi. Pioneer Scientist of the Southern United States,* ed. Mrs. Dunbar Rowland. Jackson: Press of the Mississippi Historical Society, 1930.

Elliott, Stephen. *A Sketch of the Botany of South-Carolina and Georgia,* 2 vols. Charleston: J. R. Schenk, 1821.

Ewan, Joseph, ed. *William Bartram: Botanical and Zoological Drawings, 1756–1788.* Philadelphia: Memoirs of the American Philosophical Society 74. Philadel-phia: APS, 1968.

Gordon, Harry. "The Journal of Captain Harry Gordon." In *Travels in the American Colonies,* ed. Newton D. Mereness. New York: Macmillan Com-pany, 1916.

Gray, Robert. "Colonel Robert Gray's Observations on the War in Carolina." *South Carolina Historical and Genealogical Magazine* 11 (1910): 139–159.

Hamer, Philip M., et al., eds. *The Papers of Henry Laurens.* 14 vols. Columbia: University of South Carolina Press, 1968–1994.

Hawkins, Benjamin. *The Collected Works of Benjamin Hawkins, 1796–1810,* ed. H. Thomas Foster II. Tuscaloosa: The University of Alabama Press, 2003.

———. "A Sketch of the Creek County in the Years 1798 and 1799." *Collections of the Georgia Historical Society,* vol. 3, no. 1, 1938. Reprint. Americus: Americus Book Company, 1938.

Hemperley, Marion R., comp. *English Crown Grants in St. Paul Parish in Georgia, 1755–1775.* Atlanta: State Printers, 1974.

Hudson, Frank Parker, comp. *A 1790 Census for Wilkes County, Georgia.* Spartan-burg, S.C.: Reprint Company, 1988.

Hulbert, Archer Butler. *The Crown Collection of Photographs of American Maps: A Collection of Original Photographs, Carefully Mounted, of maps important histori-cally yet hitherto unpublished, contained in the British Museum and other foreign Archives especially chosen and prepared to illustrate the early history of America.* Cleveland: Arthur H. Clark Co., 1909.

Hutchins, Thomas. *An Historical Narrative and Topographical Description of Loui-siana and West Florida.* Philadelphia: Robert Aitken, 1784. Reprint. Gaines-ville: University of Florida Press, 1968.

Lamarck, Jean Baptiste Pierre Antoine de Monet de. *Encyclopédie Méthodique: Botanique.* 8 vols. Paris: Panckoucke, 1797.

Lee, William. *The True and Interesting Travels of William Lee.* York, England: T. & R. Hughes, 1818.

Linné, Carl von. *Species plantarum: exhibentes plantas rite cognitas, ad genera rela-*

tas, cum differentiis specificis, nominibus trivialibus, synonymis selectis, locis natali- bus, secundum systema sexuale digestas. Holmiae: Impensis Laurentii Salvii, 1753.

Lister, Martin. *Historiae Sive Synopsis Methodicae Conchyliorum.* London: 1685– 1692.

Milfort, Louis LeClerc. *Memoirs: or a Quick Glance at My Various Travels and My Soujourn in the Creek Nation,* ed. Ben C. McCary. Reprint of 1802 edition. Savannah: Beehive Press, 1959.

Mooney, James. Letter to Isaac Minis Hays; Washington, December 16, 1899. American Indian Manuscript 4167. American Philosophical Society, Philadelphia. Available on-line: http://www.amphilsoc.org/library/guides/indians/info/cha.htm

Mylne, William. *Travels in the Colonies in 1773–1775,* ed. Ted Ruddock. Athens: University of Georgia Press, 1990.

Phelps, Matthew. "Appendix to the Memoirs and Adventures of Captain Phelps." In *Memoirs and Adventures of Captain Matthew Phelps . . . Particularly Two Voyages from Connecticut to the River Mississippi, From December 1773 to October 1780.* Bennington, Vt.: Press of Anthony Haswell, 1802.

Pursh, Frederick. *Flora Americae Septentrionalis.* London: White, Cochrane, and Co., 1814.

Romans, Bernard. *A Concise Natural History of East and West Florida.* ed. and with an Introduction by Kathryn E. Holland Braund. Tuscaloosa: The University of Alabama Press, 1999.

Schöpf, Johann David. *Travels in the Confederation, 1783–1784,* trans. and ed. Alfred J. Morrison. Philadelphia: William J. Campbell, 1911.

Stone, William L., trans. *Letters of Brunswick and Hessian Officers During the American Revolution.* Albany, N.Y.: Joel Munsell's Sons, 1911.

Swan, Caleb. "Position and State of Manners and Arts in the Creek, or Muscogee Nation in 1791." In Volume 5 of *Information Respecting the Condition and Prospects of the Indian Tribes of the United States,* ed. Henry Rowe Schoolcraft, 251–283. Philadelphia: J. B. Lippincott, 1852–1857.

Taitt, David. "David Taitt's Journal to and through the Upper Creek Nation." In *Documents of the American Revolution, 1770–1783,* vol. 5, *Transcripts, 1772,* ed. K. G. Davies, 251–272. Dublin: Irish University Press, 1974.

Temple, Sarah B. Gober. *Georgia Journeys: Being an Account of the Lives of Georgia's Original Settlers and Many Other Early Settlers from the Founding of the Colony in 1732 until the Institution of Royal Government in 1754,* ed. Kenneth Coleman. Athens: University of Georgia Press, 1961.

Wight, Sargeant. "Journal of the Passage of Serj't Wight to the Upper Creek Nation 1771." In *Colonial Captivities, Marches and Journeys,* ed. Isabel M. Calder, 236–243. Port Washington, N.Y.: Kennikat Press, 1967.

Woodward, Thomas. *Woodward's Reminiscences of the Creek, or Muscogee Indians.* Montgomery, Ala.: Barrett & Wimbish, 1859.

Secondary Sources

Alden, John Richard. *John Stuart and the Southern Colonial Frontier: A Study of Indian Relations, War, Trade, and Land Problems in the Southern Wilderness, 1754–1775.* 1944. Reprint. New York: Gordian Press, 1966.

Allen, Ginger M., Michael D. Bond, and Martin B. Main. "50 Common Plants Important in Florida's Ethnobotanical History." Circular 1439. Wildlife Ecology and Conservation Department, Florida Cooperative Extension Service, Institute of Food and Agricultural Sciences, University of Florida, 2002. (Available on-line at http://edis.ifas.ufl.edu/UW152.)

Andres, T. C., and G. P. Nabhan. "Taxonomic Rank and Rarity of *Cucurbita okeechobeensis.*" *FAO/IBPGR Plant Genetic Resources Newsletter* 75/75 (1988): 21–22.

Arnade, Charles. *The Siege of St. Augustine in 1702.* Gainesville: University of Florida Press, 1965.

Ashley, Keith H. "Interaction, Population Movement, and Political Economy: The Changing Social Landscape of Northeastern Florida (A.D. 900–1500)." Ph.D. diss., University of Florida, 2003.

Aten, Lawrence E., and Jerald T. Milanich. "Clarence Bloomfield Moore: A Philadelphia Archaeologist in the Southeastern United States." In *Philadelphia and the Development of Americanist Archaeology,* ed. Don D. Fowler and David R. Wilcox, 113–133. Tuscaloosa: The University of Alabama Press, 2003.

Aufmuth, Joseph L. "Mark Catesby's Travels in La Florida 1722–1726: A Present-Day Mapping Retrospective." In *Opening the Door to a New World: Mark Catesby's Travels in La Florida, 1722–1726,* ed. Arlene Fradkin and Mallory McCane O'Connor. Exhibition catalogue, Schmidt Center Gallery, Florida Atlantic University. Boca Raton: Florida Atlantic University, 2001.

Bailey, L. H. "Species of *Cucurbita.*" *Gentes Herbarium* 6 (1943): 266–322.

Bartram Heritage: A Study of the Life of William Bartram by the Bartram Trail Conference. Montgomery, Ala.: Bartram Trail Conference, 1979.

Beasley, Virgil R., III. "The Location of Edelano, a Timucua Village Encountered by the French Huguenots: 1564–1565." Paper presented at the Southeastern Archaeological Conference, November 5–8, Baton Rouge, Louisiana, 1997.

Berkeley, Edmund, and Dorothy Smith Berkeley. *The Life and Travels of John Bartram: From Lake Ontario to the River St. John.* Tallahassee: University Presses of Florida, 1982.

Bosland, Paul W., and E. J. Votana. *Peppers: Vegetable and Spice Capsicums.* Crop Production Science in Horticulture, #12. New York: CABI Publishing, 2000.

Bradley, Chad O. "The Yuchi Town Site, 1RU63, A Summary of the 1958–1962 Excavations." Report to the National Park Service by Southeastern Archaeological Services, Athens, Georgia, 1994.

Brandon, William P. "The Galphin Claim." *Georgia Historical Quarterly* 15 (1931): 113–141.

Brannon, Peter A. "Report on Trip to Foosichichi, Elmore County, May 1, 1920." Alabama Department of Archives and History, Brannon Manuscript Collection, Report Files.

Braund, Kathryn E. Holland. *Deerskins and Duffels: Creek Indian Trade with Anglo-America, 1685–1815.* Lincoln: University of Nebraska Press, 1993.

Brigham, David R. "Mark Catesby and the Patronage of Natural History." In *Empire's Nature: Mark Catesby's New World Vision,* ed. Amy R. W. Meyers and Margaret Beck Pritchard, 91–146. Chapel Hill: University of North Carolina Press, 1998.

———. "Mark Catesby: The Man and His Work." In *Opening the Door to a New World: Mark Catesby's Travels in La Florida, 1722–1726,* ed. Arlene Fradkin and Mallory McCane O'Connor. Exhibition catalogue, Schmidt Center Gallery, Florida Atlantic University. Boca Raton: Florida Atlantic University, 2001.

Brooks, Richard D., Mark D. Groover, and Samuel C. Smith. *Living on the Edge: The Archaeology of Cattle Raisers in the South Carolina Backcountry.* Columbia: University of South Carolina, 2000.

Brown, James A. "The Mississippian Period." In *Ancient Art of the American Woodland Indians,* 93–140. New York: Harry N. Abrams, 1985.

Brown, Richard Maxwell. *The South Carolina Regulators: The Story of an American Vigilante Movement.* Cambridge, Mass.: Harvard University Press, 1963.

Brown, Wallace. *The Good Americans: The Loyalists in the American Revolution.* New York: William Morrow, 1969.

Calhoon, Robert M. *The Loyalist Perception and Other Essays.* Columbia: University of South Carolina Press, 1989.

Calloway, Colin G. *The Scratch of a Pen: 1763 and the Transformation of North America.* New York: Oxford University Press, 2006.

Capron, Louis. "Notes on the Hunting Dance of the Cow Creek Seminole." *Florida Anthropologist* 9 (1956): 67–78.

Cardwell, Harold D., Sr. "Coontie Root: The Dangerous Blessing." *Florida Anthropologist* 40 (1987): 333–335.

Cashin, Edward J., ed. *Colonial Georgia: "Key of the Indian Country."* Macon, Ga.: Mercer University Press, 1986.

———. *Governor Henry Ellis and the Transformation of British North America.* Athens: University of Georgia Press, 1994.

———. *Lachlan McGillivray, Indian Trader.* Athens: University of Georgia Press, 1992.

———. "Sowing the Wind: Governor Wright and the Georgia Backcountry on the Eve of the Revolution." In *Forty Years of Diversity: Essays on Colonial*

Georgia, ed. Harvey H. Jackson and Phinizy Spalding, 233–250. Athens: University of Georgia Press, 1984.

———. *The King's Ranger: Thomas Brown and the American Revolution on the Southern Frontier.* Athens: University of Georgia Press, 1989.

———. *William Bartram and the American Revolution on the Southern Frontier.* Columbia: University of South Carolina Press, 2000.

Chesnutt, David R. *South Carolina's Expansion into Colonial Georgia, 1720–1765.* New York: Garland Publishing, 1989.

Cofer, Loris D. *Queensborough or the Irish Town and Its Citizens.* Louisville, Ga.: The Author, 1977.

Coile, N. C. *Florida's Endangered and Threatened Plants.* Florida Department of Agriculture and Consumer Services, Division of Plant Industry, Bureau of Entomology, Nematology, and Plant Pathology, Botany Section Contribution No. 29. Gainesville, Florida, 1993.

Cottier, John W. "The Display and Analysis of Spatial Data from Hoithlewaulee. In *Cultural Change on the Creek Indian Frontier,* ed. Gregory A. Waselkov, 34–55. Report to the National Science Foundation (Grant No. BSN-8305437). Auburn University, 1985.

———. "Field Records, Hickory Ground Site (1EE89) Archaeology Investigations." Auburn University: Auburn University Archaeology Laboratory, 2006.

———, and Craig T. Sheldon, Jr. "Field Records, Fusihatchee (1EE191) Archaeological Investigations." Auburn and Montgomery, Ala.: Auburn University Archaeological Laboratories, 1996.

Cox, Isaac Joslin. *The West Florida Controversy, 1798–1813.* Gloucester, Mass.: Peter Smith, 1967.

Culin, Stewart. "Games of the North American Indians." In *Twenty-fourth Annual Report of the Bureau of American Ethnology.* Washington, D.C.: Government Printing Office, 1907.

Cumming, William P. *British Maps of Colonial America.* Chicago: University of Chicago Press, 1974.

Davis, Harold. *The Fledgling Province: Social and Cultural Life in Colonial Georgia, 1733–1776.* Chapel Hill: University of North Carolina Press, 1976.

Davis, Mary B. *Field Notes of Clarence B. Moore's Southeast Archaeological Expeditions, 1891–1918: A Guide to the Microfilm Edition.* Bronx, N.Y.: Huntington Free Library, 1987.

Davis, Robert S. "A Frontier for Pioneer Revolutionaries: John Dooly and the Beginnings of Popular Democracy in Original Wilkes County." *Georgia Historical Quarterly* 60 (Fall 2006): 315–349.

———. "George Galphin and the Creek Congress of 1777." *Proceedings and Papers of the Georgia Association of Historians 1982.* Atlanta: GAH, 1982.

———. "Lessons from Kettle Creek: Patriotism and Loyalism at Askance on the

Southern Frontier." *Journal of Backcountry Studies* 1 (1) (May 2006), n. p. (online journal): http://www.uncg.edu/~rmcalhoo/jbs/.

Decker, D. S., and L. A. Newsom. "Numerical Analysis of Archaeological *Cucurbita pepo* seeds from Hontoon Island, Florida." *Journal of Ethnobiology* 8 (1988): 35–44.

DeRosier, Arthur H., Jr. *William Dunbar: Scientific Pioneer of the Old Southwest.* Lexington: University Press of Kentucky, 2007.

DeVorsey, Louis, Jr. "Early Maps as a Source in the Reconstruction of Southern Indian Landscapes." In *Red, White, and Black: Symposium on Indians in the Old South,* ed. Charles M. Hudson, 12–30. Southern Anthropological Society Proceedings, no. 5. Athens: University of Georgia Press, 1971.

———. *The Indian Boundary in the Southern Colonies, 1763–1775.* Chapel Hill: University of North Carolina Press, 1966.

De Vries, Hugo. "Mass mutations and twin hybrids of *Oenothera grandiflora* Ait." *Botanical Gazette* 65 (May 1918): 377–422.

Dictionary of American Biography. Ed. Dumas Malone. 22 vols. (New York: Charles Scribner's Sons, 1932), vol. 9.

Earnest, Ernest. *John and William Bartram, Botanists and Explorers.* Philadelphia: University of Pennsylvania Press, 1940.

Elman, Robert. *First in the Field: America's Pioneering Naturalists.* New York: Mason/Charter, 1977.

Fabel, Robin F. A. "An Eighteenth Colony: Dreams for Mississippi on the Eve of the Revolution." *Journal of Southern History* 59 (November 1993): 647–672.

———. *The Economy of British West Florida, 1763–1783.* Tuscaloosa: The University of Alabama Press, 1988.

Fairbanks, Charles H. "The Function of Black Drink Among the Creeks." In *Black Drink: A Native American Tea,* ed. Charles M. Hudson, 120–149. Athens: University of Georgia Press, 1979.

Faulkner, Charles H. "Chapter 14: Structural Analysis." In "Following in the Footsteps of Gordon R. Willey, Excavations at the Town of Kasita (9CE1)," 439–461. Report to the Headquarters United States Army Infantry Center by Panamerican Consultants, Inc. (Contract No. DABT10-01-D-017), 2004.

———. "The Winter House: an Early Southern Tradition." *Midcontinental Journal of Archaeology* 2 (1977): 41–59.

Feduccia, Alan, ed. *Catesby's Birds of Colonial America.* Chapel Hill: University of North Carolina Press, 1985.

Fendly, Owen. "George Galphin." In Kenneth Coleman and Charles Stephen Gurr, eds., *Dictionary of Georgia Biography,* 2 vols. Athens: University of Georgia Press, 1983.

Fradkin, Arlene, and Mallory McCane O'Connor, eds. *Opening the Door to a*

New World: Mark Catesby's Travels in La Florida, 1722–1726. Exhibition catalogue, Schmidt Center Gallery, Florida Atlantic University. Boca Raton:
Florida Atlantic University, 2001.

Frazier, Charles. *Cold Mountain: A Novel.* New York: Atlantic Monthly Press,
1997.

Frick, George Frederick, and Raymond Phineas Stearns. *Mark Catesby: The Colonial Audubon.* Urbana: University of Illinois Press, 1961.

Fry, Joel T. "An International Catalogue of North American Trees and Shrubs:
The Bartram Broadside, 1783." *Journal of Garden History* 16, 1 (January–March
1996): 3–66.

————. "Historic American Landscapes Survey, John Bartram House and Garden (Bartram's Garden), HALS No. PA-1, History Report," MS report,
U.S. Department of the Interior, National Park Service, HABS/HAER/
HALS/CRGIS Division, Washington, D.C., 2004. Available on-line at:
http://memory.loc.gov/cgi-bin/query/S?ammem/
hh:@FIELD(OTHER+@od1(+fry,+joel+t+,+historian+)).

Fusihatchee (1EE191), Archaeological Field Records, Auburn University Montgomery Archaeological Laboratory, Montgomery, Alabama.

Gallay, Alan. *Jonathan Bryan and the Southern Colonial Frontier: The Formation of
a Plantation Elite.* Athens: University of Georgia Press, 1989.

Galloway, Patricia, ed. *The Southeastern Ceremonial Complex: Artifacts and
Analysis.* Lincoln: University of Nebraska Press, 1989.

Gannon, Michael, ed. *The New History of Florida.* Gainesville: University Press
of Florida, 1996.

Garrison, Webb. *Oglethorpe's Folly: The Birth of Georgia,* Lakemont, GA: Copple
House Books, 1981.

Gates, R. R. "Early Historico-Botanical Records of the Oenotheras." *Proceedings
of the Iowa Academy of Science for 1910.* Vol. 17:85–124.

Godfrey, Robert K. *Trees, Shrubs, and Woody Vines of Northern Florida and Adjacent Georgia and Alabama.* Athens: University of Georgia Press, 1988.

————, and Jean W. Wooten. *Aquatic and Wetland Plants of Southeastern United
States: Dicotyledons.* Athens: University of Georgia Press, 1981.

————. *Aquatic and Wetland Plants of Southeastern United States: Monocotyledons.*
Athens: University of Georgia Press, 1979.

Goff, John H. "The Buffalo in Georgia." *Georgia Review* 11 (January 1957): 19–29.

Goggin, John M. *Space and Time Perspectives in Northern St. Johns Archeology,
Florida.* Yale University Publications in Anthropology 47. New Haven, Conn.:
Yale University Press, 1952.

————. *Spanish Majolica in the New World.* Yale University Publications in Anthropology 72. New Haven, Conn.: Yale University Press, 1968.

Gums, Bonnie L. "Earthfast (Pieux en Terre) Structures at Old Mobile." In

"French Colonial Archaeology at Old Mobile: Selected Studies," *Historical Archaeology* 36 (1): 13–25.

Hahn, Steven C. *The Invention of the Creek Nation, 1670–1763.* Lincoln: University of Nebraska Press, 2004.

Halbert, H. S. "Bernard Romans' Map of 1772." In *Publications of the Mississippi Historical Society*, vol. 6, ed. Franklin L. Riley, 415–439. Oxford, Miss.: Printed for the Society, 1902.

Hallock, Thomas. *From the Fallen Tree: Frontier Narratives, Environmental Politics, and the Roots of a National Pastoral, 1749–1826.* Chapel Hill: University of North Carolina Press, 2003.

Hally, David J. "Archaeology and Settlement of the King Site" In *The King Site: Continuity and Contacts in Sixteenth-Century Georgia*, ed. Robert L. Blakely, 3–16. Athens: University of Georgia Press, 1988.

———. "As Caves Below the Ground; Making Sense of Aboriginal House Form in the Protohistoric and Historic Southeast." In *Between Contacts and Colonies*, ed. Cameron B. Wesson and Mark A. Rees, 90–109. Tuscaloosa: The University of Alabama Press, 2002.

Hanley, Wayne. *Natural History in America: From Mark Catesby to Rachel Carson.* New York: Quadrangle/The New York Times Book Co., 1977.

Hann, John H. "Summary Guide to Spanish Florida Missions and Visitas with Churches in the Sixteenth and Seventeenth Centuries." *The Americas* 46 (1990): 417–513.

Harper, Francis. "Other Early Investigations by Naturalists on Bartram's Route of 1765–66." In Introduction, "Diary of a Journey Through the Carolinas, Georgia, and Florida, from July 1, 1765, to April 10, 1766," edited and annotated by Francis Harper, *Transactions of the American Philosophical Society*, new series, vol. 33, part 1, 5–8. Philadelphia: APS, 1942.

———. "Proposals for Publishing Bartram's *Travels*." *American Philosophical Society Library Bulletin 1943–1945*, 27–28.

Hendrick, J. Edwin. *Charles Thomson and the Making of a New Nation.* Canbury, N.J.: Associated University Presses, 1979.

Herbst, Josephine. *New Green World.* New York: Hastings House, 1954.

Hicks, Theresa M. *South Carolina Indians and Indian Traders.* Spartanburg, S.C.: Reprint Company, 1998.

Hindle, Brooke. *The Pursuit of Science in Revolutionary America, 1735–1789.* Chapel Hill: Published for the Institute of Early American History and Culture, 1956.

Hine, Robert V. *Community on the American Frontier: Separate but not Alone.* Norman: University of Oklahoma Press, 1980.

Hitz, Alex M. "The Earliest Settlements in Wilkes County." *Georgia Historical Quarterly* 40 (1956): 261–265.

Hoffmann, Nancy E. "The Construction of William Bartram's Narrative Natural History: A Genetic Text of the Draft Manuscript for 'Travels through North and South Carolina, Georgia, East and West Florida'." Ph.D. diss., University of Pennsylvania, 1996.

——, and John C. Van Horne, eds. *America's Curious Botanist: A Tercentennial Reappraisal of John Bartram, 1699–1777.* Philadelphia: Publications of the American Philosophical Society, 2004.

Horsman, Reginald. *Josiah Nott of Mobile: Southerner, Physician, and Racial Theorist.* Baton Rouge: Louisiana State University Press, 1987.

Howard, Clinton. "Colonial Natchez: The Early British Period." *Journal of Mississippi History* (July 1945): 163–170.

Howard, James H. *The Southeastern Ceremonial Complex and Its Interpretation.* Memoir of the Missouri Archaeological Society, No. 6. Columbus: Missouri Archaeological Society, 1968.

Howard, Richard A., and George W. Staples, "The Modern Names for Catesby's Plants." *Journal of the Arnold Arboretum* 64 (1983): 511–546.

Hudson, Charles M. *Elements of Southeastern Indian Religion.* Leiden: E. J. Brill, 1984.

——, ed. *The Black Drink: A Native American Tea.* Athens: University of Georgia Press, 1979.

——. *The Southeastern Indians.* Knoxville: University of Tennessee Press, 1976.

Irmscher, Christoph. *The Poetics of Natural History from John Bartram to William James.* New Brunswick, N.J.: Rutgers University Press, 1999.

Jackson, Jason Baird. *Yuchi Ceremonial Life: Performance, Meaning, and Tradition in a Contemporary American Indian Community.* Lincoln: University of Nebraska Press, 2003.

Jackson, Paul D., ed. "Following in the Footsteps of Gordon R. Willey, Excavations at the Town of Kasita (9CE1)." Report to the Headquarters United States Army Infantry Center by Panamerican Consultants (Contract No. DABT10-01-D-0017), 2004.

Johnson, Sherry. "Hurricanes in Cuba." George E. Pozzetta Lecture, 1 December 2006. History Department, University of Florida, Gainesville.

Jones, B. Calvin, and Louis D. Tesar. *1985–1995 Survey, Salvage and Mitigation of Archaeological Resources within the Mount Royal Site (8PU35) Village Area, Putnam County, Florida.* Tallahassee: Florida Bureau of Archaeological Research, 2001.

——, and Jonathan Lammers. "Calvin Jones: Comments and Commentary, Video-Taped Interview Excerpts." Transcription by Louis D. Tesar and Jonathan Lammers. *Florida Anthropologist* 51 (1998): 79–128.

Jones, Charles C., Jr. *Antiquities of the Southern Indians, Particularly of the Georgia Tribes.* D. New York: Appleton Company, 1873.

Jones, George Fenwick. *The Salzburger Saga.* Athens: University of Georgia Press, 1984.

Jones, Mark H. "Herman Husband: Millenarian, Carolina Regulator, and Whiskey Rebel." Ph.D. diss., Northern Illinois University, 1982.

Kartesz, John T. *A Synonymized Checklist of the Vascular Flora of the United States, Canada, and Greenland.* 2nd ed. 2 vols. Portland, Ore.: Timber Press, 1994.

Kastner, Joseph. *A World of Naturalists.* Great Britain: John Murray, 1978.

Kierner, Cynthia A. "Hospitality, Sociability, and Gender in the Southern Colonies." *Journal of Southern History* 62 (August 1996): 449–480.

Klinkenberg, J. "Seeds of Doubt." *St. Petersburg Times,* November 28, 1993, Section F, 1 & 6.

Knight, Vernon James, Jr. "Feasting and the Emergence of Platform Mound Ceremonialism in Eastern North America." In *Feasts: Archaeological and Ethnographic Perspectives on Food, Politics, and Power,* ed. Michael Dietler and Brian Hayden, 311–333. Washington, D.C.: Smithsonian Institution Press, 2001.

———. "The Institutional Organization of Mississippian Religion." *American Antiquity* 51 (1986): 675–687.

———. "Symbolism of Mississippian Mounds." In *Powhatan's Mantle: Indians in the Colonial Southeast,* ed. P. H. Wood, G. A. Waselkov and M. T. Hatley, 279–291. Lincoln: University of Nebraska Press, 1989.

———. "Tukabatchee: Archaeological Investigations at an Historic Creek Town, Elmore County, Alabama." Report of Investigations 45, Office of Archaeological Research, Alabama Museum of Natural History, The University of Alabama, 1985.

Kiernan, Vincent. "An Encyclopedic Data Base about Plants Will Soon Flower on the Internet." *Chronicle of Higher Education* 46, 1 (1999): A33.

Laird, Mark. *The Flowering of the Landscape Garden, English Pleasure Grounds, 1720–1800.* Philadelphia: University of Pennsylvania Press, 1999.

Logan, John H. *A History of the Upper Country of South Carolina from the Earliest Period to the Close of the War of Independence,* 2 vols. Charleston, S.C.: S. G. Courtney & Co., 1859.

Lorant, Stefan. *The New World, the First Pictures of America.* New York: Duell, Sloan & Pearce, 1946.

Maier, Charles S. *Among Empires: American Ascendancy and Its Predecessors* (Cambridge, Mass.: Harvard University Press, 2006.

McBurney, Henrietta. *Mark Catesby's Natural History of America: The Watercolors from the Royal Library, Windsor Castle.* London: Merrell Holberton, 1997.

———. "Mark Catesby's Techniques as a Draftsman and Printmaker." In *Opening the Door to a New World: Mark Catesby's Travels in La Florida, 1722–1726,* ed. Arlene Fradkin and Mallory McCane O'Connor. Exhibition catalogue, Schmidt Center Gallery, Florida Atlantic University. Boca Raton: Florida Atlantic University, 2001.

MacDougal, D. T., A. M. Vail, and G. H. Shull. *Mutations, Variations, and Relationships of the Oenotheras,* Publication No. 81. Washington, D.C.: Carnegie Institution of Washington, 1907.

———, and J. K. Small. *Mutants and Hybrids of the Oenotheras.* Publication No. 24. Washington, D.C.: Carnegie Institution of Washington, 1905.

Magee, Judith. *The Art and Science of William Bartram.* University Park: Pennsylvania State University Press in association with the Natural History Museum, London, 2007.

Manning, Harvey. *Mountaineering: The Freedom of the Hills.* Seattle, Wash.: Mountaineers Books, 1967.

Manning, Martin J. *William Wadden Turner.* American National Biography Online. http://www.anb.org/articles/20/20-01644-article.html

Martin, Jack B., and Margaret McKane Maudlin. *A Dictionary of Creek/ Muskogee.* Lincoln: University of Nebraska Press, 2000.

Meltzer, David J. "Introduction: Ephraim Squier, Edwin Davis, and the Making of an American Archaeological Classic." In *Ancient Monuments of the Mississippi Valley,* ed. E. G. Squier and E. H. Davis, 1–98. Washington, D.C.: Smithsonian Institution Press, 1998.

Merrill, E. D. "In Defense of the Validity of William Bartram's Binomials." *Bartonia* 23(1944): 10–35.

Meyers, Amy R. W. "'The Perfecting of Natural History': Mark Catesby's Drawings of American Flora and Fauna in the Royal Library, Windsor Castle." In Henrietta McBurney, *Mark Catesby's Natural History of America: The Watercolors from the Royal Library, Windsor Castle,* 11–25. London: Merrell Holberton, 1997.

———. "Sketches from the Wilderness: Changing Conceptions of Nature in American Natural History Illustration: 1680–1880." 2 vols. Ph.D. diss., Yale University, 1985.

———, and Margaret Beck Pritchard. "Introduction: Toward an Understanding of Catesby." In *Empire's Nature: Mark Catesby's New World Vision,* ed. Amy R. W. Meyers and Margaret Beck Pritchard, 1–33. Chapel Hill and London: University of North Carolina Press, 1998.

Meyers, Amy R. Weinstein. "Sketches from the Wilderness: Changing Conceptions of Nature in American Natural History Illustration: 1680–1880." 2 vols. Ph.D. diss., Yale University, 1985.

Milanich, Jerald T. *Archaeology of Precolumbian Florida.* Gainesville: University Press of Florida, 1994.

———. *The Timucua*. Oxford: Blackwell Publishers, 1996.

———, ed. *Famous Florida Sites: Mt. Royal and Crystal River*. Gainesville: University Press of Florida, 1999.

———. *Frolicking Bears, Wet Vultures, and Other Oddities: A New York City Journalist in Nineteenth-Century Florida*. Gainesville: University Press of Florida, 2005.

Miller, Charles A. *Jefferson and Nature: An Interpretation*. Baltimore: Johns Hopkins University Press, 1988.

Miller, James J. *An Environmental History of Northeast Florida*. Gainesville: University Press of Florida, 1998.

Mitchem, Jeffrey M. "Introduction: Clarence B. Moore's Research in East Florida, 1873–1896." In *The East Florida Expeditions of Clarence Bloomfield Moore*, ed. Jeffrey M. Mitchem, 1–52. Tuscaloosa: The University of Alabama Press, 1999.

Moore, Clarence B. "Certain Shell Heaps of the St. John's River, Florida, hitherto Unexplored." (Second Paper) *American Naturalist* 27 (1893): 8–13, 113–117.

———. "Certain Sand Mounds of the St. John's River, Florida, Part I." *Journal of the Academy of Natural Sciences of Philadelphia* 10 (1894): 5–128.

———. "Certain Sand Mounds of the St. John's River, Florida, Part II." *Journal of the Academy of Natural Sciences of Philadelphia* 10 (1894): 129–246.

Moore, L. Hugh. "The Aesthetic Theory of William Bartram." *Essays in Arts & Sciences* 12 (March 1983): 17–35.

Morton, Samuel G. *Crania Americana*. Philadelphia: Dobson, 1838.

Mráček, Jaroslav. "Investigation of interspecific genome-plastome incompatibility in Oenothera and Passiflora." Ph.D. diss., Biology Faculty, Ludwig-Maximilians University, Munich, 2005.

Muller, Dianne S. "Intrasite Settlement at the Historic Creek Town of Hickory Ground (1EE89), Elmore County, Alabama (1990–1991)." *Journal of Alabama Archaeology* 41 (1995): 107–136.

Myers, Ronald L., and John J. Ewel, eds. *Ecosystems of Florida*. Orlando: University of Central Florida Press, 1990.

Nahbah, Gary Paul. "Lost Gourds and Spent Soils on the Shores of Okeechobee." In *Enduring Seeds: Native American Agriculture and Wild Plant Conservation*, 135–203. San Francisco: North Point Press, 1989.

Natural History Museum. *The John Clayton Herbarium*. London: Natural History Museum. http://www.nhm.ac.uk/research-curation/projects/clayton-herbarium/ (accessed 2008).

———. *The Linnaean Plant Name Typification Project*. London: Natural History Museum. http://www.nhm.ac.uk/research-curation/projects/linnaean-typification/ (accessed 2008).

Nichols, Ashton, ed. *Romantic Natural Histories: William Wordsworth, Charles Darwin, and Others*. Boston: Houghton Mifflin, 2004.

O'Malley, Therese. "Mark Catesby and the Culture of Gardens." In *Empire's Nature: Mark Catesby's New World Vision,* ed. Amy R. Meyers and Margaret Beck Pritchard, 147–183. Chapel Hill: University of North Carolina Press, 1998.

Overmyer, Grace. *America's First Hamlet.* New York: New York University Press, 1957.

Parrish, Susan Scott. *American Curiosity: Cultures of Natural History in the Colonial British Atlantic World.* Chapel Hill: University of North Carolina Press, 2006.

Porter, Charlotte M. "An Eighteenth-Century Flower Child: William Bartram." In *Paradise Lost? The Environmental History of Florida,* ed. Jack E. Davis and Raymond Arsenault, 47–71. Gainesville: University Presses of Florida, 2005.

———. "Mark Catesby's Audience and Patrons." In *Opening the Door to a New World: Mark Catesby's Travels in La Florida, 1722–1726,* ed. Arlene Fradkin and Mallory McCane O'Connor, 12–13. Exhibition catalogue, Schmidt Center Gallery, Florida Atlantic University. Boca Raton: Florida Atlantic University, 2001.

———. "William Bartram's Travels in the Indian Nations." *Florida Historical Quarterly* 70, 4 (April 1992): 436–440.

Porter, Robert Shig, II. "The Noblest Offspring: Concerning the British Origins of the Eighteenth-Century Colony of Georgia." M.A. thesis, Armstrong Atlantic State University, 2005.

Presley, Delma E. "The Crackers of Georgia." *Georgia Historical Quarterly* 60 (Summer 1976): 102–116.

Quattrocchi, Anna Margaret. "Thomas Hutchins, 1730–1789." Ph.D. diss., University of Pittsburgh, 1944.

Quinn, David B., ed. "Major Spanish Searches in Eastern North America: Franco-Spanish Clash." In *Florida: The Beginnings of Spanish Florida. New American World: A Documentary History of North America to 1612,* vol. 2. New York: Arno Press, 1979.

Randolph, J. Ralph. *British Travelers Among the Southern Indians, 1660–1763.* Norman: University of Oklahoma Press, 1973.

Ready, Milton L. "Philanthropy and the Origins of Georgia." In *Forty Years of Diversity: Essays on Colonial Georgia,* ed. Harvey H. Jackson and Phinizy Spalding, 46–59. Athens: University of Georgia Press, 1984.

Robertson, Heard. "The Second British Occupation of Augusta." *Georgia Historical Quarterly* 58 (1974): 422–446.

Rodning, Christopher B. "William Bartram and the Archaeology of the Appalachian Summit." In *Between Contacts and Colonies,* ed. Cameron B. Wesson and Mark A. Rees, 67–89. Tuscaloosa: The University of Alabama Press, 2002.

Peterson, Roger Tory. *A Field Guide to the Birds: A Completely New Guide to All the Birds of Eastern and Central North America.* 4th edition. Boston: Houghton Mifflin, 1980.

Russell, Bertrand. "A Free Man's Worship." was first published in 1903. *Modern History Sourcebook,* http://www.fordham.edu/halsall/mod/1917russell-worship.html (accessed October 2008).

Sangster, Dess L., and Tom Sangster, comps. *Fort Mims and the Tensaw Settlement.* 3rd printing, 2nd revision. Bay Minette, Ala.: Lavender Publishing, 1998.

Schorger, A. W. *The Passenger Pigeon: Its Natural History and Extinction.* Norman: University of Oklahoma Press, 1973.

———. *The Wild Turkey: Its History and Domestication.* Norman: University of Oklahoma Press, 1966.

Schroedl, Gerald F., ed. "Overhill Cherokee Archaeology at Chota-Tannasee." University of Tennessee, Department of Anthropology, Report of Investigations 38. Knoxville: University of Tennessee, 1986.

Scott, Robert J. "Chapter 15: Characterizing Domestic Activities." In "Following in the Footsteps of Gordon R. Willey, Excavations at the Town of Kasita (9CE1)," 463–475. (Contract No. DABT10-01-D-0017.) Report to the Headquarters United States Army Infantry Center by Panamerican Consultants, 2004.

Sheldon, Craig T., Jr. "The Council Houses of Fusihatchee." In *Archaeological Excavations at the Early Historic Creek Town of Fusihatchee (Phase I, 1988–1989),* ed. Gregory A. Waselkov, John W. Cottier, and Craig T. Sheldon Jr., 45–76. Report to the National Science Foundation 1990. Grant no. BNS-8718934.

———. "Historic Creek 'Summer' Houses of Central Alabama." Paper presented at the 40th meeting of the Southeastern Archaeological Conference, Nashville, Tennessee, 1997.

———. "Public Architecture of the Historic Creeks." Paper presented at the 33rd meeting of the Southeastern Archaeological Conference, Mobile, Alabama, 1990.

———. "The Square Ground at Fusihatchee in Central Alabama." Paper presented at the 45th meeting of the Southeastern Archaeological Conference, Biloxi, Mississippi, 2002.

———, Ned J. Jenkins, and Gregory A. Waselkov. "French Habitations at the Alabama Post, ca. 1720–1763." *Archéologiques, Collection Hosr-Série* 2 (2008): 112–127.

Sherman, Stuart. *Telling Time: Clocks, Diaries, and English Diurnal Form, 1660–1785.* Chicago: University of Chicago Press, 1996.

Shi, David E. *The Simple Life: Plain Living and High Thinking in American Culture.* New York: Oxford University Press, 1985.

Shy, John. *A People Numerous and Armed: Reflections on the Military Struggle for American Independence.* Rev. ed. Ann Arbor: University of Michigan Press, 1990.

Slaughter, Thomas P. *The Natures of John and William Bartram.* New York: Alfred A. Knopf, 1996.

Small, J. K. "Exploration in the Everglades and on the Florida Keys." *Journal of the New York Botanical Garden* 15 (1914): 63–79.

———. "Narrative of a Cruise to Lake Okeechobee." *American Museum Journal* 18 (1918): 685–700.

———. "The Okeechobee Gourd." *Journal of the New York Botanical Garden* 31 (1930): 10–14.

———. "Wild Pumpkins." *Journal of the New York Botanical Garden* 23 (1922): 19–23.

Smith, Andrew F. *The Turkey: An American Story.* Urbana: University of Illinois Press, 2006.

Squier, Ephraim G. *Aboriginal Monuments of the State of New York.* Smithsonian Contributions to Knowledge, vol. 2. Washington, D.C.: Smithsonian Institution, 1851.

———. "Observations on the Uses of the Mounds of the West, with an Attempt at their Classification." *American Journal of Science and Arts* 3 (1847): 237–248.

———. "Serpent Symbol and the Worship of the Reciprocal Principles of Nature in America." *American Archaeological Researches,* vol. 1. New York: Putnam, 1851.

———, and Edwin H. Davis. *Ancient Monuments of the Mississippi Valley.* Edited and with an Introduction by D. J. Meltzer. Washington, D.C.: Smithsonian Institution Press, 1998.

Stearns, Raymond Phineas. *Science in the British Colonies of America.* Urbana: University of Illinois Press, 1970.

Stubbe, W., and E. Steiner. "Inactivation of Pollen and other effects of genome-plastome incompatibility in Oenothera." *Plant Systematics and Evolution* 217 (1999): 259–277.

Swanton, John R. "Coonti." *American Anthropologist,* New Series 15 (January–March 1913): 141–142.

———. "Social Organization and Social Usages of the Indians of the Creek Confederacy." In *Forty-Second Annual Report of the Bureau of American Ethnology,* 27–472. Washington, D.C.: Government Printing Office, 1928.

———. "The Creek Indians as Mound Builders." *American Anthropologist* New series, 14 (April–June 1912): 320–324.

———. "The Interpretation of Aboriginal Mounds by Means of Creek Indian Customs." In *Forty-First Annual Report of the Bureau of American Ethnology,* 495–506. Washington, D.C.: Government Printing Office, 1927.

Sweet, Julie Anne. "The Thirteenth Colony in Perspective: Historian's Views on Early Georgia." *Georgia Historical Quarterly* 85 (Fall 2001): 435–460.

Taylor, R. J., Jr. Foundation. *An Index to Georgia Colonial Conveyances and Confiscated Land Records, 1750–1804.* Atlanta, Ga.: The Author, 1981.

University of Florida Digital Library Center. *The Bartrams' Florida.* Gainesville: University of Florida Libraries. http://www.uflib.ufl.edu/digital/collections/bartram/default.htm. (accessed 2008).

University of Florida Libraries. *The Roving Naturalist.* Gainesville: University of Florida Libraries. http://www.uflib.ufl.edu/UFDC/?s=bart. (accessed 2008).

Vail, Anna Murray. "*Onagra grandiflora* (Ait.): A Species to be Included in the North American Flora." *Torreya* 5 (1905): 9–10.

Volmer, Stephanie. "Planting a New World: Letters and Languages of Trans-atlantic Botanical Exchange, 1733–1777." Ph.D. diss., Rutgers University, 2008.

Waller, Donna. "Mark Catesby's Legacy." In *Opening the Door, Opening the Door to a New World: Mark Catesby's Travels in La Florida, 1722–1726,* ed. Arlene Fradkin and Mallory McCane O'Connor, Exhibition catalogue, Schmidt Center Gallery, Florida Atlantic University. Boca Raton: Florida Atlantic University, 2001.

Walters, T. W., and D. S. Decker-Walters. "Systematics of the Endangered Okeechobee Gourd (*Cucurbita okeechobeensis: Cucurbitaceae*)." *Systematic Botany* 18 (1993): 175–187.

Walters, T. W., D. S. Decker-Walters, and S. Katz. "Seeking the Elusive Okee-chobee Gourd." *Fairchild Tropical Garden Bulletin* (January 1992): 22–30.

Ward, D. B. "Okeechobee Gourd." In *Rare and Endangered Biota of Florida,* ed. Peter C. H. Pritchard, 6 vols., 5:81–83. Gainesville: University Presses of Florida, 1979.

———, and Marc C. Minno. "Rediscovery of the Endangered Okeechobee Gourd (*Cucurbita okeechobeensis*) along the St. Johns River, Florida, where last reported by William Bartram in 1774." *Castanea* 67 (2002): 201–206.

Waselkov, Gregory A. "A History of the Alabama Anthropological Society." *Southeastern Archaeology* 13 (1994): 64–76.

———. "Changing Strategies of Indian Field Location in the Early Historic Southeast." In *People, Plants, and Landscapes, Studies in Paleobotany,* ed. Kristen J. Gremillion, 179–195. Tuscaloosa: The University of Alabama Press, 1997.

———. "Historic Creek Architectural Adaptations to the Deerskin Trade." In *Archaeological Excavations at the Early Historic Creek Town of Fusihatchee (Phase I, 1988–1989),* ed. Gregory A. Waselkov, John W. Cottier, and Craig T. Sheldon Jr., 39–41. Report to the National Science Foundation, 1990. Grant no. BNS-8718934.

———. "Introduction: Recent Archaeological and Historical Research." In

Fort Toulouse: The French Outpost at the Alabama on the Coosa, ed. Daniel H. Thomas, vii–xlii. Tuscaloosa: The University of Alabama Press, 1989.

———. "Lower Tallapoosa River Cultural Resources Survey, Phase I Report." Report to Alabama Historical Commission, Montgomery, 1981.

———, and Bonnie L. Gums. *Plantation Archaeology at Rivère aux Chiens, ca. 1725–1848.* Mobile: University of South Alabama Center for Archaeological Studies, 2000.

———, and Marvin T. Smith. "Upper Creek Archaeology." In *Indians of the Greater Southeast, Historic Archaeology and Ethnohistory*, ed. Bonnie G. McEwan, 242–264. Gainesville: University Press of Florida, 2000.

Weeks, Stephen B. *Southern Quakers and Slavery: A Study in Institutional History.* New York: Bergman, 1896.

Wilbur, Robert L. "Identification of the Plants Illustrated and Described in Catesby's *Natural History of the Carolinas, Florida and the Bahamas.*" *SIDA, Contributions to Botany* 14 (1990): 29–48.

Williams, Mark. *Archaeological Excavations at Scull Shoals Mounds.* Cultural Resources Report 6. U.S. Forest Service, Southern Region, 1984.

———. *Archaeological Excavations at Scull Shoals Mounds (9GE4): 1983–1985.* LAMAR Institute Publication 1. Watkinsville, Ga.: LAMAR Institute, 1992.

———. *Archaeological Excavations at Shoulderbone Mounds and Village, 9HK1.* LAMAR Institute Publication 3. Watkinsville, Ga.: LAMAR Institute, 1990.

Wilson, Alexander. *American Ornithology: or, The natural history of birds of the United States. With a sketch of the author's life, by George Ord.* New York: Harrison Hall; Philadelphia: Collins & Co., 1828.

Wilson, David Scofield. *In the Presence of Nature.* Amherst: University of Massachusetts Press, 1978.

Wilson, James Grant, and John Fiske, eds. *Appleton's Cyclopedia of American Biography.* 6 vols. New York: D. Appleton and Company, 1887. Online at http://www.famousamericans.net/.

Wood, Betty. *Slavery in Colonial Georgia, 1730–1775.* Athens: University of Georgia Press, 1984.

Worral, Arthur J. *Quakers in the Colonial Northeast.* Hanover: University Press of New England, 1980.

Worth, John E. *The Timucuan Chiefdoms of Spanish Florida*, vol. 2. *Resistance and Destruction.* Gainesville: University Press of Florida, 1998.

Wright, J. Leitch, Jr. *Creeks and Seminoles: Destruction and Regeneration of the Muscogulge People.* Lincoln: University of Nebraska Press, 1986.

Wright, Muriel H. "American Indian Corn Dishes." *Chronicles of Oklahoma* 36 (1958): 155–166.

Wunderlin, Richard P. *Guide to the Vascular Plants of Florida.* Gainesville: University Press of Florida, 1998.

———, and B. F. Hansen. *Atlas of Florida Vascular Plants.* Tampa: Institute for Systematic Botany, University of South Florida. http://www.plantatlas.usf .edu/. S. M. Landry and K. N. Campbell (application development), Tampa: Florida Center for Community Design and Research, University of South Florida (accessed 2005). A newer beta test version is available at http:// www.plantatlasbeta.usf.edu/ (accessed 2008).

Wyman, Jeffries. "Fresh-water Shell Mounds of the St. Johns River, Florida." *Peabody Academy of Science Memoir* 4:3–94. Salem, Mass., 1875.

Contributors

Michael Bond is a county Extension agent for the Seminole Indian Tribe of Florida. He works on youth and plant related projects and is regularly asked to speak to audiences about the Florida Seminoles and their history of plant use. He is also coauthor of *50 Ethnobotanical Plants That Played an Important Role in Florida's History*.

Kathryn E. Holland Braund, professor of History at Auburn University, specializes in the early history of the Creek and Seminole Indians. She is the author of *Deerskins and Duffels: Creek Indian Trade with Anglo-America, 1685–1815* and coauthor, with Gregory Waselkov, of *William Bartram and Southeastern Indians*. She is the current president of the Bartram Trail Conference.

Edward J. Cashin was professor emeritus of History at Augusta State University and the founding director of the Center for the Study of Georgia History. Dr. Cashin was the author of numerous books, including *William Bartram and the American Revolution on the Southern Frontier*. A dedicated member of the Bartram Trail Conference, Dr. Cashin died suddenly in September 2007.

Robert S. Davis, director of the Family & Regional History Program, Wallace State College, Hanceville, Alabama, has published several articles and books on Georgia genealogy, history, and records. He is currently coauthoring with Dr. Robert Calhoon a collection of essays on new research on the American Loyalists.

Arlene Fradkin, associate professor in Archaeology at Florida Atlantic University, specializes in zooarchaeology, the study of animal remains from archaeological sites, with a geographical focus on the southeastern United States and especially Florida. She is the author of *Cherokee Folk Zoology* and has published a number of papers on pre-Columbian subsistence patterns. She also has curated several natural history museum exhibitions and was curator, with

Mallory O'Connor, for the traveling exhibition, *Opening the Door to a New World: Mark Catesby's Travels in La Florida, 1722–1726.*

Joel T. Fry has been curator at Bartram's Garden, the home of John and William Bartram, since 1992. He studied anthropology, historical archaeology, and American Civilization at the University of Pennsylvania, and specializes in garden archaeology and garden history. He has completed numerous articles on the history of Bartram's Garden and the Bartram family plant collections.

Stephanie C. Haas is currently the assistant director of the Digital Library Center at the University of Florida. She has worked as a librarian at museums, botanic gardens, and in academia. She is interested in integrative technologies that permit cross-disciplinary data retrieval and in the spatial referencing of information.

Burt Kornegay has been a reader of William Bartram for twenty years and he was president of the North Carolina Bartram Trail Society for twelve. He is the owner of Slickrock Expeditions and has run many backpacking trips on the North Carolina Bartram Trail. He has a B.A. in History from the University of Oregon and an M.A. in English from UNC-Chapel Hill.

Robert J. Malone, is the executive director of the History of Science Society and an associate scholar at the University of Florida. His research focuses on science in the Old Southwest, with a special emphasis on the planter naturalists William Dunbar and Benjamin L. C. Wailes.

Jerald T. Milanich is curator emeritus in archaeology at the Florida Museum of Natural History in Gainesville. Presently he serves as a contributing editor for *Archaeology* magazine, dividing his time between Roxbury, New York, and New York City. He is the author or editor of more than twenty books describing the Indian societies of the Americas and their interactions with Europeans during the colonial and postcolonial periods. His most recent book is *A Remarkable Curiosity: Dispatches from a New York City Journalist's 1873 Railroad Trip across the American West.*

Marc C. Minno, Ph.D., Zoology, University of Florida, and M.S., Entomology, UC Davis, works as a senior regulatory scientist for the St. Johns River Water Management District in Palatka, Florida. Dr. Minno has written or coauthored numerous scientific and popular articles on butterflies and moths, including *Butterflies through Binoculars: Florida* and *Florida Butterfly Caterpillars and Their Host Plants.*

Maria Minno is coauthor of *Florida Butterfly Gardening* and *Handbook to Schoolyard Plants and Animals of North Central Florida,* and with her husband, Marc, owns and operates Eco-Cognizant, Inc., an environmental consulting and education firm specializing in endangered plant and butterfly research and land management for biodiversity.

Mallory McCane O'Connor, professor emerita of Art History at Santa Fe College, Gainesville, Florida, has written extensively on pre-contact Indians of the Southeast and on artist-naturalists of the same region. She is the author of *Lost Cities of the Ancient Southeast* and coauthor, with Gary Monroe, of *Florida's American Heritage River: A Visual History of the St. Johns Region*. She was curator, with Arlene Fradkin, for the traveling exhibition, *Opening the Door to a New World: Mark Catesby's Travels in La Florida, 1722–1726*.

Kent D. Perkins, manager of the collection, University of Florida Herbarium, Florida Museum of Natural History, manages the daily operations of the Herbarium including specimen accessions, loans, and exchanges. His research interests are in plant systematics, collection informatics, endangered species, and economic plants. He is actively digitizing the collections of the University of Florida Herbarium.

Charlotte M. Porter, Ph.D., is a curator at the Florida Museum of Natural History at the University of Florida, Gainesville. She teaches and supervises graduate students in the History of Science and Museum Studies. A lover of books, Porter publishes on the history of natural history and serves on the executive committee of the University Libraries Leadership Board. She has worked with the Bartram Trail Conference since its inception.

Craig T. Sheldon Jr., Distinguished Research Professor, Auburn Montgomery, is an archaeologist concentrating on the protohistoric and early historic periods in the Southeast. He prepared an introduction to *Southern and Central Expeditions of Clarence B. Moore* and recently coauthored an article, with Ned J. Jenkins and Gregory A. Waselkov, on the "French Habitations at the Alabama Post, ca. 1720–1763."

Stephanie Volmer is the managing editor of *Raritan Quarterly*. She recently completed a dissertation at Rutgers University titled "Planting a New World: Letters and Languages of Transatlantic Botanical Exchange, 1733–1777."

Mark Williams, senior academic professional in Anthropology at the University of Georgia, specializes in Georgia archaeology and ethnohistory. He is coauthor of *Lamar Archaeology* with Gary Shapiro, and *A World Engraved* with Dan Elliott. He is also director of the UGA Laboratory of Archaeology.

Index